Praise for Janet Wallach's

FLIRTING WITH DANGER

"A compelling story that pulsates with the energy of a thriller."
—*The Wall Street Journal*

"Suspense, élan, and a generous helping of glamour: Think George Smiley in a mink-trimmed coat."
—*The New York Times Book Review*

"Janet Wallach delivers an enthusiastic portrait of a Baltimore socialite who defied expectations."
—*The Washington Post*

"It was a life well-lived. Baltimore socialite, journalist, author, intrepid explorer, and filmmaker—and a spy for American military intelligence—Marguerite Harrison broke all the rules for a young woman in the early twentieth century. Biographer Janet Wallach has brilliantly rediscovered this fabulous life and spins a colorful tale of a smart, beautiful young woman who was too bored to stay at home. Instead, she runs off to revolutionary Russia, interviews Leon Trotsky in Moscow, befriends John Reed, and considers Emma Goldman 'a sympathetic soul.' Twice imprisoned by the Bolsheviks, Harrison manages to survive for more wild adventures in the Middle East, the Far East, and Mongolia. Wallach's heroine is a feisty feminist—but her espionage, working under the cover of a journalist, underscores the lost art of human intelligence collection in the modern spy business."
—Kai Bird, Pulitzer Prize–winning biographer and director of the Leon Levy Center for Biography

"Janet Wallach weaves together the almost unbelievable adventures of a fearless American socialite, Marguerite Harrison, who operated as a spy, reporting to military intelligence during the precarious years between the two world wars. Scrupulously researched but reading like a page-turning novel, the aptly titled *Flirting with Danger* takes us from the debutante balls in Baltimore to Harrison's dangerous exploits in Baghdad, the Far East, and Moscow, where she is incarcerated in the notorious Lubyanka prison before being released to whatever is next."
—Eden Collinsworth, author of *What the Ermine Saw: The Extraordinary Journey of Leonardo da Vinci's Most Mysterious Portrait*

"Wallach's in-depth portrayal of Harrison's complex personality deftly reveals the socialite spy's intrepid character through a masterly crafted narrative and detailed anecdotes."   —*Historical Novels Review*

"A remarkable tale of intrigue and daring."   —*Publishers Weekly*

"Wallach's expert storytelling, which has the suspense and pacing of a good spy novel, is clearly her own, and it makes for engaging reading."
—*Kirkus Reviews*

JANET WALLACH

FLIRTING WITH DANGER

Janet Wallach is the author of ten books, including *Desert Queen: The Extraordinary Life of Gertrude Bell*, which has been translated into twelve languages and was a *New York Times* Notable Book.

Also by Janet Wallach

Seraglio

Chanel: Her Style and Her Life

Desert Queen

The Richest Woman in America

Arafat: In the Eye of the Beholder
(with John Wallach)

The New Palestinians
(with John Wallach)

*Still Small Voices: The Real Heroes
of the Arab-Israeli Conflict*
(with John Wallach)

FLIRTING

· WITH ·

DANGER

The Mysterious Life of

Marguerite Harrison, Socialite Spy

JANET WALLACH

VINTAGE BOOKS

A Division of Penguin Random House LLC

New York

Published by Vintage Books, a division of Penguin Random House LLC, 1745 Broadway, New York, NY 10019. Originally published in hardcover by Doubleday, a division of Penguin Random House LLC, New York, in 2023.

Vintage and colophon are registered
trademarks of Penguin Random House LLC.

Pages 323–24 constitute an extension of this copyright page.

The Library of Congress has cataloged the Doubleday edition as follows:
Names: Wallach, Janet, 1942– author.
Title: Flirting with danger : the mysterious life of Marguerite Harrison, socialite spy / by Janet Wallach.
Other titles: Mysterious life of Marguerite Harrison, socialite spy
Description: First edition. | New York : Doubleday, 2023.
Identifiers: LCCN 2022043114 (print)
Subjects: LCSH: Harrison, Marguerite, 1879–1967. | United States. War Department. Military Intelligence Division—History. | Espionage, American—Germany—History—20th century. | Espionage, American—Soviet Union—History—20th century. | Soviet Union—Politics and government—1917–1936. | Spies—United States—History—20th century. | Women intelligence officers—United States—Biography. | Journalists—Maryland—Baltimore—Biography. | Intelligence officers—United States—Biography. | Baltimore (Md.)—Biography.
Classification: LCC C H379 2023 (print) | DDC 327.12730092—dc23
LC record available at https://lccn.loc.gov/2022043114

Vintage Books Trade Paperback ISBN: 978-0-525-56685-4
eBook ISBN: 978-0-385-54509-9

Author photograph © Vance Jacobs
Book design by Maria Carella
Maps designed by Mapping Specialists, Ltd.

penguinrandomhouse.com | vintagebooks.com

Printed in the United States of America
1st Printing

The authorized representative in the EU for product safety and compliance is Penguin Random House Ireland, Morrison Chambers, 32 Nassau Street, Dublin D02 YH68, Ireland, https://eu-contact.penguin.ie.

To Jordan, who fills me with joy

Contents

PART TWO

PART THREE

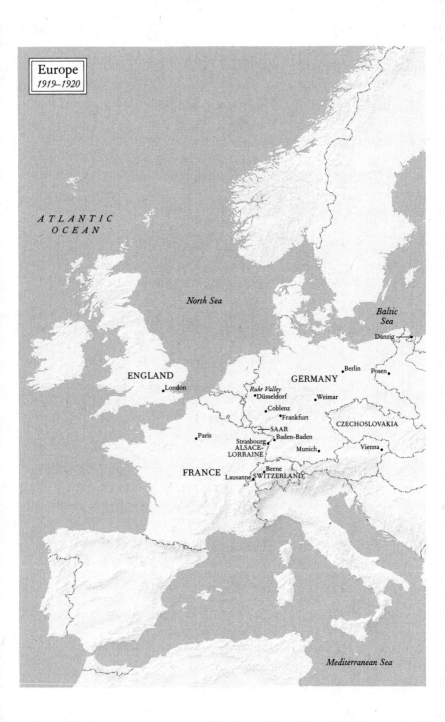

Europe
1919–1920

ATLANTIC
OCEAN

North Sea

Baltic
Sea

Danzig

ENGLAND

London

GERMANY

Berlin

Posen

Ruhr Valley

Düsseldorf

Weimar

Coblenz

Frankfurt

CZECHOSLOVAKIA

Paris

SAAR

Strasbourg

Baden-Baden

ALSACE-
LORRAINE

Munich

Vienna

FRANCE

Berne

Lausanne

SWITZERLAND

Mediterranean Sea

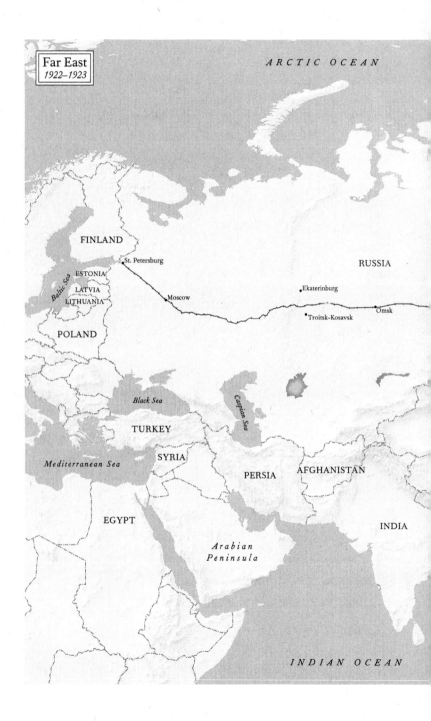

Far East
1922–1923

ARCTIC OCEAN

FINLAND

St. Petersburg

ESTONIA

LATVIA

LITHUANIA

Baltic Sea

POLAND

RUSSIA

Ekaterinburg

Moscow

Troitsk-Kosavsk

Omsk

Black Sea

Caspian Sea

TURKEY

SYRIA

Mediterranean Sea

PERSIA

AFGHANISTAN

EGYPT

INDIA

Arabian
Peninsula

INDIAN OCEAN

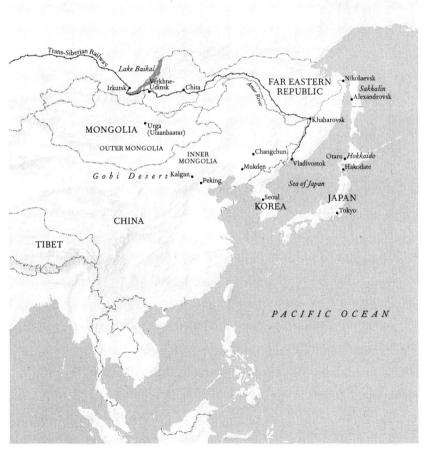

Siberia

Trans-Siberian Railway

Lake Baikal

Verkhne-
Udinsk

Irkutsk

Chita

Amur River

FAR EASTERN
REPUBLIC

Nikolaevsk

Sakhalin
Alexandrovsk

Khabarovsk

MONGOLIA

Urga
(Ulaanbaatar)

OUTER MONGOLIA

INNER
MONGOLIA

Changchun

Mukden

Otaru *Hokkaido*

Vladivostok

Hakodate

Gobi Desert Kalgan

Peking

Sea of Japan

JAPAN

Seoul
KOREA

Tokyo

CHINA

TIBET

PACIFIC OCEAN

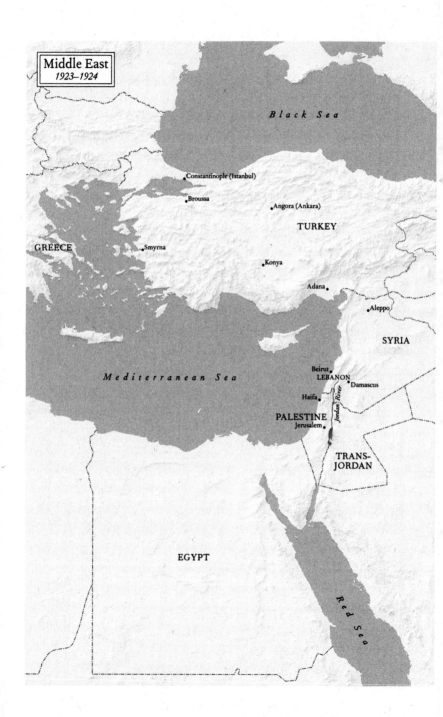

Middle East
1923–1924

Black Sea

Constantinople (Istanbul)

Broussa

Angora (Ankara)

TURKEY

GREECE

Smyrna

Konya

Adana

Aleppo

SYRIA

Mediterranean Sea

Beirut
LEBANON
Damascus

Haifa

PALESTINE
Jerusalem

Jordan River

TRANS-
JORDAN

EGYPT

Red Sea

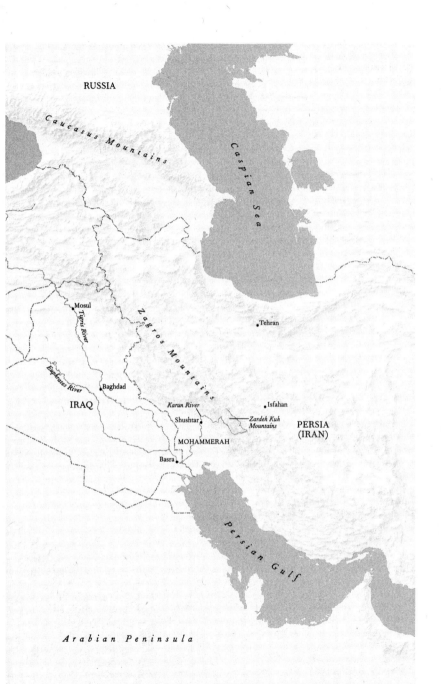

FLIRTING WITH DANGER

Prologue

She was always drawn to adventure, lured by the blurry beyond. She traveled by ship, by train, by horse, by donkey, by car, by cart, and by foot through windstorms, blizzards, and blazing heat. She loved the salty spray of the ocean, the sweep of sand in the desert, the crunch of mountain snow. It all made her feel content.

On this trip she had sailed from New York to France on the SS *Lafayette* and overnighted to Turkey on the Orient Express, stopping in Constantinople and then continuing on to Ankara, by animal and araba to Anatolia, and by ancient car to Damascus and across the Syrian Desert to Iraq.

Now on a rain-soaked day in March 1924, she was in Baghdad, a smartly dressed American woman in a British colonial building with a letter introducing her, Mrs. Marguerite Harrison, to the British High Commissioner, Sir Percy Cox.

Sir Percy may have been too polite to ask, but surely he wondered why she was actually here, where she had been, and what her real intent was. The arrival of an American woman in Baghdad was an uncommon event. Then again, she was an uncommon woman.

A privileged child of the Gilded Age, she married a man her mother despised, and when she was left a widow at thirty-seven, she rebelled again. She refused to wear widow's weeds and went to work as a reporter, a culture critic, an author, a filmmaker, and a spy. An insatiable traveler and relentless explorer, she overcame sickness, hunger, cold, heat, and wet and risked her life through war zones in

Europe, contested lands in Far Eastern Asia, and unmapped regions of the Middle East. With an unusual passion for history, she saw the world with a prescient view and a rare understanding of political consequences. Her top secret reports won high praise.

Thanks to her good looks and advice she received in her youth, she hid her intellect, turned on her charm, and never lacked for male companions, whether platonic or otherwise. "Be intellectual if you must," she was taught, "but learn to be charming. It will take you much farther."

Her escapades began at Radcliffe with a secret fiancé, and continued to Rome where, as a debutante, she was courted by a dreamy-eyed diplomat who turned out to be a rebellious Young Turk. Much later, she traveled to Berlin as a foreign correspondent, the first American woman to arrive in the enemy country after the Great War. She smoked, she drank, she wore her best evening dresses, dined with monocled counts, and danced with ardent socialists. Then she stole into Moscow, where she had a brief encounter with Trotsky at the Kremlin and a lengthy stay in prison at the infamous Lubyanka. But why?

She sipped tea in Tokyo with the emperor of Japan and drank sour milk in Outer Mongolia with natives who had never bathed in their lives. She joked with generals, flirted with foreign ministers, and amused businessmen, some of whom fell madly in love with her. And all the while she trod on dangerous turf. But how? And why?

Her British host suggested at once that she see Miss Gertrude Bell, a confidante of King Faisal. Mrs. Harrison had an image in mind of the well-known Miss Bell: a hard masculine type, with a formidable facade and an even more resilient interior. As she waited in Miss Bell's office, with its high ceilings and tall French windows overlooking the Tigris, the surroundings seemed to confirm her thoughts. Never had she seen such a disorderly place, unladylike to say the least, with papers everywhere: books, pamphlets, reports strewn across the enormous desk, piled on the upholstered divan, stacked on the straight-backed chairs.

Miss Bell swept in, looking as different from her mental picture as Baghdad looked from New York. She was the essence of femininity:

her features were fine, her hair well coiffed, her gray velvet frock fresh from Paris. She was not so different, in fact, from her American guest.

They eyed each other carefully and sized each other up with some suspicion. Miss Bell rarely found women to match her standards; Mrs. Harrison rarely encountered women known to be so tough. Each, however, quickly found a soulmate.

.   .   .

They were two daughters of the Gilded Age, scions of prominent families with gobs of money and generations of good lineage. Physically similar at five foot six, with auburn hair and blue-gray eyes, the British piercing, the American sparkling, each had a shapely figure, stiff spine, and self-assured bearing. Each was highly intelligent, fluent in at least five languages, well educated with an interest in world affairs, a strong knowledge of European literature, and an appreciation of the arts. Each loved riding, hiking, and flowers, and each had a passion for stylish clothes.

Both were indefatigable travelers and stalwart explorers, but driven by what? Was it to escape their domineering mothers? Or to follow in the adventuresome steps of their fathers? Or was there something more? Each of them was patrician. Was each of them also a spy?

Feminists not by their words but by their deeds, they did a man's work in mapping new territory and mining new information. In addition, Miss Bell was a worthy diplomat, Mrs. Harrison a worthwhile reporter who had recently interviewed Mustafa Kemal, soon to be known as Ataturk, the new ruler of the new Turkish republic.

Questions flew, from conditions in Turkey to the issues of Mosul and the situation in Iraq.

Mrs. Harrison was eager to meet King Faisal, newly created monarch of the newly created state of Iraq, who relied on Miss Bell for much of his political life. She did not, however, have much success in posing her questions. Miss Bell fired hers as rapidly as shots from a rifle. But Mrs. Harrison would have another chance.

"I am having a dinner this evening," Miss Bell announced. "You must come to my house." There would be a handful of guests, all of them important men, with good conversation in the proper dining room, continuing afterward over coffee and brandy on the chintz-covered chairs in front of a fire in the cozy drawing room.

Miss Bell would wear her blue velvet gown, and the talk would ramble on among her friends: Late into the night, Mrs. Harrison held them all under her spell. "She is an American traveler and writer and an exceptionally brilliant woman," Miss Bell wrote home to her father.

Another discussion in the office was arranged for the following day, and after two hours the American was asked to dine again. This time the group would be larger and would go off to a ball at the British Residency, where the king would be in attendance. He had mentioned that he wanted to meet the American woman. Like Scheherazade, she beguiled her new acquaintances with her tales. But which were true? And which were missing large pieces? Spies have their own truths.

She would have more tales to tell, more secrets to hide after she left Iraq, on her way to Iran in search of a wild nomadic tribe. In a day or so she would be off, hearing the call of her mysterious past and heeding the cry of her future.

Part One

CHAPTER 1

Willkommen

The Anhalter Bahnhof, Berlin's gateway to the kaiser's once mighty realm, seemed a shadow of itself on this January night in 1919. The crackle of guns was too far off to be heard, but the silence of fear muffled the usual hurly-burly and pervaded the ghostly hallways of the Romanesque railway station. No welcome mat greeted the few arriving passengers, only armed soldiers who guarded their path.

Diplomats in derbies and soft dove gloves, movie stars in silks and feathers, bankers with waxed moustaches and starched collars had once disembarked here from Prague, Vienna, Paris, and Rome. Tonight the tired travelers who emerged from the Cassel train were mostly demobilized German soldiers returning from the war or businessmen hoping to find orders for their wares and services, but there was one smartly dressed American woman. Her shapely figure wrapped in a fur coat, auburn hair tucked in a fur hat, and manicured hands warmed in a muff, Marguerite Harrison moved through the soaring arches on her way to adventure.

Outside the station's entrance, moonlight beamed from a clear dark sky, revealing empty streets where lines of taxis once stretched. Fatigued, yet exhilarated, she sat down on her leather luggage, crossed her legs at her ankles, and waited. Something would come along. It always did.

She had made the trip to Berlin via Paris to Coblenz and then to Frankfurt in an unheated train filled with shivering workers on their way to factories in the east. Arriving on the enemy soil of Frankfurt in the pitch black of five a.m., she had had no pass, no permission, and no credentials; she could easily be imprisoned or expelled. Yet, with her perfect command of the German language, and a self-assurance that stemmed from patrician roots, she had confidence that, somehow, she would be allowed to stay.

The hotel clerk in Frankfurt told her she was the first American he had seen in four years. All he wanted, he said, was *"Ruhe und Ordnung,"* peace and order, the national chant of the German people. He brought her an ersatz coffee made of chicory and peas and directed her to the office of the Workmen's and Soldiers' Council, where she asked for permission to travel to Berlin. With the cocksure knowledge he and his fellow Bolsheviks would soon take over the world, the bureaucrat in charge stamped a paper and handed it to her: Frau Marguerite Harrison of Baltimore had an official pass to travel as a journalist unhindered to Berlin. The next morning when she left, she learned she could go only as far as Cassel; Berlin was closed to all but the military.

Crammed on a train with twice the usual number of passengers, a ride that took eight hours instead of the scheduled two, she arrived in Cassel, marched into military headquarters, and asked for permission to travel the two hundred miles to Berlin. She was turned down. Luckily, the major in charge succumbed to her flirtations. The military card he gave her was the gilded key to every city in the country. Storing the official pass safely in her purse, she was on her way to Berlin. Now, at the Anhalter Bahnhof, Marguerite Harrison, newspaper correspondent and secret agent, waited for a cab.

.   .   .

Born Marguerite Elton Baker, daughter of a shipping magnate and his noted hostess wife, Elizabeth Livezey, cared for by governesses and schooled by tutors, she was the privileged offspring of one of Baltimore's richest families. Keenly intelligent, always daring and eager for challenge, she relished danger and was willing to accept the consequences so long as they delivered a more interesting life. As a red-haired sprite she climbed towering spruce trees; as a Radcliffe student she nearly ran off with her landlady's son; as a debutante she was courted by princes; as a beautiful heiress she was betrothed to an impoverished man.

Still eye-catchingly pretty at forty-one, she was no longer the social butterfly, Miss Marguerite Baker, who loved to drink champagne and flirt at parties. Nor was she Mrs. Thomas Harrison, wife of a prominent stockbroker/sportsman/clubman, who was a devoted father to their son. She was, instead, Mrs. Marguerite Harrison, young-looking widow, hardworking correspondent, undercover spy.

Determined to tread the unmarked path, she craned her neck a little too far around corners and sniffed out trouble wherever it lurked. Her independence made her chafe at the rules, defiant toward authority. The first American woman to enter Germany since the start of the war in 1914, she was not only one of the first foreign correspondents in Germany after the Armistice; she was, more importantly, an American espionage agent. She faced far greater risks than ever before.

Soon enough the slow clop-clop of a worn-out horse sounded on the street. She halted the driver perched atop the old droshky and instructed him in German to take her to the Bristol. The hotel was a palace of fond memories, of youthful summers spent on the Continent with her family.

The ancient man looked at her, astounded. "The Hotel Bristol is *abgesperrt*!" Impossible, he cried out. "Only the *Militar* can pass through the Brandenburger Tor at this hour of the night, *Gnadige*." The hotel may have been closed off to others, but not to the determined Madame Harrison.

Undaunted, she pierced him with her steely gray-blue eyes and announced, "*Ich gehöre zum Militar*" (I belong to the military), and with the authority of an army officer she flashed her official pass from Cassel and swung her two bags and typewriter into the open carriage. Climbing onto the seat, she demanded the man get under way.

An order was an order. The military ruled the fatherland. As German field marshal and military writer Colmar von der Goltz had written a generation earlier: "We have won our position through the sharpness of our sword, not through the sharpness of our mind." So it was then; so it was now.

Despite his grumbles about distant guns, the driver set off, nudging his weary horse down the Budapester Strasse. Within a few minutes, the sounds of rifle rat-a-tat-tat and machine-gun fire brought the man to a pause. "Shall I go on, fraulein?" he asked fearfully.

"*Gewiss*," she answered firmly. The carriage continued to the Brandenburg Gate, where a chariot driven by the Goddess of Victory reigned over the gate's massive columns and looked down on its statue of Mars. Vehicles were verboten, but the soldier on guard, shocked at the sight of a woman alone and much impressed by her pass, allowed the droshky onto the Unter der Linden.

The famed boulevard, lined with chestnut and lime trees, was home to the Kaiser's Palace, the Opera House, embassies, and ministries. The carriage followed along the broad avenue to the Wilhelmstrasse, site of both the Reichstag and Reich Chancellery, where the national assembly and the chancellor carried out their work. Again, the woman heard the ominous sounds of guns bursting the air, but now the explosions were close.

Crashes came from the rooftops, where government troops, their bodies bent low, their heads covered in steel helmets, aimed their machine guns downward. The rapid bullets bounded onto buildings and pavements; in return, the shots of Spartacists' rifles ripped and snapped across the streets, and the droshky was almost caught in the crossfire.

The driver wrapped his big fur collar around his head and whipped his old horse to go on; the American woman ducked down in her seat and used her suitcase to buffer herself from the bullets. It was a long few minutes until the cab came to a halt at number 5-6 Wilhelmstrasse; the elegant Bristol, the only hotel she had ever stayed at in Berlin, looked as deserted as a cemetery at midnight.

Curtains were drawn, shutters locked, iron doors were bolted tight. She rang the night bell and waited in fear until she heard the click of a turning key. It wasn't a cemetery ghost, but the night porter: "*Um Gottes willen, Fräulein!*" ("For God's sake, miss"), he said, shaking his head as he pulled her inside.

Glowing chandeliers lighted the lobby, and strains of Offenbach's *Tales of Hoffmann* swirled through the air, assuring her that life went on here as she remembered, at least at the Bristol. "*Willkommen zurück*," a clerk said, and relieved to hear the welcome back, she signed her name to the register. She joined the handful of guests brave enough to remain in Berlin, and while the orchestra entertained, she supped in the dining room, then retired to the quiet of her chamber. In the morning, she would get straight to work.

.   .   .

The coffee was hot and strong the way she liked it, the *brötchen* freshly baked, and the newspapers she ordered were stacked high. She took a bite of the crunchy roll and chewed over the articles. The news was grim.

Two months earlier Kaiser Wilhelm II had been forced to abdicate. Germans witnessed chaos as competing politicians turned their backs on the king and thrust themselves to the forefront. On November 9, 1918, three different men pronounced the monarchy at an end. Philipp Scheidemann, the white-haired, white-goateed minister of the Social Democrats and a supporter of the monarchy, stood at the balcony window of the Reichstag, while his colleague Friedrich Ebert listened in surprise: "The old and rotten, the monarchy has collapsed," Scheidemann announced. "Long live the German Republic!"

That same day, the moustachioed Max von Baden, moderate chancellor and member of the ruling family, surprised everyone by proclaiming the end of both the German monarchy and the German empire; and Karl Liebknecht, the pince-nezzed Marxist leader of the Spartacists, surprised no one when he spoke out from the palace of the ruling Hohenzollerns: "The day of revolution has come," he declared. "We proclaim the free Socialist Republic of Germany."

Like many citizens, from poor laborers to successful professionals, the artist Käthe Kollwitz had been loyal to the empire: even the death of her younger son on the battlefield did not destroy her fealty. As von der Goltz had written, the German people, with their "passionate love for the Fatherland," were "determined not to shrink from the hard trials" of war and were ready for the "self-denial and self-sacrifice that may wax mightier in our hearts."

But like Marguerite Harrison, Käthe Kollwitz was moved by authors such as Dickens who wrote of the injustices pressed upon the weak and the poor. As the war went on and she learned of its huge financial costs and human losses, and as she watched the growing despair of the hungry masses, her sympathies turned even more to the socialists. But she worried they might turn too far to the left.

She had been strolling through the Tiergarten, Berlin's sprawling park, to the Brandenburg Gate on that November afternoon when a copy of *Vorwarts*, the Social Democrats' newspaper, was thrust at her. Reading the headline, she learned of the kaiser's abdication. The fevered crowds pushed her forward to the Reichstag, and then to the Unter der Linden, where soldiers celebrated, throwing their cockades on the ground, shouting, "Long live free Germany!"

Two days later, on November 11, the Germans asked for an armistice, and the Allies answered with a resounding "yes." But they had their conditions for the vanquished, one of which, from the Americans, was that the Germans form a democratic state.

With peace in mind, the members of the Reichstag, the German parliament, organized a provisional government led by the Social Democrats. Looming on the left were the Spartacists, named for the slave who led a rebellion against the Romans, ready to give their lives for the masses; hovering on the right were the loyal officers and militant monarchists, ready to die for the king. The result of all this had been an onslaught of strikes, demonstrations, and armed clashes.

The German people may have survived the end of the kaiser, they may have smiled when he escaped to Holland, they may have cried when their own sons and husbands came home ravaged from the front, or didn't come home at all; but now, in the throes of revolution, they did not know how to react, whether to laugh or cry. They were fighting after the reign of Wilhelm and the beginning of . . . who knew what?

Tense as amateurs balanced on a tightrope, Berlin's population greeted the last day of December with a sigh of relief and a gulp of trepidation. "The year 1918 ended the war and brought the revolution," Kollwitz wrote in her diary. "We have finally crawled through the narrow shaft in which we were prisoned, in which we could not stir." She, for one, felt hopeful. "We see light and breathe air."

.   .   .

Days later, Germany was again at war, not with its enemies' forces but with itself. Its socialists and Spartacists, militants and monarchists, nationalists and imperialists were wrestling inside their own tents and outside their own camps. Compounding the problems, the Spartacist leaders, Karl Liebknecht and his brilliant partner Rosa Luxemburg, founders of the Communist movement in Germany, were murdered.

Rosa Luxemburg, a Polish-born Jew, had defied convention: a graduate of the University of Zurich and the rare woman to earn a doctorate, she was a leading thinker and activist of the socialist movement in Germany and a threat to the status quo. Her short stature seemed to grow when she spoke, her voice sang warm and melodic, her words cried out with passion to help the oppressed.

Her lover, Karl Liebknecht, the only member of the Reichstag to vote against entering the war, had an intellectual air emphasized by his high forehead, thick brown hair, and spectacles. A born orator, his poetic images roused affection, his fiery speeches rallied the crowds to action.

At the beginning of 1919, the pair founded the Communist Party in Germany and were arrested two weeks later. As the car taking them to prison drove through the Tiergarten, militant volunteers, part of a *Freikorps*, or anti-Communist militia made up of former soldiers, stopped the vehicle, yanked them both out, and beat them with rifle butts. Rosa Luxemburg was bashed in the skull; Karl Liebknecht was shot several times in the back.

The attackers threw Luxemburg's corpse in the Landwehr Canal, where it went undiscovered for two months. The same militia dumped Liebknecht's body on the doorstep of the morgue. News of the leaders' brutal deaths enraged their followers. The furious battle between the Spartacists and the government-supported Freikorps was under way when Marguerite arrived at the Anhalter Bahnhof in Berlin.

. . .

After the untimely death of her husband in 1915, Marguerite became a reporter for the *Baltimore Sun*, first as a socialite covering afternoon teas and charity dinners, then as a music and drama critic writing reviews and interviewing performers. In 1917, when the United States joined the Allies in Europe, she turned her attention to the war.

She worked for the Maryland Board of Motion Picture Censors to protect movie audiences from German propaganda. She wrote avidly for the *Sun* to encourage support for the American effort in the war. She visited the Red Cross offices in Washington and wrote a series hailing the organization for its hard work and devoted staff. She traveled to New York and rode in the sidecar of a motorcycle to a secret army air camp on Long Island.

Dressed in a helmet, goggles, and a leather coat, she was strapped into a seat on a small propeller plane. With the pilot seated behind her, the plane soared to thirty-five hundred feet and flew at ninety-six miles an hour, and she was thrilled. But then "it humped and bumped, then ceased," and they plummeted into a field. "Engine trouble," said the pilot. With the help of some mechanics, they soon took off again and made a proper landing two miles away at the hangar. She looked ruefully at her grease-covered white stockings and white shoes, but the experience left her enthralled and she had only praise for the pilots and the program.

In her endeavors to promote patriotism, she won a front-page place for a series on women's capability to work. Americans need not worry, she assured the public: women could support their families when their men went off to fight. To prove her point, she found jobs as a stenographer, salesgirl, and streetcar conductor. Then came the toughest work of all.

Bethlehem Steel employed seven thousand laborers at their shipbuilding yard at Sparrows Point, Maryland, and every single worker was a man. Until, that is, Marguerite Harrison, "with great trepidation," convinced the division head that she could do their jobs. In May 1918, the daughter of one of the country's richest and most famous shipowners became the first and only woman in America to work as a laborer at a shipbuilding plant.

With a show of bravado, she stepped out of her silk peignoir and into a rugged uniform of khaki cloth overalls, laced up a pair of ankle-high, brown leather boots, snapped a cap on her head, and reported to work. For one week she toiled from early morning to evening, full time and overtime, doing what no one believed a woman could do: she tackled pneumatic drills, climbed towering ladders, swung hammers, dug with chisels, and pounded twenty-five rivets into steel. With every rivet, she said, "I felt I was helping to drive another nail in the Kaiser's coffin."

She ached in muscles she never knew she had, but her strength convinced the doubting public. On her last day, when she stopped to say goodbye to the policeman at the gate, he told her: "I've got a new opinion about the nerve of women. I always said that women could never do the things I've seen you do . . . I'm ready now to believe all of 'em could do it if they had the chance."

She had proven to her readers that if their men were drafted to fight overseas, women could take their place at home; mouths would be fed, essential jobs would be filled. What's more, she said of the adventure: "I have had the most wonderful, the most unforgettable experience of my whole life."

. . .

Despite the paper's prominent display of her series, she no longer felt gratified by her work: typing patriotic stories in the newsroom was adequate, but she was eager to take on a more active role. She informed the government of suspected spies at home and, restless to report from the frontlines, she offered to cover the war in Europe. But she ran into a firewall when she learned that women were officially barred from the war zone. Refusing to give up, she explored a different route.

As a child of the Gilded Age, she had traveled to Europe annually with her parents and younger sister, meeting people from all walks of life, from the queen of England to the quartermasters on her father's fleet, the Atlantic Transport Line. As a girl she visited the London home of J. P. Morgan; as a worldly adolescent she had tea with Sir Henry Lucy, the editor of *Punch*. She lunched with the author of *Dracula*, Bram Stoker; had drinks with the Shakespearean actors Henry Irving and Ellen Terry; and dined with Arthur Sullivan, who, with W. S. Gilbert, created *The Pirates of Penzance* and other comic operas.

By the time she was a debutante she was dining and dancing with Winston Churchill. Four years older than her, he had a paternal ancestry of British aristocrats and elites and a maternal pedigree of Jeromes, an American family of princely wealth. A graduate of Sandhurst, Winston had already been elected to serve in Parliament.

He was the handsome, fair-skinned son of her mother's friend Jennie, and her ambitious mother's candidate for the man she wanted her daughter to marry. Each time Marguerite set off for a party where Winston was also invited, Elizabeth Baker offered simple advice: "Be nice," she urged her daughter. Marguerite tried. But the romantic young deb was not impressed.

He invited her out to suppers, but instead of paying her compliments he furrowed his brow and bored her with somber talk of the Boer War, from which he had just returned. "He was too serious," she said. When the music played, he asked her to dance, but proceeded to step on her feet. "He was an awful dancer," she added, conceding years later, "he is undoubtedly one of the greatest men in the world today."

There were evenings with barons and earls and prized invitations to other events, the most treasured of which arrived in August 1900: an invitation to Buckingham Palace for the Royal Garden Party. After hours of practice sweeping her right foot behind her left, back straight, knees bent, and holding out her skirts, she joined a lawnful of ladies fluttering about the palace grounds. Parasols in hand, hats blooming with feathers and flowers, pastel dresses ruffling in the breeze, they tittered and tottered and queued up to be presented to the queen. The short, chubby royal Victoria, Queen of the United Kingdom of Great Britain and Ireland and Empress of India, was the longest-reigning British monarch in history.

Marguerite described the moment: "I curtsied to a little old lady in black wearing a hat like an inverted bowl and sitting in a Bath chariot drawn by a small donkey attended by an old Scotsman in Highland costume," she said drily. The old woman "bowed slightly and uttered something unintelligible, and then drove on." It was three years after the Golden Jubilee, and Victoria was the most powerful woman in the world. But the younger woman was not impressed. "She was not my idea of Queen Empress," the American declared.

.   .   .

Marguerite may have had a sharp tongue, but wherever she was, she was cosmopolitan and self-assured, unusually fluent in languages, with exceptional recall and an ability to listen as well as to speak, all qualities essential to work in intelligence. She knew when to be sweet and when to be tart: she could charm a duke over cocktails, banter with a workman over a beer, or discuss art and literature with an intellectual. In the summer of 1918 she applied to the navy to be a spy.

The secretary of the navy turned down her application. He refused to hire a woman. With help from friends she tried again, this time with the army, and this time she was invited for an interview. If she passed, she acknowledged, she would be taking on "a career that promised nothing but danger and uncertainty." If she succeeded, "my effort would never be publicly recognized." But if she failed, "I would be repudiated by my government and perhaps lose my life." For a woman who savored adventure, the prospects were delicious.

Her first encounter with military intelligence had the spicy whiff of undercover work. Instructed to appear at the Hotel Emerson at the corner of Calvert and Baltimore Streets in downtown Baltimore at three p.m. on Saturday, September 28, she arrived at the smart hotel, entered the grand lobby with its soaring marble columns and chandeliers, sidestepped the ladies in large hats and flowing dresses, observed the men in fedoras, and waited until she was approached by an unknown man.

Armed with her name and description, clad in civilian clothes, Colonel Martin introduced himself and led her off to a quiet space for conversation. In the modulated tones Marguerite had learned from her stern yet caring governess, Miss Gillet, she spoke with ease. Chatting for a few minutes about this and that, Colonel Martin asked a series of questions and she answered, poised and self-assured, comfortable within the guidelines set by Miss Gillet, who insisted that small talk was as important as grand ideas.

"Be intellectual if you must," the stout, corseted woman insisted, "but do not let anyone see it. It is fatal. Learn to be charming. It will take you much farther."

On the forms, the colonel said, she had referred to her facility with languages: "I have an absolute command of French and German, am very fluent and have a good accent in Italian and I speak a little Spanish. Without any trouble I could pass as a French woman and after a little practice, as Swiss German," she had written.

And so, he tested her ability. "She spoke German with such fluency that I questioned her as to where she learned it," he said in his report. Might she have lived in Germany? he asked. Oh no, she assured him graciously, she had always lived in Maryland. Did she have German ancestors? he wanted to know. Shaking her head, she replied that her family went back eight generations in America. Her father's side arrived from England before the Revolution; her mother's side sailed with William Penn and the Friends.

Why was she so eager to get involved in the war? he wondered. She was fond of adventure, she said in the clipped style of St. Timothy's, the exclusive girls' school she had attended from the age of twelve. Was she afraid? Not at all, she answered, waving off the notion with a manicured hand; she was fearless. Most importantly, she had an intense desire to do something for her country. But what about romance? Love affairs? There were many, she could have said, but mostly in the past.

They started at seventeen, when her mother suggested she attend Radcliffe, where she could complete her education and, more importantly, polish her social skills. The new school offered young women the same collegiate experience as Harvard offered to men. At the onset of the academic year in Cambridge, Massachusetts, Elizabeth found her daughter a suitable room in the home of a highly respected family.

The college lectures began, but Marguerite's attention soon drifted from the classroom to the drawing room. Her landlady's son, attractive, alluring, and claiming to love her, became the object of her studies. They walked together along the narrow cobblestone streets, whispered sweet words behind the elm trees, and by Christmas they were secretly engaged.

At home for the holidays, he wrote her romantic letters that her mother discovered. When Elizabeth sniffed through the pages, a battle ensued. Weeks later Marguerite was yanked out of Radcliffe and hauled off to Italy, where she trekked around the museums and perfected her Italian. Back in Baltimore, two years later another romance arose. Swept up in the arms of a popular southern gentleman, she danced on puffs of dreams, but her mother saw only clouds. The handsome young man may have had social assets, but he also carried financial liabilities. This time when her mother towed her off to Italy, the trip took a different turn.

Soon after boarding the ship, Marguerite was pursued by a dashing man with parted black hair and sweeping black moustaches. Vittorio Emanuele, the count of Turin and grandson of the king of Italy, paid her lavish compliments, and she, despite her proclamations of love for the man back home, batted her eyes and made clever comments in response.

Suave, sophisticated, and famous throughout Europe, the count had defended his country's reputation and defeated Prince Henri of Orleans in a sword duel. It didn't take long before a romance blossomed. Her mother's hopes may have run high, but for Marguerite the liaison was only an amusement. "All men were fair game, to be bagged for sheer sport," she later said.

Days after, ensconced at the Grand Hotel in Rome, she noticed a dark-haired man with pale skin and smoldering brown eyes. He was "different" and "exotic," and his looks were tantalizing. Seated near him in the dining room, she could hardly turn away. And he took notice of her.

When she and her mother arrived for tea at the home of a family friend, there he was. The clever fellow had done some sleuthing, found a mutual acquaintance, and asked for an introduction to the beautiful young American. He bowed and kissed her hand: he was Reshid Sadi Bey, secretary of the Turkish embassy in Rome, an aristocrat and a diplomat, and poison for her mother's dreams.

He was political and poetic, an important member of the rebellious Young Turks, a writer who left her spellbound. His voice made her tremble; his letters "were poems of prose." He taught her philosophy and quoted John Stuart Mill; he was a Muslim and taught her about spirituality and religion; he was an expert on Ottoman politics and taught her about foreign affairs of all sorts.

He took her on long drives and spoke to Marguerite in tones that made her feel "indecent," she said. "He fascinated me more than any man I have ever known." It was as if he put a spell on her. When he pleaded with her to marry him, she felt bewitched, as though she could not give him up. But his charms were lost on her mother, and Elizabeth Baker drew the line. Besides, the young man in Baltimore was drawing her back. She daydreamed of life with him: a cozy home in Maryland, a family of their own, a prominent place in the social set.

.   .   .

Now, here at the Hotel Emerson with Colonel Martin of Army Intelligence, she was a Baltimore socialite indeed, but also a widowed reporter restless for something more in life. She was eager to visit the battlefront in France, and even more, to find out what was occurring in Germany, the source of so much reputed evil. Behind the enemy barriers, she sensed "momentous movements in progress." She craved the opportunity to uncover the truth about the country she had visited many times in her youth and the people she felt she had once known well.

She would not only have the chance to bring the war home to readers sitting in their living rooms, she would have the means to inform men in government whose decisions could affect the fate of multitudes. Working for Military Intelligence would provide her with the ability to observe the war and unlock its mysteries; more importantly, it would enable her to help "make the world safe for democracy."

She focused her attention on Colonel Martin. Intent on his questions, she heard him ask worriedly, would she get caught in a compromising situation? She shook her head and refuted his suggestion. She was "callous to love affairs," she said, and long past the foolish stage at the age of thirty-nine. "She could easily be considered 15 years younger," he wrote.

"She is a cultured lady," he stated, "of very attractive personality and of high intelligence." He confirmed she was a staff reporter for the *Baltimore Sun* and noted that she had an appointment that very afternoon to interview the widow of President Cleveland. She said she could go to Europe as a correspondent for the *Baltimore Sun*, writing "harmless feature stories," and assured him her editor would be the only one to know of her secret work.

Hired! declared General Marlborough Churchill, head of the Military Intelligence Division of the United States Army. She met the general in his office at Military Intelligence, not far from the White House at Sixth and B Streets. He presented a commanding figure, elegant and trim, with piercing gray eyes, a firm chin, and a straight mouth slow to smile.

She found him delightful and charmed the Harvard graduate,

a commissioned field officer, with her easy conversation. They had much in common, from his friendship with her father-in-law, Joseph Ames, an aeronautics adviser to the military, to their shared memories of school days in Cambridge, Massachusetts. She even knew his distant relative Winston Churchill. Most importantly, they were aligned in their admiration for the president and agreed with Wilson's belief it was America's manifest destiny to be a world leader.

Her orders were to go to Switzerland, where she would be given a new identity, and with a new name and new passport, she was to sneak behind enemy lines. But her fantasy of high drama was erased when the Germans called for an armistice. Along with most of the world she felt relief; nevertheless, she also felt disappointment. She paced the floor waiting to hear from MI, but knew in her heart that her efforts were no longer needed.

As Woodrow Wilson told Congress: "We know only that this tragic war, whose consuming flames swept from one nation to another until all the world was on fire, is at an end." It was too soon to assess the outcome.

The world lost twenty million people in the Great War, and although governments around the globe suppressed the news, tens of millions more died from an outbreak of influenza. Those who survived lost their footing: regimes were toppled, revolutionaries seized power. Hunger, disease, and unemployment took hold, pushing desperate people to overthrow their governments. Empires crumbled like chunks of coal into ash. Fatigued from the battlefield, haggard from starvation and the search for scraps of food, demoralized by the disappearance of jobs, men and women young and old, peasants and townspeople, uniformed and civilian, searched for answers. What would come next?

The call from Marlborough Churchill took her by surprise. She was to go to Paris, where the peace talks were soon to begin, report to Colonel Alexander Coxe, speak to no one else, and receive her new orders.

CHAPTER 2

Undercover

Masses of Very Important People filled the French city. Presidents and prime ministers flanked by their minions, four-star generals and full admirals bursting with brass, discreet diplomats and inconspicuous spies, tense note takers, anxious interpreters, and pink-cheeked clerks had all gathered for the discussions. Seated at long tables in chandeliered halls, huddled in quiet corners of hotel bars, or convening on slushy streets, they were there to discuss the aftermath of the war. The subject on every agenda, whether written or implied, was: how will the winners be rewarded and how will the losers pay?

From the point of view of the American president, Woodrow Wilson: "There shall be no annexation, no contributions, no punitive damages" for the enemy. "National aspirations must be respected," he said, "'self-determination' is . . . an imperative principle of action, which statesmen will henceforth ignore at their peril."

France, England, and Italy had harsher ideas. The French, led by Prime Minister Georges Clemenceau, were still licking their wounds over their bitter defeat by the Germans in 1870; the British, led by Prime Minister David Lloyd George, and the Italians, headed up by Vittorio Emanuele Orlando, were carrying long lists of grievances from the more recent, very rotten war.

With all due respect to President Wilson, whatever the end results, certain information was needed to make judicious decisions on reparations, limitations, and amends. But the disposition of Germany was unknown. Under direct orders from General Churchill, now working in Paris, Marguerite Harrison was to assess the weaknesses and strengths of the enemy.

Her assignment was to determine with an objective eye the political, economic, social, and psychological conditions in Germany. Who was in power and who was most likely to take control? How strong were the socialists? The Bolsheviks? The centrists? How much food was available? How much fuel? How productive were the factories? What was the mood of the people? How did they feel about making peace? Would the Germans feel remorseful or recalcitrant? Humbled or humiliated? Would they seek retribution or renewal? With her covert assignment imprinted on her mind, and her typewriter close to her side, she arrived in Berlin under cover as a special correspondent for the *Baltimore Sun*.

.   .   .

After she finished working in her room, scouring the newspapers, clipping some articles and translating others for her MI reports, Marguerite left her hotel and sauntered onto the Unter der Linden, not far from where Käthe Kollwitz had stood. There was much she wanted to do, but because of the fighting, the Wilhelmstrasse was barricaded and government bureaus, cold and dark from lack of heat and electricity, were shut. She had a list of people to contact and offices to visit for her press pass and papers; they would have to wait. Instead, she wrapped her coat tight against the January chill and strolled the city, observing the mood of the people.

Her orders had been to analyze who was in power, who was a threat, who would come out on top. The popular street was a good place to start. How different it was from Paris, where she had stopped before coming here; the French capital ached from months of aerial bombardments and cannon assaults. The Place de la Concorde and other hallowed areas were strewn with guns, tanks, shrapnel, and the shards of conflict. The facades of some buildings, like the faces of some soldiers, had been blown off; other buildings under construction stood half naked and abandoned.

Oddly, the war had left Berlin unscathed. No enemy bombers had strafed the city, no Allied tanks had touched its avenues. Yet, here too, a pall of mourning covered the streets as widows and mothers grieved for their lost men, and the men who returned home hunted for jobs and rummaged for food. The city was filled with detritus of another kind.

The light that Käthe Kollwitz had seen at the end of the tunnel was clouded with gunpowder; the air suffused with the smell of death. War had come on its own terms, from the German people themselves. Steel-helmeted soldiers stood with fixed bayonets, grenades in their hands, machine guns at the ready. Blood still smeared the sidewalks, and traumatized veterans sat on the ground like the living dead.

Marguerite walked past mournful widows and children shrunken from hunger, past angry strikers and fuming demonstrators, past curious onlookers and confused observers, and inserted herself into their groups, a *frau* easing her way into their conversations. She heard denials that the Germans had been defeated by the Allies, despair that the Kaiser had stepped down, disgust with those who still wanted a monarchy, mutterings against the Jews, and utter dread of the Bolsheviks. If she heard nothing else, it was clear that the German people felt it was the end of the world as they knew it. But as Kollwitz had said, it may have held the promise of something better.

.   .   .

The Social Democrats in charge of the provisional government had pledged universal health care and free elections for all German citizens, male and female, from the age of twenty-one. Voting was called for January 19, 1919, marking the start of German democracy: it was the first election for representatives to the new parliament and the first time that German women were permitted to vote. American women had not yet won universal suffrage, and Marguerite was eager to watch the historic event in Berlin.

Smoothing the way with butter and chocolates, she was already friends with Johanna, her lively chambermaid at the Hotel Bristol, and on Sunday they went together to the polls in Charlottenburg. Despite the soldiers in the streets, long lines had already formed. With so many men killed in the war, the queue they joined was composed mostly of widows and grieving mothers, some poor and wearing old coats made of rabbit, others well off in mink, some with clear opinions of the candidates, some with no idea whom to vote for.

A woman in the line told her that there were three men in her household, and each one favored a different politician: she was so confused, she could not remember which name to choose. One thing was for certain: the turnout was huge, and all were eager to cast their vote. Marguerite could report that the most popular group was the center Catholic party, and that German women were no more conciliatory than the men.

As soon as the government offices reopened, she headed to the press bureau. The endless questions about how and why she was in the city tested her patience, but knowing a misstep could cause her serious problems, she flashed a smile, piled on her charm, and kept her temper in check. A few hours later she possessed her press card, a Berlin residency permit, and a ration card needed to purchase weekly provisions: a half pound of meat, three ounces of barley, less than an ounce of butter, a little margarine, and some bread. It was no wonder Johanna was pleased by her gifts of food.

The press card gave her access to government buildings and barricaded streets but did not protect her from government patrols, who saw everyone with suspicion. Soldiers were quick to stop vehicles and question their passengers. One night when Marguerite was crossing the canal where Rosa Luxemburg's body had been thrown, her car was halted. The soldier asked if she was carrying any arms. In a good mood after a dinner with friends, she laughed and answered that she only had two hand grenades.

Her humor hardly pleased the soldier. She was ordered out of the cab while he searched her pockets and her muff. Not finding anything there, he lifted the seat cushions and poked them with his rifle. Still unsuccessful, he cross-examined her until, finally convinced she was innocent, he sent her on her way. In a city boiling with rage, any expedition or digression, even a cab ride or a joke, had its risks.

.   .   .

The struggle for power turned Germans into a family divided in crisis: they may have valued blood over water, had common loyalties and mutual enemies, but rivalries were rampant and jealousies unbridled, and each side viewed the other as an existential threat.

On one flank stood the supporters of the monarchy, former officers and landowners, staunch defenders of the fatherland and their old way of life. Militaristic and aggressive, eager to install a new king and revive the empire, they were ready to throw their fists and aim their firepower at any threats to their turf.

At the other end stood the Bolsheviks who called for radical change. With an intense drive to improve the lives of workers who had suffered under the kaiser's thumb, the Spartacists were ready to take the revolution to the streets. Their Workmen's and Soldiers' Councils, now running the cities, were only the first step. They aimed for a Bolshevik government like the one in Russia.

In the center were the Social Democrats. Like adolescents searching for their identity, they were impatient for their independence, ready to test democracy, but anxious about giving up their past. The fierce belligerence of the leftists threw them off keel, and in their fear, they turned to the right, calling on the Freikorps to stop the Bolsheviks from taking over.

It was Marguerite's goal to meet with them all, assess their strengths, analyze their ideas, and report the information to Military Intelligence. She carried a list of contacts from all sides, names given to her by MI officers and by friends and associates, that ranged from retired officers to young radicals.

Her letters of introduction included a note to Nina Bryce Turnbull, a Philadelphia socialite married to an aristocratic German officer. The well-respected general Hans von Below had led fourteen divisions against the Allies on the Western Front. Marguerite sensed their meeting might be uncomfortable, but she knew it was worth reaching out to them: the couple had many influential friends in Berlin.

With a slight case of jitters, she joined the couple for tea and cakes and found the taste more bitter than sweet, as she met the enemy face-to-face. The white-moustached Prussian, bullet headed and thickly built, greeted her with a stiff bow and a cold shoulder. She stayed silent while the general addressed her with contempt, acknowledging the Americans' weaponry but berating the incompetence of their men, especially at the Argonne. She listened while the tea in her cup went cold.

It was, indeed, the costliest battle the Americans had ever fought, not only in equipment and materiel, but in the loss of twenty-six thousand lives. Yet the Germans had lost even more. In the end, exhausted and demoralized, with over two million dead and twice as many wounded over the course of the war, they had held up a white flag and called for an armistice.

Frau von Below held her nose high and kept her opinions to herself. She was, Marguerite thought, a handsome woman who, before the war, was noted in the social pages of the *Washington Post* for her royal friendships, her lavish wardrobe, and her diamond tiara. Divorced in 1906 and married to von Below a few months later in Buenos Aires, where he was advising the Argentine army, she was a loyal fan of the kaiser and a member of the court. To help the war effort, she told a Dutch journalist, she had taken cooking lessons, and she remarked that the German *hausfrau* had become "the strongest ally of her husband in the field."

The erstwhile American was more condescending than her German husband, angrily scorning President Wilson for joining the Allies and scoffing at the notion that the Germans had lost the war. As irritating as her comments were, Marguerite held back her annoyance and turned on her charm, amiably comparing notes on mutual friends and friends of friends, tossing in a little gossip, bringing her hostess up to date on their lives. Her politesse paid off: a few days later she was invited to dine at their home.

· · ·

The group that gathered at the von Belows looked as stylish as any at a smart Parisian dinner: ladies shimmering in silk evening dresses, jewels sparkling on their ears and arms and around their necks; the men, starched and polished, standing stiff and straight, their hair gleaming with pomade, their moustaches waxed and combed to a point.

The dinner table, equally brilliant, glowed with shiny silver and

Bavarian crystal, and the food brought in by the servants was plentiful and well prepared. But it was the distasteful conversation that caught Marguerite's attention.

The guests, all former officers and their wives, subscribed to the nineteenth-century theory of pan-Germanism, which asserted that all German-speaking people should live under the same red, white, and black imperial German flag. They swore their fealty to the kaiser, followed orders without question, and would proudly lay down their lives for the fatherland. Together with them, Marguerite lifted her glass of *Sekt* to toast the hosts and joined the nationalist conversation. Sipping her German champagne, she nodded and smiled and laughed in all the right places, taking mental notes for the report she would send to MI.

They began their discussion with the Social Democrats, waving them off as left-wing socialists. Their greatest concern, they affirmed, was the Bolsheviks, who were spreading "the poison of the Russian revolution." Like many Europeans and Americans as well, they were convinced that the Communists, with help from Russia, were plotting to invade the West and overthrow its governments.

Between bites, the guests sprinkled spice on their meal, peppering the conversation with anti-Semitic remarks. The Jews, they insisted, were to blame for everything: they were the leaders of Marxist thinking, they had profited from the war, they had caused problems for the economy, and they were behind the new government.

Marguerite kept a cool front while she boiled inside. Some of her father's closest colleagues were Jews, men like Albert Ballin, the Hamburg shipping magnate, who until his recent death had been a strong supporter of the kaiser, and Gustav Wolff, whom she had known from her childhood. The German-born shipbuilder had given her "a lasting friendship and respect for the Jewish race," she wrote. Though Judaism was a religion, not a race, her sympathies were clear.

Still, it was important for her to befriend the von Belows and their guests, to learn more about their thinking and what they planned to do. Showing her interest, she joined her new acquaintances for concerts and cabarets. More often, she dined with them in the best hotels. Food and wine were plentiful for those who could afford it: at the Bristol and the Excelsior, she chose from menus that offered thick soups and eggs, fowl, game, and filet of beef, fresh salads, and rich ice cream smothered in chocolate sauce. On more than one occasion, the oysters slid down like silk, but as she bit into her main course of wiener schnitzel, the talk grew more difficult.

Carefully, she poked at the conversation. Like the Americans, her new friends bit their nails worriedly over the Bolsheviks. In Washington, the very term "Bolshevik Revolution" shook the ground like Vesuvius and officials shuddered in its wake. References to the Red Terror taking place in Russia made them tremble more.

Indeed, before she arrived in Germany, Marguerite was ordered to find evidence against a leading American cartoonist known for his Bolshevik sympathies. The man was promoting Communist propaganda and inciting American troops stationed abroad. But it was believed in Washington and Berlin that containing the Communists was as important as trying to halt their work.

With a little prodding, the German nationalists told her the way to block the Bolsheviks was to use the Freikorps, the volunteer militias growing in their ranks. A militant German response was not what the Americans had in mind. But the nationalists were stalwart, exaggerating the threat posed by the Bolsheviks, using them as the excuse to bolster the German army.

When she dug some more, she unearthed the names of secret societies such as the Deutschen Trutz und Schutz Bund or the Deutsche Bund. Formed by right-wingers, they were made up exclusively of those with pure Teutonic blood. Reporting this to MI, she was ordered to infiltrate the groups and join under a fictitious name. The literature she received from the League of German Men and Women for the Defense of Personal Liberty and the Rights of Wilhelm II made it clear that personal liberty and rights did not apply to Jews.

.   .   .

Like a chameleon who easily changed her colors, she slid from groups on the right to those on the left. Yet, if the dark conduct and conversation of the reactionaries made Marguerite uneasy, the discussions of the radicals also gave her pause. The Bolsheviks' tactics were no less militant, their defiance no more moderate than the angry army of nationalists. She found some comfort, however, in the liberal intellectuals. An introduction to Paul Cassirer, the well-known art dealer, led to invitations to his home and into a stimulating world of prominent artists, musicians, writers, and scholars.

In his gallery Cassirer held exhibitions for artists such as Max Beckmann, Oskar Kokoschka, and Käthe Kollwitz, their modern works all painful reflections on the grimness of war. Cassirer's broad circle included longtime Marxists, left-wing socialists, and moderates like Count Harry Kessler, former German ambassador to Poland, and now a member of the government. At home in Cassirer's dining room overlooking the Hohenzollern Palace, political leaders and thinkers often debated the ideas that set the course for the future.

Her hair cut in a stylish bob, her dress falling fashionably at her calf, her cheeks lightly rouged, and her nails polished red, Marguerite joined other guests at the art dealer's soirees. Drinking coffee or *Sekt* and nibbling pastries in the drawing room, she watched the host, round-faced, cigarette dangling from his lips, glide from one group to another, eliciting "conversation that was always brilliant, often cynical, sometimes witty."

The American journalist, who was well versed in politics and the arts, who knew and interviewed writers, artists, and politicians and could hold her own in clever conversation, called the evenings "the nearest to the salons of the 18th century I have ever seen." Cassirer was a master at provoking exchanges and encouraged his guests to cast their progressive ideas into the churning waters, with the hope that some would stay afloat.

Later, Marguerite passed on the information she garnered from both the left and the right to her contact from MI. Her drop-off point was the Adlon, an imposing hotel with an impressive mansard roof located on the Unter der Linden near the British, French, and Russian embassies. The Adlon had welcomed guests as illustrious as the czar and as industrious as Thomas Edison.

"Spies, counter-spies, and agents were thick as peas in Germany," Marguerite wrote, and the Adlon was their most important haunt, a stewpot swirling with savory and unsavory characters. The English-speaking, frock-coated manager who stood inside the entrance eyeing the visitors and bowing to guests shook her hand and did the same with the foreign diplomats, government agents, journalists, and moles who congregated in the grand lobby. Marguerite often stopped by the busy bar or lounged over a coffee in the palm court, a correspondent seeing old friends and making new ones, and, surreptitiously, an espionage agent delivering her reports to Colonel Bouvier, her contact for MI.

One of those she met was an attractive German woman married to an English naval officer. Under instructions from MI, who believed the lady was a German spy, Marguerite became a friend and frequent visitor to her home. The gracious hostess paid close attention to the Allied officers who were her guests, making sure their glasses were filled and their information flowing. Marguerite listened as well and, taking small sips of *Sekt*, discreetly tossed most of her drinks into a palm plant behind her. Her assignment was to change the course of conversation and stop Allied secrets from escaping Allied lips.

Other sources provided more information, such as the countess Hetta Treuberg, a dark-eyed beauty and friend of Paul Cassirer and Count Kessler who supplied valuable news and introductions to prominent people. Born to a cultured Jewish family, she had been married off in her youth to a titled Bavarian, but his arrogance was overbearing and she divorced him. In further revolt, she openly supported the socialists.

The countess enjoyed playing a role in politics. An intellectual, she knew everyone from the former German chancellor Bernhard von Bülow to Herr Stompfer, the editor of the Social Democrats' newspaper, *Vorwarts*, and from Albert Einstein to radical leftists. Ensconced at the Adlon, she entertained influential acquaintances in her drawing room, organized meetings for political leaders, and introduced Marguerite to anyone she wanted to meet.

At her salon, Marguerite met Theodor Wolff, the liberal editor of the *Berliner Tageblatt,* who helped found the German Democratic Party; George Bernhard, an economist who espoused a mix of socialism and capitalism; and Helmut von Gerlach, pacifist editor of the *Die Velt am Montag,* concerned about the monarchists and the rise of the right wing. She interviewed others as well, including Matthias Erzberger, head of the powerful Catholic Party and the first to propose a United States of Europe.

One of her most valued contacts was Walter Rathenau, the Jewish industrialist whose father had obtained the patent rights for the electric bulb from Thomas Edison. The owner of the General Electric Company of Germany was a capitalist, a socialist, and an intellectual.

She smiled when, at the start of an interview at his office, he offered her a pack of the Virginia cigarettes he kept hidden during the war. With a deep inhale of the rich tobacco, he told her how he felt about the peace talks. He recognized the desire of the French to punish the Germans for the demeaning way they were treated in 1870, he said, but, more important, he trusted the Americans to be fair.

Rathenau supported President Wilson's Fourteen Points and emphasized the urgent need to enact America's plans for peace. He wanted the Allies to understand that without the proper remedies, Germany would collapse, and other countries would fall like dominoes in its footsteps. "Germany is ill with an infectious disease that she will spread to others," he said. It was critical that she be given "food, work, means of communication and means of obtaining credit." Without them, hope would disappear, and anarchy would follow.

The conversation gave Marguerite much to think about, but for many people, their thoughts were only of food. The German people had suffered for years, starting with the Turnip Winter of 1916, when the only vegetable available was the fleshy white root. The combination of the British blockade and a failed potato harvest had brought many to starvation. Meager rations were put into effect throughout the war, and the Allied blockade continued; although peace was now in the air, the working class had little to show for it on their table.

Diners at the Bristol Hotel were indulging in desserts of ice cream coated in chocolate, but factory workers were eating cakes made of potatoes, with icing composed of saccharine and chalk. Marguerite wanted to see for herself what meals were like in an average working home and asked her chambermaid for an invitation to her sister's house. "You couldn't eat our food—*ausgeschlossen*," it's impossible, she replied. But the American journalist, always generous to Johanna, insisted, and was soon invited to the bleak neighborhood of factories and tenements where the family lived.

She wanted to know how it felt to live for a day on rations. Beginning with an early breakfast in her room, she asked Johanna to bring her the same sort of food she had eaten: some slices of black bread made of bran, rye, and straw; marmalade made with beets and apple peel sweetened with saccharine; and ersatz coffee made of acorns flavored with chicory. A glance at Marguerite's windowsill revealed the eggs, butter, and tea she had bought on the black market, but showing restraint, she refused to touch them that morning.

Walking through a maze of alleyways that led from one courtyard to another, Marguerite arrived at the tidy apartment of Johanna's sister and heard an infant's insistent cries. The baby was suffering from dysentery, the mother explained; her breasts were dry because there was little food for herself or for her husband and their two other children, a toddler and a seven-year-old girl.

The only vegetables available for the family were turnips, rough carrots and, occasionally, cabbage, and the bits of meat she could buy were mainly bones. The husband's working hours had been cut because his factory lacked enough fuel, and they gave their allotment of potato bread that night to their children.

The dinner consisted of watery soup with a few slices of carrots and thin shreds of meat, and some boiled potatoes. Yet, "there were plenty of people in Berlin not nearly so well off as this family," Marguerite wrote. She had visited a People's Kitchen where thousands of others relied on only potato soup for daily sustenance. The agony of hunger and despair led to a fury of demonstrations and strikes in Berlin. Yet for some, life went on as if the violence had never happened.

While angry crowds filled the streets, some enjoyed movies at the De Luxe, operas at the Staatsoper, concerts at the Philharmonie, and plays at the Schauspielhaus and the Wintergarten. Marguerite carried out her interviews and continued to build her friendships, and on more than one occasion, she and her friends listened to a chanteuse at the Schwarzer Kater or the Linden Cabaret, or shimmied to Alexander's Ragtime Band on the dance floor, while in the background the sounds of gunfire shattered the air.

In the smartest part of town, shoppers smoothed their hands over the fine linens at Mosse Brothers, compared the new clothes at Tietz's and Wertheim's, the two department stores on Leipziger Platz, and stopped to relax with a coffee and *Apfelkuchen* at Bauer or Josty on the Unter der Linden.

The most stylish women had their clothing made by dressmak-
ers who smuggled the patterns in from France. On the advice of a
friend who confided that Drecoll's, a favorite of the royal court, had
the latest fashions, Marguerite stopped by the pink-swathed shop on
Budapester Strasse.

Mannequins strolled through the salons, showing smart Parisian
styles to prosperous clients. Out of the dressing rooms stepped a well-
known movie star in a form-fitting evening gown made of tulle and
sapphire-blue paillettes; a young matron tried on a red chemise gown
to wear to a spring ball; and a mother watched her not-so-innocent
debutante daughter twirl in a décolleté dress.

The shop's patrons, often enriched by war profiteering and black-
market enterprise, stuffed their closets with new leather shoes, patent leather boots, and brocaded slippers. But not far away, Marguerite
noted, the poor struggled in paper shirts and paper shoes.

Since the Armistice in November 1918, she wrote, "twenty percent of the people were living in luxury, thirty percent were spending
all their income for food, and fifty percent were pretty close to starvation. Half the population was going to bed hungry." She reported on
the disparity of wealth to her superiors at MI in Paris, but American
officials at the peace talks were listening to a different story.

The French were determined to seek revenge on the Germans,
not just for their shaming defeat fifty years earlier, but for the enormous destruction inflicted on France during the Great War. Besides
the heavy damage to Paris, vast numbers of their farms and factories
had been demolished. France had lost more lives than any other country: at least one and a half million were dead, and more than four million were wounded. The cost to the nation, physically and mentally, as
well as emotionally, had been excruciating.

The French government demanded heavy retaliation and restitu-
tion. Although the Americans were asking for reparations of $22 bil-
lion, and the British $120 billion, the French demanded more: $220
billion, nearly twice as much as England. Their vengeance was taking its toll, causing unrest across Germany. Many Germans looked to
America for help.

CHAPTER 3

The Birth of Weimar

The new snow that fell in February brought with it a coating of fresh ideas. In art, in design, and in politics, change was under way. In architecture, Walter Gropius introduced his new Bauhaus school, wiping away the gilded extravagances of empire. Artists including Otto Dix, George Grosz, and Käthe Kollwitz, along with playwrights and composers such as Berthold Brecht and Kurt Weill erased the romantic excess of the royal era, replacing it with realistic portrayals of a world wrenched by war. And in politics, although mayhem replaced the monarchy, out of the rubble of revolution crawled an infant state.

The elections that Marguerite had witnessed when she first arrived culminated in the official birth of the German Republic on February 6, 1919. But the arrival of a democratic parliamentary system led by the Social Democrats was met at first with apprehension, not elation. If in some ways it was a symbol of hope, it was also wrapped with suspicions and doubt. Germany was still a battleground: Bolsheviks continued to fight for a new, radical leftist form of government, and monarchists resisting change continued to fight to maintain the royal order.

In Düsseldorf, Hamburg, and Bremen, government forces, reinforced by the Freikorps, battled against the Spartacists, who encouraged railway workers, factory workers, restaurant employees, and office clerks to go on strike. In Berlin, the threat of violence hung over plans for where to hold the meetings of the new provisional government. After some deliberation, the conference was set in Weimar, the city known for its most famous residents, Friedrich Schiller, who wrote of the inequities of wealth, class, and religion, and Johann von Goethe, the poet and playwright who warned of selling one's soul to the devil.

Marguerite Harrison, the only female foreign correspondent with permission to attend the National Assembly meetings, arrived by special train and made her way through the snow-covered streets of Weimar. The gatherings were taking place at the Goethe Memorial Theater, where Faustian deals could prove fatal. A coalition of centrists was essential for democracy to succeed.

Weaving through masses of people milling outside, she flashed her pink pass to the National Assembly and, like the others who entered, was stopped straightaway, ordered to take off her hat, unpin her hair, and stand still while she was searched for bombs.

Inside, thousands of people filled the hall. She noted the throngs of representatives, including forty newly elected women, lined up politically from right to left and seated at desks that replaced the orchestra seats in the theater. Her interviews with the women representatives were featured in the *Sun*.

Upstairs in the balconies, where dignitaries were assigned, she showed her dark-blue press card and joined three rows of correspondents crammed at long tables. Among the reporters in attendance was her close friend Gordon Stiles, reporting for the *Chicago Daily News*, along with Ben Hecht, also of the *Chicago Daily News*, Sidney Greenwald of the *London Express*, and Arno Dosch-Fleurot of the *New York World*. Her own work entailed stories for the *Baltimore Sun* and the *London Times* as well as covert reports for Military Intelligence. She was pleased to find a spot from which she could hear and observe everything.

An air of expectation filled the theater, and promptly at three p.m. church bells rang and the proceedings began. Looking down at the stage, she watched the leader of the Provisional Assembly, Friedrich Ebert, "squat and dumpy in his tightly buttoned frock coat." A "homely figure" with thick features, moustached, with a rectangular patch of beard on his chin and leathery skin that hinted at his earlier work as a harness maker. Nonetheless, the head of the Social Democrats spoke slowly "with a certain rough eloquence and obvious sincerity," she acknowledged.

Addressing the somber crowd, he declared the German people were "done forever with princes and nobles." In place of royalty, he announced, "We will be an empire of justice and truth." His use of *Reich*, meaning "empire," rather than *Republik*, did not escape her keen ear; she noted he repeated the term *Reich* throughout his thirty-minute speech.

She was pleased to hear Herr Ebert confirm his belief in President Wilson's Fourteen Points and the League of Nations, but he went on to blame the Allies for his country's continued lack of food and supplies. He denounced the French for taking back the coal-mining region of Alsace and declared that Germany would not be a slave to its enemies.

His remarks were met with mixed emotions; socialists booed some of his points and monarchists jeered at others. But his firm stands vis-à-vis the Allies appealed to the German parliamentarians; they cheered his cry for a union of Germany and Austria. A few days later Ebert was formally elected president of Germany and head of state. He chose Philipp Scheidemann as head of government, and Gustav Noske, who called on the Freikorps to fight the Spartacists, as minister of defense.

Ebert's cabinet laid out a program that stressed the immediate negotiation of a fair peace; a relaunch of the economy by "creating peace and order, bread and work"; a democratic structure; and a rejection of Communist-led violence. The buds of a strong democratic state had surfaced: the burden was on the Allies to help make them bloom.

.   .   .

To mark their presence at Weimar, Marguerite joined a group of correspondents and posed for a photograph outdoors. Standing near her on the steps of a government building was Robert Minor, the cartoonist she had been ordered to help convict for sedition. Tall and serious, with dark hair and dark brows, the son of a Texas judge was newly arrived from Moscow, where, it was known, he had been assisting the Bolsheviks, and he was working now in Weimar as a freelance journalist.

Asked about conditions in Moscow, the noted left-winger told a correspondent, "If you're heading for Russia, take my advice and stay out. The whole place has gone crazy." The American looked surprised. "So has Germany," he said. "No," replied Minor, "I know the Russians. And I tell you that the Germans are a fine, sane people—by comparison."

Over the course of three days, Marguerite followed her orders and befriended Bob Minor, showing interest in his activities and offering a sympathetic ear. He told her about his work for the Bolsheviks in Russia, the strength of their party in Germany, and their efforts in America. Later, she wrote up their conversation in a confidential report.

A few blocks from where they met, a different revolution was under way: the architect Walter Gropius was creating the new Bauhaus school. Founded in an old arts institute, its modernist and minimalist philosophy combined craftmanship with art. Its aim was to advance equality among the classes, and to unite the practicality of function with the clarity of form.

The simplicity of Bauhaus design eventually developed into buildings distinguished by right angles and composed of unpainted concrete and glass panes. Those, along with brightly colored paintings of abstract figures floating in space; tubular steel furniture; and geometrically shaped teapots, lamps, and other functional items expressed a new version of freedom and beauty. The spirit of innovation produced by Bauhaus artists such as Mies van der Rohe, Marcel Breuer, and Paul Klee would leave an indelible imprint on art and architecture.

But the opening of the school was two months away, too late for Marguerite to witness. Instead, she left behind the aspirations of Weimar and returned to Berlin where the Spartacists were threatening new attacks.

.   .   .

The latest unrest had begun in Munich, the capital of Bavaria, on February 21, when nationalists assassinated the Jewish Communist Kurt Eisner, a minister in the new government. In response, Sparta-

cists in central Germany declared a general strike that spread, trig-
gering chaos across the country. The turmoil increased fears among
a public already concerned that the Russians were working to spread
anarchy throughout Germany and Europe. The "peace and order"
proclaimed by Ebert were nowhere to be found. Yeats's ceremony of
innocence was drowned. The blood-dimmed tide would follow.

The revolution had not improved the economy, nor had it delivered more to eat. German men struggled to find jobs, and German
women strained to find food for their tables. The country was deeply
in debt, with $35 billion in war loans, and provisions were in short
supply, due in part to the continued Allied blockades. The demoralized citizens had lost their sense of hope. The dreary winter shrouded
dreams and increased despair. No one knew what to do.

In early March 1919, the Arbeiter Rath, the city Workmen's and
Soldiers' Council, hoping to revive the revolution, voted for a general strike. The decision sent twenty thousand people into the streets
demonstrating for higher wages and attacking newspaper buildings.
Berlin became a combat zone.

On the evening of the vote, as shopkeepers shuttered their windows and office managers turned the key in their doors, the city's
trams, buses, and underground trains came to a stop. Store clerks,
office workers, mothers carrying young children and clutching heavy
packages, wounded soldiers hobbling on crutches, and others trying
to reach their homes far from the center of town had no means of
transportation.

In the morning, drivers of droshkies, wagons, trucks, and carts
fitted out their vehicles with benches or plank seats and organized in
the big squares, shouting out their routes for those who needed rides.
Droves of people grabbed a place on the improvised benches and
crude chairs and returned to the main streets, where restaurants and
shops opened to greet them.

Marguerite climbed on one of the wagons, squeezed onto one
of the crowded benches, and rode to the Alexanderplatz. Hundreds
of people stood in groups in the big square, while political speakers,
some demanding greater socialism, others arguing in favor of ending
war loans, took turns defending their case.

Fearful of the strike, the government declared a state of siege and ordered the paramilitary Freikorps to guard Berlin. For four days Berliners withstood a civil war; newspapers were shut, leaving people without reliable information, and troops occupied Leipziger Strasse, the site of department stores and publishing houses. Spartacist fighters, joined by former navy officers armed with mortars and automatic guns, positioned themselves on rooftops and shot at soldiers in the streets. Government airplanes dropped bombs, Freikorps troops fired into the crowds, and machine guns blasted in major squares.

Gangs looted stores, splintered the windows of Tietz's, and shattered a ball-gowned wooden mannequin into sawdust. Marguerite gasped at the horrors and hid in a doorway, shielding herself from a barrage of bullets whizzing by. She shuddered, seeing an innocent man shot and a harmless girl murdered, her head blown to bits.

Later, on a visit to the Santa Maria Hospital, she came face-to-face with many wounded and mutilated men: the worst, she said, were "two boys whose eyes had been cut out with a knife as neatly as you would stone a cherry." By the end of the revolt, over twelve hundred people were dead.

In the midst of it all, the Dada artist George Grosz played with absurdist ideas, plastering the city with posters that asked, "Who has the prettiest legs in Berlin?" and inviting "would-be movie stars" to come to his studio at eight p.m. When a mob showed up, they were ordered to take off their clothes, and the male artists who were already there hid in the kitchen. A few minutes later the kitchen doors opened: the men remained dressed, the rest of the crowd was naked, and a sprawling, drunken orgy began. Too many people were too dazed, too depleted to care; fun was the order of the day. "*Je m'en fous,*" people said, and it was true: they did not give a damn.

During the fighting "Berlin went about its pleasures," Marguerite reported with nonchalance. "If you were invited out to dinner, as I was, you simply made a detour." Taxi drivers changed their routes to dodge machine guns; pedestrians searched for quiet streets to walk along. On her way back from one dinner, unable to find a taxi, she strode bravely through the Tiergarten, watching nervously for robbers active at night in the unlighted park.

Suddenly she heard footsteps and saw a well-dressed young man pass her by, then slow down and let her catch up to him. "May I accompany you home, fraulein?" he asked, not inquiring where she lived. "With pleasure," she replied.

She knew he was looking for a good time, but she was looking for something too: protection in the dangerous park. They strolled together along the Tiergarten, through the Brandenburg Gate and onto the Unter der Linden.

Arriving at the Hotel Bristol, she stopped. "This is where I live, and I am American," she announced. The fellow's mouth dropped as she went on: "I was really rather nervous about that lonely walk through the Tiergarten and I want to thank you for your chivalry in succoring an alien enemy." Later she said, "His face was a study!"

Other nights she taxied with friends to theatrical plays and musical performances. A frequent operagoer, she saw works by Richard Strauss, heard a well-known tenor who had sung at New York's Metropolitan Opera, and listened happily to Max von Schillings's *Mona Lisa*.

As much as she appreciated the performers, she had an acerbic view of the audience. Before the war, formal dress was obligatory, she said, but "the revolution swept away all such conventions. The stalls and boxes were full of plainly dressed bourgeois, elbowing great ladies in furs and satins and the imperial box was usually filled with friends of President Ebert who had formerly occupied places in the peanut gallery."

The performances lasted from 6:30 to 10:00 p.m., and to her disgust, "most of the spectators brought their dinner along—thick sandwiches of black bread wrapped in newspaper, which they munched between acts." Instead of champagne, they chugged beer.

Dramas, comedies, and musicals were all popular. When the Künstler Theatre presented *As You Like It*, she found it "superbly put on," and thought a revival of Hans Pfitzner's opera *Der Arme Heinrich* "delightful." Audiences were so intrigued by the plays that when the Spartacists dropped a bomb on the roof of the People's Theatre, no one budged, and the actors continued onstage.

"Berlin has gone mad for dancing, cabarets, and restaurants," Marguerite wrote. Rich women were spending recklessly on lavish gowns, modish hats, and shoes, ready to flounce on the arms of their escorts into the cabarets at the big restaurants, the tea dances at the big hotels, the nightly public balls, and the fancy balls in the Zoological Gardens. After the lights went out at 11:30 p.m., those in the know went out the front door and returned at the back.

At the Palais de Danse, the band carried on until the early morning as customers shook off their fears, shimmying to ragtime or dancing to the music of John Philip Sousa. It seemed like everyone had a craze for dancing. And drinking. And drugs. Homosexuals, lesbians, transvestites, sado-masochists and pedophiles curled a sinister finger and licked their lips or smacked their whips at the jeweled and furred patrons eager to soak in their sinister world. Anything to escape reality.

Like big-breasted women in corsets pulled too tight, Berliners burst through their restraints, releasing their stress, sliding their bodies together in tangoes and foxtrots, or watching women perform nude in the cabarets, sometimes joining in, eager to break the boundaries.

Ben Hecht, invited to a German army officers' club, watched monocled army officers, perfumed and pomaded and high on heroin or cocaine, show their ardor and kiss openly on the dance floor. At other times, he noted, aristocratic nymphomaniacs with burned and scarred thighs or child prostitutes wearing rouged cheeks, baby doll dresses, and shiny boots were added to the mix.

It felt to many like the country was in shock. Noted Count Kessler in his diary: "The German people, starved and dying by the hundred thousand, were reeling deliriously between blank despair, frenzied revelry and Revolution. Berlin had become a nightmare, a carnival of jazz bands and rattling machine guns."

Late one night when Marguerite and a British officer dashed to the back door at Kuttner's, they declared the secret password, "member of the club," and were permitted to enter. Climbing the back stairs, they made their way through the kitchen and stepped into the ornate red salon where guests were gulping down French champagne as though it were *wasser*.

Foreigners enjoyed the atmosphere as much as the locals, but they were not as welcome; the Germans suspected the Allies were selling them out in Paris. Gustav Noske, minister of defense, lectured Marguerite about the stipulations in the peace talks. Tall and stooped, with a giant black moustache and gold-rimmed glasses, he warned her, "Go home and tell your people that they are to blame for the fact that Bolshevism threatens the world today. Tell the Americans the shameful conditions will make it impossible for us. Unless the Allies allow us to protect ourselves the dam will be broken."

On this particular evening at Kuttner's, Marguerite's date was told that no British officers were allowed on the dance floor, and the pair was forced to leave. A few weeks later Berliners went on a strike of silence against the Americans, refusing to speak with anyone from the United States.

On another night she went to the Blaue Drele with Gordon Stiles, who drank "more *sekt* than was good for him." When the American Stiles became embroiled in an argument with a Bulgarian, he found himself face-to-face with a group of Germans. "It looked like there would be a free-for-all," Marguerite said. Taking matters into her own hands, she convinced them it was only a small misunderstanding, charmed her friend into a taxi, and barely avoided a brawl.

At the movies, which Berliners attended frequently, sex, drugs, and violence permeated the screen. "To sit through one of these was to wallow in filth," she said. "There was no vice too low, no situation too nasty to be exploited."

Even the Adlon, official home to the Allied officers, served as a den for wheelers and dealers. Currency traders and drug sellers offered her big commissions to smuggle out their goods, as did airplane motor inventors and playwrights, and owners of jewels who hoped she would find them buyers in New York and Paris.

"Everywhere there was a breakdown of standards," she wrote. "The big demand for luxuries" and the craze for dancing were "an indication of the widespread demoralization in Berlin. It was appalling to me."

If Germany was to return to normalcy and become a member of the family of nations once again, she advised, it had to be treated like a person who had had a nervous breakdown and "given a chance to come back and recover her balance."

In every report she sent to Military Intelligence, she stressed her concerns: "The Germans would recover eventually but whether with a warped mind would depend on their treatment by the Allies."

In the midst of it all, rumors swirled like sandstorms: One journalist heard that Trotsky was coming from Russia on a black horse to lead the Bolshevik Revolution; others claimed a member of the monarchy would return, perhaps on a white horse, to run the empire. Socialists moved further to the left to side with the Spartacists; Social Democrats moved nearer to the right, relying on the Freikorps to prevent a Red Terror like the one occurring in Russia. The fanaticism of the left-wing revolutionaries was no less dangerous than the fervor of the right-wing reactionaries.

At the Paris peace talks, officials spread stories to the American press encouraging fears of Russian activists. Headlines with Paris datelines cried out that Bolshevism was spreading, that Communist propaganda was proliferating, and that extremist socialists were encouraging revolution in America.

Isolationism replaced globalism as Americans shrank back, fearful that the radicals, helped by labor movements, would overthrow the United States government. Nationalism took hold in Congress, where the Republicans refused to accept President Wilson's proposal for a League of Nations. Feelings were so strong that members banged their fists at the idea. "American questions shall be settled by Americans alone," Henry Cabot Lodge, Republican chairman of the Foreign Relations Committee, told Congress.

In Germany, Marguerite was tasked by MI with assessing how much support the Communists had gained and how great a role the Freikorps played in stifling the insurrection. People were concerned where the clash would lead. Marguerite worried about real revolution.

Her reporting led to a series of newspaper articles for the *Sun*, forwarded to the paper by Dennis Nolan, chief of staff for the American Expeditionary Forces in Germany. In an accompanying letter to Marlborough Churchill, Director of Military Intelligence in Washington, he stated: "Mrs. Harrison has proved to be a most valuable agent. Her reports are full of information largely derived by conversation with officials of the German government." Those officials included a wide range of leaders from left-wing socialists to centrists to right-wing nationalists.

Naturally, she discussed the political situation with other correspondents. Her circle included Karl von Weigand, the German-born correspondent for the *New York Sun*, whom she considered a valuable source of guidance, George Young of the *London Daily News,* and Ben Hecht of the *Chicago Daily News.* She was also close to Gordon Stiles of the *Chicago Daily News.* He had been a flyer for the British army during the war and they became intimate friends, sharing the pleasures of good food, theater, and concerts, and even escaping the city for weekend respites together in the country.

As much as she enjoyed his company, she never allowed herself to become enmeshed in her emotions. She dined and danced and flirted as readily as a moth darts around a flame, but refused to fly close enough to be burned. She did, however, feel the need for female companionship and mentioned this at lunch one afternoon with George Young. In her early days at the *Sun,* she had made friends with the society editor, Mary McCarty, and, so long as Marguerite was in Baltimore, they remained chums. But after several months away with only male colleagues in a war-torn foreign country, she longed for a female confidante. When George Young suggested she contact his British acquaintance, Constance "Stan" Harding, she jumped at the chance. Little did she know she was jumping into a quagmire.

CHAPTER 4

Entanglements

On the one hand, Mrs. Stan Harding Krayl, as she was known in Germany, and Mrs. Marguerite Harrison had much in common. Well bred, well educated, and well traveled, both were reddish-haired beauties with mischievous gray-blue eyes, engaging smiles, and keen intellects. They were both fluent in French and German and interested in the arts, and both worked as journalists. Both were alone in Berlin: Stan, because she was seeking a divorce from her husband, a German doctor; Marguerite because she was widowed and working.

Each of them was rebellious and unafraid: As a young woman on holiday in Florence, Stan Harding broke away from her controlling parents and fled to a group of English expats. It made her feel "like a song-bird released from a cage." Marguerite broke away from her mother's social ambitions by marrying Thomas Bullitt Harrison.

Scion of an elite Baltimore family and twenty-five years old when she first laid eyes on him, Tom Harrison was considered the handsomest bachelor in Baltimore. Tall and strongly built, he rode well, danced like a dream, and was adored by all the debs. He was a regular, "a member," of the bachelor balls, who stood attired in his tailcoat, aloof from anyone on his trail.

Twenty-year-old Marguerite Baker, a ripe, bright-eyed beauty and one of the "birds" at the debutante cotillion, stood out from the others in her blue tulle gown sparkling with silver. She claimed she had no serious interest in Tom, but his apathy was a conundrum and she took his disinterest as a dare.

The competition was keen. An abundance of rich, pretty girls would do most anything to win him over. It was known that he had already broken off one engagement, but then again, so had Marguerite. She was determined to snag a fiancé before the winter was over, and Tom was her target. "I had chosen my victim," she said. She made up her mind to use the same tactics on Tom that he used on all the girls. While the others threw themselves at his feet, she "snubbed him, abused him, ignored him." Her wicked methods just might work.

She lured him in, and then treated him with detachment. He sent her flowers and she thanked him politely; he took her for drives and she smiled sweetly; he asked her to dances and she accepted, then sometimes broke the dates and showed up with someone else. "He was piqued by my indifference," she said.

The cooler she acted, the more heated his interest until, finally, he succumbed and fell in love with her. It was a surprise to Marguerite that the better she knew him, the more she found him "gallant and chivalrous," "loveable and charming." It wasn't long before she fell madly in love with him. In the early spring they told her parents they wanted to marry. Her father noted calmly that she was still young and might change her mind. Her mother reacted more sharply. She "ranted, raved and stormed and had hysterics," said Marguerite.

Tom may have come from a prominent family, but he was five years older than her and his bank account was slim. True, he had a circle of rich friends and good connections. But he was a struggling stockbroker, not a landed nobleman, as her mother would have preferred. As far as Mrs. Bernard Baker was concerned, Tom was "a nobody." Like the popular Houdini performing his magic tricks, she would have liked to make Tom disappear. Instead, for the second time she made her daughter vanish by dragging her off to Europe.

When they returned to Maryland, Marguerite found her charming fiancé as warm and caring as ever. He was the love of her life, she realized, and she was his love, his "Mardie." They looked forward to their future together. But her mother put up barriers at every step along the way. When she tried to entice her daughter with a Scottish marquis, Marguerite laughed it off and helped the man get drunk. When her mother stormed around the house, Marguerite hid in the closet. When she threatened suicide, Marguerite barricaded herself in her room.

Her mother's theatrics reached the breaking point. The couple announced to her father that they were going to wed and offered a choice; they would either be married with her parents' permission, or they would elope. When Elizabeth Baker realized she might not even have the chance to produce a wedding, she conceded and spared no expense.

Marguerite selected a bridal wardrobe and gown fit for a princess: her trousseau of forty outfits included elaborate silk sleepwear, morning peignoirs and jackets, and afternoon lingerie dresses of linen and lace embellished with ruffles and bows; reception gowns and loose tea gowns, dinner dresses, décolleté evening dresses, and lavishly decorated ball gowns; twenty-four hats; nineteen pairs of shoes; and gloves, belts, shawls, and enough handbags to accessorize each outfit. For her wedding gown she chose a dress of heavy ivory satin embellished with Belgian lace, set off with a veil that floated from the crown of her head to the hem of her train.

A brilliant Baltimore sun gleamed on Marguerite Elton Baker the morning of June 5, 1901. With her father, who just returned home from England while arranging a merger with J. P. Morgan, standing beside her, the bride posed at the entrance to the Emanuel Protestant Episcopal Church. White roses and lilies blossomed everywhere, from the bride's bouquet to the bunches tied with white ribbons attached to the end of each pew, forming a path to the masses of flowers on the chancel. A chorus of the Wedding March from *Lohengrin* rang out, and ten bridesmaids in yellow dresses and white picture hats alongside ten groomsmen in tailcoats marched down the aisle.

Beatific in her satin bridal gown and lace veil, her auburn hair crowning her face, her eyes dancing like soft clouds in a dazzling sky, with her hand on the arm of her father, Marguerite glided down the carpeted path.

Reaching the altar, she stood alongside the adoring groom, and as the chorus sang out "O, Perfect Love," they were officially wed by two reverends and blessed by the bishop. Newly anointed husband and wife, Mr. and Mrs. Thomas Harrison returned down the aisle while a grand chorus from *Aida* filled the church. At a cost of sixty thousand dollars, the wedding was one of the most sumptuous ever held in the city.

A breakfast followed at the Bakers' brick town house on St. Paul's Street, where the rooms were adorned with roses and marguerites, and the stairs were covered in laurels. The bride and groom welcomed the guests in the drawing room and then led them upstairs, where twenty-four people were seated at the bride's table, others at small tables scattered around the room. Family and friends feasted on oysters and birds, the bride cut the first slice of wedding cake, the couple was toasted with champagne, and cablegrams including congratulatory messages from the Lord Chief Justice of England and the famed British actor Sir Henry Irving were read aloud.

Among an array of gifts laid out for show, the guests ogled a pearl collar necklace with diamond clasp from the groom and strands of pearls with diamond bows from the father of the bride; unseen was a thousand-dollar check from her grandfather Elias Livezey. The festivities concluded, the bride and groom waved farewell and left on her father's ship, *Knight Commander,* for their three-month, round-the-world honeymoon while Elizabeth Baker collapsed in her bed. The relationship between mother and daughter had sunk to its nadir.

.   .   .

Mr. and Mrs. Tom Harrison settled into their new four-story town house on elegant North Charles Street with a cook, a maid, and a new perspective. Pregnant just days after their wedding, Marguerite, who considered travel an indispensable part of her life, fixed her attention on home. Her interests, once worldwide, turned domestic.

Rather than reading literature she read recipes; in place of concerned conversations on foreign affairs, she focused on sewing curtains and cushions and making her own clothes. No longer staying at grand hotels and viewing the latest art exhibitions in Paris and London, she went shooting and fishing with Tom, bagging piles of canvasbacks, spending weekends in a rough cabin on the Eastern Shore. And instead of flirting with men, she doted on her husband and her son, Tommy, born in March 1902.

While Tom Harrison worked to build his brokerage business, Marguerite took on the role of a proper young married: she played the piano with exceptional skill, made a good partner at bridge, entertained graciously, and dished up gossip over lunch with the ladies. Monday nights she and Tom attended the "germans," the society dances where they waltzed, danced the quadrilles, and joined in the party games. Some evenings they attended concerts and theater; other times they welcomed guests at home or dined at the homes of friends.

As expected in their set, she volunteered for charity work. Following in family footsteps, she worked first for the Home of the Friendless, but the cause's "mournful name" disheartened her. Bored with the Volunteer Nurses, she started a charity of her own.

After learning that children hospitalized for long stays were not receiving their education, she raised funds for their cause: she leaned on her father to donate part of a large farm he was selling, beseeched friends to contribute money, organized bake sales, and borrowed furniture. With the help of her son's physician, in 1905 she opened the doors of the Children's Hospital School. It became one of her proudest achievements.

Despite occasional troubles, from the time of her marriage and for more than a decade, Marguerite was completely absorbed in her own domestic bliss. The debutante who once chatted with princes was now more engrossed in family matters. The young woman who once sparkled as an intellectual now cared more about the sparkling crystal on her table. The lady concerned with international issues now gossiped about local affairs.

One of those affairs, and the most important political event for Baltimore, took place in June 1912 when the National Democratic Party held its convention in the city. The Harrisons' good friend Albert Ritchie, a groomsman at their wedding and afterward the husband of Marguerite's sister, was active in the party and invited them to attend.

Marguerite was intrigued by the political machinations taking place at the Fifth Regiment Armory. She listened to the brilliant orator William Jennings Bryan, who declined the offer of vice president, and she heard Governor Woodrow Wilson of New Jersey, the dark-horse candidate who won the party's presidential nomination. He had been, she noted dryly, "an undistinguished classmate of my distinguished father-in-law at Johns Hopkins."

Other than the convention, there was little beyond daily life that roused her attention: she had caught the brass ring and remained content riding the carousel. She and Tom may not have been as rich as some of their friends, and certainly not as rich as her mother would have liked, but they lived on his earnings and money did not concern her. She was an heiress, after all. Some day, she knew, she would inherit a substantial sum from her father and grandfather. The couple never thought to save, never worried about the rainy day. They had their love and that seemed enough. But rumbles of war brought the carousel to a halt.

. . .

Ever since their victorious battles against France in 1870, the German states, under the guidance of Prime Minister Otto von Bismarck, had been united. At the Hall of Mirrors in Versailles, where the German conquerors announced their demands while the French hung their heads in shame, Bismarck declared Wilhelm II the kaiser of a new German empire. The domain brought together the areas of Prussia, and its capital Berlin, in the east; Bavaria, with Munich as its capital, in the south; Hanover in the west; and Holstein in the north. Combined, "they had become a world power and demanded their share of world markets and raw materials," Marguerite explained.

For years she had heard friends in England talk about the Germans' need to expand economically, though they insisted on England's need to keep control of the seas. She knew that the kaiser was ready to rattle his saber at England or France or Russia or any given country at any hour of the day, but it was said that he feared confrontation and did not want to fight a war.

Then, on June 28, 1914, her attention turned to faraway places. Americans learned that a nationalist student with an unpronounceable name committed an appalling act in an obscure European city against two people with incomprehensible titles.

The Austrian archduke Franz Ferdinand and his wife, the Duchess of Hohenberg, who earlier that same day had escaped a bomb attack, were killed in a double homicide. The murder took place in Sarajevo, Bosnia, and was carried out by Gavrilo Princip, a Serbian member of a terrorist organization called the Black Hand.

Around the country, headlines proclaimed the news: "Peace of Europe Endangered by Servian Hate," cried the *Baltimore Evening Sun*. "Heir to Austrian Throne, Archduke Ferdinand, and his Wife Slain by Assassin," said the *Washington Post*.

For Marguerite the significance of the Austrian assassination was clear. The double murder changed everything. Not only were the Balkans familiar to her, she knew Bismarck had predicted that "some damn foolish thing in the Balkans" would set off a great European war.

As days passed, she watched tensions increase. The world waited to see if Austria, which had seized control of Bosnia from the Ottoman Turks, would declare war on Serbia, which wanted Bosnia for itself. Leaders worried whether Germany would come to the aid of Austria, with which it had signed an agreement, and whether Russia, which supported the Serbs, or France, which had lost land to the Germans, would become involved, and, if so, whether those two countries, signatories to a pact, would ally against Germany. The assassination was, Marguerite believed, one of the most momentous events in history.

.   .   .

One month after the murder of its heir apparent, Austria took its revenge. On July 28, 1914, it declared war on Serbia and the next day it bombed the Serbian capital, Belgrade. That same day Russia mobilized forces on its border with Austria, and on August 1, 1914, Germany declared war on Russia. All of Europe was on the brink of war.

Hungry for information, Marguerite followed events in Europe "with passionate interest." As she read the news, she thought of people she knew throughout the Continent. Along with her close friends in England and France, she felt deeply for her "beloved Austrians," even knitting socks for them, and cared about "all the gentle, kind Germans" she had known.

As concerned as she was with events in Europe, nothing brought home the war more than a telegram from Tom. She was on vacation in Atlantic City with her son and her mother-in-law when, a few days after the start of the fighting, her husband sent her a message to say that the New York Stock Exchange had shut down. Worried that the new technology of wire cables would speed worldwide sell-off orders on U.S. stocks, and that U.S. businesses might be forced to pay back the vast sums of money they had borrowed from Europe, the members of the stock exchange moved defensively and, like countries around the world, stopped their trading.

Tom's income derived from his commissions as a stockbroker, and his earnings were already suffering from the long, steep drop in the market caused by the recession in 1913. Now, with the stock exchange closed and not opening until four months later, in December 1915, his business came to a halt. The Harrisons found themselves with little cash to cover their expenses. To make ends meet, they rented out their house, Marguerite started a home decorating business with a friend, and Tom made some high-risk investments, using large amounts of money borrowed from his sister.

It was an uneasy time in their life, and Marguerite was aware of the pressure on her husband. As a young boy, he had suffered the tragic loss of his father, who, tormented by severe losses in the stock market, his mood blackened by depression, had committed suicide. If Tom was not as lively now as he had been when his earnings were strong, Marguerite understood.

It surprised her, nonetheless, when her spirited husband, a dedicated sportsman, became lethargic; ordinarily proud of his good health, he started complaining of pains over his left eye. As the days and weeks wore on, his personality changed drastically, and she felt hurt that the man she knew, sometimes quick tempered with others, was turning violent at home, lashing out at her and their son in brutal temper tantrums.

In February 1915, her mother died. Marguerite had dismissed their relationship years before. "I admired her very extravagantly," she said. "I thought she was beautiful," but "she often suppressed her feelings and seemed cold and exacting. . . . Perhaps if she had loved me less and petted me more it would have been better for both of us."

She felt little emotion over her mother's death and focused her thoughts on Tom. In April, when he complained of excruciating headaches, she was taken aback.

After consultations at Johns Hopkins Hospital with several doctors who could not identify the problem, Tom was sent to see Harvey Cushing, the foremost brain specialist in America. It was then that

Marguerite understood the seriousness of his illness. Tests showed a tumor on the brain, and over the course of six weeks he underwent ten difficult operations that affected his mind and left him partially blind and paralyzed.

As his condition worsened, Marguerite moved into the hospital to be closer to Tom. Before one of the surgeries, she turned to her husband and asked if he wanted her to be with him while he was given the anesthesia. "I want you with me always," he answered. "Those were the last intelligent words he spoke," she said later.

His death was devastating. Unable to accept that he was gone, she fell into a state of denial and refused to admit to her fourteen-year-old son that his father had died; rather, she told him Tom had taken another form. When she realized what she was saying, she questioned her own words and asked herself if she was feeding lies to her son. But she could not allow herself to think logically, and she could not let herself feel the loss. She felt no anger, no sorrow, nor any other emotion. She was dazed.

"I mustn't think. I mustn't feel," she told herself. "I have suffered too much. I will never suffer like this again. I think I am numb, quite numb. I must stay that way, I must not care for anyone like that again." As a result, she distanced herself from her son as her mother had distanced herself from Marguerite.

Despite separating herself from her mother and her sister, whom she mostly ignored, she had managed to have good friends who were women. Now, a few years later, alone in Berlin, she yearned for a female companion, someone of her own gender to confide in. When George Young suggested she get in touch with Mrs. Stan Harding, she was delighted.

The Englishwoman was in desperate circumstances, living in a chilly boardinghouse room. Her daring spirit and tales of adventure intrigued the American, who helped her with food and money and invited her out for meals. Over lunches and dinners together, they discovered they had much in common.

The attractive Mrs. Harding, whose close-cropped hair set off her fine nose and mouth, smiled brilliantly as she told tales of her exploits as a reporter for an English newspaper and as a spy for British Intelligence. Although she was now unemployed, she shared with Marguerite a deep interest in political issues and a determination to find the truth. She planned to write a book about China, where she had visited her brother, a British diplomat, and also hoped to open a shop for interior decoration, which Marguerite had done before Tom died.

But there were sharp differences in their lives. While Marguerite Baker had married at twenty-one and settled into the familiar surroundings of Baltimore society, Stan Harding, visiting Italy at age twenty-two, agreed to marry an older German man, but only if he consented to separate lives. Living apart from him in Florence, she wove her way into the avant-garde tapestry of artists and patrons. An aspiring artist herself, she befriended women such as the writer and traveler Janet Ross, and the arts patron Mabel Dodge, and met the collectors Gertrude and Leo Stein, the pianist Arthur Rubinstein, and the actress Eleanora Duse.

Whether at the Villa Medici, home to Mabel Dodge, or I Tatti, the villa of art connoisseur Bernhard Berenson, Stan Harding made friendships that bordered on scandals and sought thrills that put people in harm's way. Her suspected romances with women including Mabel Dodge and Käthe Kollwitz; her known affair with Isadora Duncan's lover, the theater director Gordon Craig; her abortion to end a pregnancy with the artist Stephen Haweis, husband of English artist Mina Loy; and her attempt to snatch the journalist John Reed away from the arms of Mabel Dodge all raised eyebrows.

Her friend Käthe Kollwitz called her "a courageous Englishwoman," noting that Stan carried a black gun in her pocket during a monthlong trek they made together across the Italian mountains. Nonetheless, said another acquaintance, she divided friendships, alienated people, and caused trouble. Wherever she went, "she slithered in and out like an adroit little snake." Still, to Marguerite, who may not have heard these stories, the introduction seemed like a good idea.

In the years leading up to the World War, she had spent time in China, trekked to India, where she took up dance, and then traveled to Berlin in 1918 to pursue a divorce. Suspected by the German government of being a spy for the Italians or the English, and unafraid to say she was a socialist, she had tried to find work. But even with the help of Käthe Kollwitz, she failed. Her small income had come as payment for news stories she gave to the foreign correspondent for the *London Daily Express*.

With introductions from Mrs. Harding in Berlin, Marguerite made valuable contacts including high-ranking British officers, German socialists, and Communists. Stan's left-wing credentials eased the way for Marguerite to attend meetings of radical groups and report on their plans. At one point she even joined the Socialist party, an act with consequences she would come to regret.

Shortly after the two women met, the plague of strikes in Berlin in early April caused people to feel the situation was worse than the January Revolution. "I had never known there could be so many different kinds of strikes," Marguerite said. "There were transportation strikes, employees' strikes, day laborers' strikes; strikes for shorter hours, higher wages, better working conditions; political strikes, protest strikes, sympathy strikes, counterstrikes."

Street battles between the socialists, who were demanding increased pay, and the Spartacists, who were intent on overthrowing the government, turned so dangerous that Marguerite was ordered by MI to move to the Adlon Hotel, where American military officers and others from the Entente, were based. She offered to share her spacious new quarters with Stan Harding, assuring her she did not have to pay, and the two became roommates.

By mid-April 1919, the fighting in the city calmed down, but new problems arose in eastern Prussia. Marguerite was ordered to travel to Danzig and Silesia to report on the situation; Stan Harding remained in Berlin.

CHAPTER 5

Ominous Hints

Eastern Europe was a source of concern for both the Allies and the Germans. In accordance with the Fourteen Points and President Wilson's emphasis on self-determination, Poland, led by the patriotic musician Paderewski, declared its independence. But the demands that went with independence raised serious problems for Prussia, the area of the Weimar Republic that stretched from Danzig in the northeast to the Saar valley in the southwest.

Warsaw remained the capital of Poland, as it had been for centuries, but the demographics were ill defined: the city was composed of Slavs, but the population around it included both Prussian Germans and Slavic Poles. The newly created country of Poland contained the provinces of Posen, part of Germany since the mid-eighteenth century; Krakow, which had belonged to Austria for almost as long; and parts of Russia that had broken away from Bolshevik rule.

The Polish government insisted that in order to survive economically it required possession of the vast coal mines in upper Silesia, and it needed a narrow stretch of land along the Vistula River. The river flowed from Krakow in the south, to Warsaw in the middle, to Danzig, which had been the largest grain market in Prussia, in the north. Polish control of the corridor along the Vistula gave the country its only access to the Baltic Sea.

That crucial area, however, sliced through Prussia, dividing it into east and west, and it was unclear to the Americans if the people who lived on the eastern side of Prussia, in the new Poland, were primarily Germans or Poles. Although Danzig itself had been part of the German empire, the population in the towns nearby was primarily Polish. Marguerite was tasked with analyzing the mindset of the people and the viability of the situation. "It was," she said, "one of the most knotty problems of the Versailles Conference—the German-Polish question."

"From the moment of my arrival at Danzig, I felt as though I had stepped into the old Germany," she said. "The whole country was an armed camp." Interviews with officials revealed that General Hans von Below, brother of her acquaintance Otto von Below in Berlin, commanded a volunteer army comprised of the Freikorps and other groups stationed all the way from Danzig down to Silesia.

In addition, in neighboring Latvia and Lithuania, two more German generals had maintained their forces of half a million men. Not only were their army corps still in place, the generals were also training new volunteer recruits: schoolboys and youths were encouraged to join; socialists and Jews were banned. The excuse for the military presence was similar to what Marguerite had heard from her right-wing dinner companions in Berlin: the loyal imperialists were determined to buttress the area against the Bolsheviks.

As Marguerite traveled the country from Danzig to Upper Silesia, she encountered a mix of Protestant Germans and Catholic Poles; some areas were overwhelmingly German, others mainly Polish, and still others, a jumble of both. She learned that access to the Baltic Sea, so necessary for Poland, would enflame the Prussians and bring about armed conflict with Germany.

With probing questions here and there, she discovered that the three German generals, headed by von Below, were plotting to defy the terms of the peace agreement with the Allies. They intended to secede from the Weimar government and create a separate state that would include the eastern portion of Prussia and Silesia, along with the newly formed states of Latvia and Lithuania. If the generals succeeded with their plans, they would present a threat to the entire balance of Eastern Europe.

Self-determination, which seemed as simple as a stroke of pen on paper, was, in reality, more a signature written in invisible ink. The results caused problems that were not so easily solvable. Indeed, she noted, "self-determination was creating a new nationalism, quite as dangerous as the old imperialism."

She felt angry and frustrated. She had worked "harder than ever before," she said, "to collect information which I hoped would strengthen the hand of the President." But her efforts to "secure a just and lasting peace . . . had been in vain. I felt like a child who builds a sandcastle only to see it undermined by the rising tide."

The material she accumulated on her trip was critical to understanding both the attitudes of the population living in Poland and the alarming plans of the Prussian generals. Her lengthy account was so important she was ordered to report in person to General Nolan, who was based in Trier. As the chief of intelligence at the headquarters of the Allied Expeditionary Forces, he would send the reports to the peace talks in Paris.

But first she stopped in Berlin. Stan Harding was out when Marguerite returned to her room at the Adlon. She took a few minutes at her desk to scrawl a brief report for Colonel Bouvier, and then tore up the copy and thoughtlessly tossed it in the wastebasket.

She wrote a note to Stan Harding, packed some clean clothes, and left. On her way to Trier, mulling over the papers she had thrown away, she realized that "anyone familiar with Intelligence work might have seen that they were an official report," and not a newspaper story.

In her verbal report to Military Intelligence, she delivered critical information confirming the confusion on the ground in Poland; the danger of dividing Prussia; and the size of the army and the strength of the German generals. Most important, she gave details of the generals' plot to secede and the turbulence that it could cause. A few weeks later her analyses of Danzig and Upper Silesia were incorporated in the Paris Peace Conference terms. But more troubling for her was the problem she encountered upon her return to Berlin.

When she opened the door to her room, Stan Harding was seated at the desk. The Englishwoman announced some news so startling, Marguerite said, it "took my breath away." It was clear that Stan had rifled through the trash, read the notes she had discarded, and "realized then and there that they were not rough drafts of newspaper articles." The Englishwoman strongly suggested that Marguerite hire her and pay for information she would provide in the future.

Marguerite was trapped. She may have been naive, or slipshod, or unconsciously showing off when she tossed the pages in the trash, but whatever the reasons, the results were clear: Stan Harding would betray her. The only way out was to pay the ransom. Keeping her composure, she smiled at her roommate, shrugged, and said, "It was very careless of me, but they say that every criminal has a blind spot. Perhaps we can cooperate. I will speak to Colonel Bouvier about it."

The Colonel agreed to go ahead with the arrangement. From then until Marguerite left Germany a few months later, she confirmed that Stan Harding "supplied me with bits of correct and valuable information for which she was duly paid with money furnished me by Colonel Bouvier." She added that Stan Harding was duly recognized and credited by name. But the incident would lead to serious consequences.

. . .

The success of her work in Poland led to orders for Marguerite to visit the Baltics. The overt excuse for her trip was to write about the American Red Cross and its good work in Lithuania. Her covert mission was to assess the area militarily.

Along with Latvia and Estonia, the area of Lithuania, located on the northern border of Poland, had been part of the Russian empire and now served as a bulwark between Bolshevik Russia and the West. Under the kaiser, the Germans had planned to incorporate the three areas into the empire and had sent occupying forces into Lithuania. Once again Marguerite was tasked with reporting on the German troops still stationed in the country and told to investigate the overall situation.

Kovno, the capital of Lithuania, had long been under the czar's thumb. Now the city was independent, but its economy was in shreds. Marguerite registered at the Hotel Metropole, the government's showplace for visiting dignitaries, and found no heat, no hot water, no sheets for the bed, no towels for the bathroom. The only thing it had in full supply was bugs. "When I retired that night, I discovered I had plenty of bedfellows," she said.

Walking around the town, she came across only a few of the ten thousand men in the newly organized Lithuanian army. Far more visible were groups of German soldiers who sauntered through the streets. Speaking with the troops and with local officials, she learned that the Germans were far from eager to fight, and either deliberately avoided any battles or disguised themselves in Lithuanian army caps when forced to confront the Bolsheviks.

Shortly after she arrived, the newspapers announced that the German delegation invited to the peace talks in Versailles had received the terms of the treaty and had been personally treated with contempt. Not only were they installed in a shabby hotel surrounded by guards and barbed wire, they were ordered to carry their own luggage to their rooms and told they could not leave the premises. Most infuriating of all, they were not allowed to negotiate the terms. The Allies, enraged by the brutality of the war with its devastating losses of men and materiel, gave the Germans an ultimatum: they could either accept the harsh conditions and formalize the peace or reject the conditions and return their country to war.

Among the Entente's many stipulations were the return of Alsace-Lorraine and the Saar Basin coal mines to France; establishment of the Saar Basin as an international zone; recognition of Danzig as an international city; and acceptance of most of Upper Silesia as part of Poland. Allied occupation of parts of Germany was to continue until reparations were made.

The German army was to be reduced from a million and a half to a hundred thousand men and conscription abolished; the German navy was reduced to six battleships, six light cruisers, twelve torpedo boats. All submarines and all of the air force were to be eliminated.

Germany was required to accept responsibility for all damages and agree to an initial payment of two hundred thousand marks; German prisoners of war were to be returned, but the officers were to be held as hostages for reparations. As for the League of Nations, Germany must accept its existence but was not allowed to be a member. The severe terms included a special trial to prosecute the former kaiser Wilhelm II and his officers accused of war crimes.

Lastly, the Germans were forced to admit their guilt: "Germany agrees to accept the responsibility . . . for causing all the loss and damage to which the Allied governments and their nationals have been subjected as a consequence of the war imposed upon them by the aggression of Germany and her allies."

Two weeks earlier the German people were celebrating Easter Sunday, watching the sun stream down like rays of hope. Now, the Entente's demands hovered with the weight of storm clouds overhead.

The contempt expressed by France, England, Italy, and the United States negated all that the Germans had envisioned. They had expected President Wilson's principles to be upheld, assumed they would be assured of justice, that they would be dealt with evenhandedly. Instead, they felt deceived. The battle was lost; all that was fair had turned foul.

The Germans believed they had behaved well: they had obeyed their leaders, sacrificed their lives, and fought mightily for their fatherland. They suffered no guilt over a war they did not think they had started and did not believe they had lost; they saw no reason to give up land they had conquered, no cause to disband a military they had built, and certainly no need to pay enormous reparations they could not afford. Resentment and anger rattled their very souls.

At a protest in the Wilhelmstrasse one morning, Marguerite watched a mob of German youth sing "Heil dir im Siegerkranz" ("Hail to thee in the victor's crown"). "This small incident was significant to me. The youth of Germany was turning nationalistic and conservative. The boys who had been children at the beginning of the war and had had no part in it were taking up the banner of the old Germany! They were the forerunners of the Brown Shirts," she recalled.

Wrote Marguerite: "Unless we wake up and face the fact that we're dealing with a defeated, but uncrushed and powerful nation, 25 years from now our children may be asking, 'Who won this war, anyway?'" But the message, which she had sent time and again from Berlin to Paris, had gone unheeded by the men setting the terms in France.

Reading the news of the treaty, the German soldiers in the streets of Kovno expressed their anger by hooting, shouting insults, and threatening members of the Allied missions. The Hotel Metropole was forced to take special precautions, stationing two men with machine guns on guard at the front door. The city warned foreign guests not to leave the hotel.

The American, French, and British missions stayed safely inside, but Marguerite had come to Lithuania to take the temperature of the people and refused to hide indoors. Always curious, and ignoring all advice, she strode past the hotel sentry and mingled with the soldiers on the street. "I heard enough to make me realize they were in an ugly frame of mind," she said.

At the risk of being caught, that evening she pretended to be the wife of a German officer and joined a massive protest at the Municipal Theatre. She listened to people rage against the peace terms and one after another take the podium to deliver their fiery speeches. When the crowd, swollen with pride, rallied to patriotic music, she, the German officer's wife, joined in, singing "Die Wacht am Rhein" ("The Watch on the Rhine"), and the national anthem, "Deutschland über Alles" ("Germany over All"). The night gave an ominous hint of the German future.

For several days afterward she explored the region. Trekking through towns and villages, she came across rage so vicious it shocked her; but the victims were not the Allies; they were poor, scholarly Jews, barely able to eke out a living, crowded into small quarters in dingy neighborhoods.

Anti-Semitism had been building since Marguerite arrived in Berlin. She had seen evidence of it in her newspaper clippings and reported it early on to Military Intelligence, who mostly denied it. Jewish citizens represented all points of view, from right-wing supporters of the kaiser to left-wing supporters of the Bolsheviks; nonetheless, in Germany and Lithuania Jews were used as scapegoats. Peasants, townspeople, and military men accused them of everything from petty thievery to controlling commerce, and from running the government to supporting its overthrow.

The bigotry showed its ugly face not just among the impoverished or uneducated but throughout German society. Even the Bauhaus founder Walter Gropius, later married to a Jewish woman, wrote to his cuckolding wife Alma Mahler about her Jewish lover: "Your magnificence has been corroded by the Jewish spirit. At some point, you will return to your Aryan origins, and then you will understand me and look for me in your memories."

But the most blatant anti-Semitism was carried out by militants. Marguerite visited one Lithuanian village where she witnessed a German officer attack an old man, accuse him of overcharging, and beat him with the flat side of a sword. When neighbors shrieked and rushed out to help, the soldier blew a whistle and called for more troops, who lashed their whips on the crowd of innocent men, women, and children.

Hiding in a house with half a dozen terrified Jews, Marguerite watched the helpless people outside run away, emptying the streets for the brazen soldiers who fired their guns in the air. It was a pogrom, as old as the czarist regimes, and a warning of things to come. She called it "anti-Semitism in its most virulent form," and said, "then and there I began to appreciate the seriousness of the Jewish problem."

In Germany, the problem intensified as groups of volunteers formed anti-Semitic organizations. In search of new members, they advertised their motto, "Germany for the Germans," and posted placards at the University of Berlin. They sought to enlist military men "of pure German blood," they announced, and warned that "no Jews or associates of Jews are admitted."

Those who signed up were trained to march together in formation: older men in their military uniforms, boys as young as sixteen in gray leather-belted jackets, with caps on their heads and puttees tucked in their boots. Their necks stretched high, they stomped with goose steps on their way to routing out Jews and Bolsheviks for the fatherland.

Some groups like the Thule Society in Munich, whose Aryan theories attracted the future Nazis Hermann Göring, Heinrich Himmler, and Rudolf Hess, had small memberships. But overall membership in the secret societies was escalating as the economy languished and unemployment grew. The league Marguerite had joined earlier expanded from a minor group to a major organization with one million members. Their pamphlets stated their goal: "to enlighten the people on the Jewish menace and to fight it with all available social, political and economic weapons. The Bund will work openly, ceaselessly and ruthlessly to break the overlordship of the Jews."

At Bund meetings, German officers asked, "Will you now stand in the front ranks in the struggle for the soul of Germany? Only if we revive the German spirit can we find the path that leads from the abyss to the heights. We need fellow fighters," they declared.

"Gradual disillusionment from sane, well-disciplined, sentimental, un-imaginative people" turned them "into bitter, neurotic, excitable creatures," Marguerite said later. "The seeds of the Nazi movement had been sewn." She noted, "Hitler used substantially the same words at brown shirt meetings."

. . .

At home in the United States, where nationalism was on the rise, "Make America Good" became the slogan of conservatives. Their war against alcohol, tobacco, gambling, prizefighting, and desecration of the Sabbath spread beyond domestic issues. Hatred and paranoia prevailed. The vigilantist movement, which had driven the hunt for German spies when the United States joined the war in 1917, now turned on the Bolsheviks.

Many believed that the greatest threat to the democratic system stemmed from Russian interference. In an attempt to destabilize the United States and foment revolution, they said, the Russians were sending spies to infiltrate America and funding thousands of radicals in the country, giving their agents as much as two hundred million rubles.

Some senators assailed the Bolsheviks for influencing newspapers and accused them of sending dangerous literature through the mails. With slogans such as "The war is over: now for the revolution" and "A little strike today means a big strike tomorrow and a revolution later," the Russians were, indeed, trying to overthrow the government. In its attempt to stop the insurrection, Washington targeted a few key people. One was W. E. B. Du Bois, who spoke out against the vile treatment of Black soldiers when they returned from the war. Another target was one of the most popular political cartoonists in the country, Robert Minor.

CHAPTER 6

Spider's Web

At the start of her trip to Europe in 1919, under orders from Marlborough Churchill, Marguerite had stopped in Paris to meet with Colonel Coxe. He, in turn, sent her to see the man in charge of American counterintelligence, Ralph Van Deman. Long-faced, with long ears, wire-rimmed glasses, thick lips covering protruding teeth, he was as unattractive as Marlborough Churchill was elegant, a grade horse to the general's thoroughbred. In one area, however, he had no peers: he was 100 percent determined to establish a permanent intelligence agency for the army. Through persistence, perseverance, and paranoia, he earned his reputation as the "father of military intelligence."

He envisioned a department with two sections: one, Positive Intelligence, would seek useful information about the enemy; the other, Negative Intelligence, would provide counterintelligence to stop enemy agents from doing harm to America. Van Deman had charge of all counterespionage for the Paris Peace Conference. In particular, he was concerned with damage from the radical left.

Before the meeting with Marguerite, he had been preoccupied with a different matter. His office at 4 Place de la Concorde was close to Maxim's, the chic restaurant on the Rue Royale, where courtesans and their well-heeled escorts clinked their champagne glasses and blew smoke rings into the Art Nouveau air.

Under the colonel's stern rules, the night spot had been placed off bounds for American personnel. But to his embarrassment, a couple of clever men on his payroll had found a trapdoor that led underground from the intelligence offices to the tables at Maxim's.

With the schoolmasterly President Wilson in town, it would not have been wise to turn a blind eye to such shenanigans. Van Deman demanded a padlock on the door and installed a soldier to guard the secret entry. Nonetheless, shortly after his orders were filled, the padlock disappeared, and the entry was reopened. The colonel was not happy.

Van Deman's main concerns, however, were the socialists and Bolsheviks he believed were infesting Europe like bedbugs invading a mattress. He worried that scores of anti-American left-wingers, disguised as members of the press, were working behind the scenes, and he feared that scores more were instigating a campaign to sabotage the army. At their meeting Marguerite agreed to keep an eye out for saboteurs and, with patriotic fever, promised to report to him on suspicious journalists. One, in particular, was high on the list.

The intelligence chief showed her a memo that had just landed on his desk: Robert Minor, one of the most famous and well-paid American political cartoonists, known for his radical sympathies, was suspected of distributing pamphlets encouraging antiwar activities among thousands of American and British soldiers in Europe.

Minor had been in Russia, working on Lenin's editorial staff, writing an English-language newspaper and circulating it to American troops based in the northern Russian seaport of Archangel. The soldiers, initially stationed there to fight the Germans during the war, were assigned afterward to combat the Bolsheviks. But it was believed that Minor was inciting them to oppose America.

From Moscow, Minor was ordered to Germany to help the Spartacists with their cause. Under instructions from the woman who ran the Spartacists' office in Düsseldorf, he had prepared a pamphlet called *Why American Soldiers Are in Europe*. It was meant to fuel discontent and stir mutiny among the American troops.

Minor became a prime target for Ralph Van Deman, who wanted him court-martialed for treason. But he needed evidence. When he mentioned this to Marguerite, she agreed to secure information in Germany that would prove the cartoonist guilty; in addition, she con-

sented to bring him to the American authorities. Her work in counterintelligence began on her first encounter with Bob Minor in February
1919.

During the three days they were together at the National Assembly in Weimar, she encouraged him to talk about the Soviet movement in Russia. He admitted he was affiliated with the Communist
Party, told her about its strength in Germany, and mentioned how it
was developing in the United States. He had high hopes for its growth
at home, and, she informed authorities, he expected "great results
from the contact of our soldiers with radical leaders in France and
Germany. He said that it was an opportunity for enlightenment that
could not be missed."

A month later, after Minor helped organize a Spartacist uprising
in the Ruhr coal-mining region of western Germany, he appeared in
Berlin, where Marguerite met him again. With a discerning question
here and a reassuring nod there, she induced him to lay out his plans.
He spoke about his work in the Ruhr Valley and discussed his relationships with the leading Communists in Germany. The time was
ripe for spreading Bolshevist propaganda among the American soldiers, he told her. Shortly afterward he left Berlin.

Now Marguerite's orders were to meet once again with Minor.
Her assignment was to find the proof that he was directly responsible
for the thousands of inflammatory antiwar leaflets distributed to U.S.
troops in Germany.

Toward the end of June, she boarded a train and headed from Berlin to Coblenz, where Minor was staying in the neutral part of the
city. On her way, she took a detour and stopped in Baden-Baden to
see an old school friend from Baltimore. Mabel Payne had married a
German baron and suffered the consequences of staying loyal to the
United States during the war.

Alone, impoverished, and sickly, she burst into tears when she
saw Marguerite arrive at the train station. The once wealthy Maryland
socialite begged her longtime friend to lend her money. Shocked by
her situation, Marguerite gave her enough to help her get by.

The baroness described the lies that had been told by the kaiser's
government. Throughout the war, she said, the German people had
been deceived into thinking they were winning battle after battle.

Only days before the Armistice did they realize the weakness of their army.

Fed government propaganda, the German women in Baden-Baden were terrified that American soldiers might enter their town and rape them. Marguerite, who in her youth spent family vacations at the spa while her father took the cure, was taken aback by their fear. Later, she conceded that the Germans' propaganda was no different than the Entente's stories of "*Schrecklichkeit*," the terror tactics said to be used by the Germans against Allied civilians during the war.

After saying goodbye to her friend in Baden-Baden, Marguerite headed for Coblenz. At a train station along the way, she caught a newspaper thrown into the compartment and read the headline: the Versailles Peace Treaty had been signed. For the rest of the ride, as the train steamed from one station to the next, she saw Germans on the platforms poring over the news, but "there was little excitement and no jubilation," she noted. Humiliation drained their spirits.

Before she set off on this part of her trip, Marguerite was told to inform Colonel Williams, the military intelligence officer in Coblenz, that she was on her way. Her mission was to lure Bob Minor across the Coblenz bridge from the neutral side of the city to the American occupied zone, where the Americans would meet him. When Marguerite arrived in Coblenz, she discovered a frustrating turn of events: Minor had been put in military prison and refused to see her.

On the hunt for incriminating evidence, she was ordered by MI to visit one of Minor's colleagues, Richard Seidel. A German Communist imprisoned near Bonn, Seidel knew the name of the man who had printed the propaganda leaflets. Her mission was to persuade him to give her the printer's name. She was also instructed to find Seidel's intimate friend, Meta Filip, the Spartacists' head of propaganda, who was based in Düsseldorf. Her first step was to see Seidel in Bonn, eighty kilometers away.

The authorities had made Seidel available to her, but before she could ask him any questions, she would have to win his trust. She anguished over how to gain his confidence. "I was compelled to do something I had never done before," Marguerite confessed. Knowing that he would be wary of divulging information to an American correspondent, she was ordered "to pose as a Socialist," and claimed to be writing for a socialist newspaper. She also professed to be friends with many German radicals and ticked off their names to Seidel. The list was true, she added, but "not exactly in the way I led him to believe."

The ploy worked. Seidel admitted he was a Communist, but insisted he was not the person who had distributed the propaganda leaflets. With that, Marguerite assured him that his name would be cleared: all he had to do was help her find witnesses to testify to his innocence. One of those witnesses was the printer in Düsseldorf, and with much encouragement, she convinced Seidel to tell her the man's name.

In addition, she persuaded Seidel to give her a letter for Meta Filip. The note urged the woman to meet with Marguerite to discuss the case and testify on Seidel's behalf.

Like a cat pursuing a mouse, Marguerite made her way through the cobblestone streets of Düsseldorf, knocking on doors until she found the printer, Mr. Berton. With the mention of Seidel's name, she gained the man's trust and drew out the information she needed: Mr. Berton confirmed he had overseen the printing process for Robert Minor's manuscript and had given Minor sixty thousand leaflets for distribution. Marguerite left with the crucial information safe in her head and the incriminating evidence, a batch of copies, grasped in her hand.

She had completed half her mission. Now she had to find Meta Filip. Before she did, she met with Communist party leaders and learned from them that Robert Minor was not just an affiliate, but an official committee member of the party. She also learned with disappointment that Meta Filip was no longer in Düsseldorf.

With an air of innocence and endless questions, she tracked the woman down to a small village a few hours away. Once again, Marguerite repeated her story that she was a friend of Seidel's and a correspondent for a socialist newspaper. She gave Meta Filip the letter from Seidel and persuaded her that her testimony was essential to save her lover. Furthermore, she insisted, it was important that Meta Filip go with Marguerite to Bonn, where she could testify on his behalf. The woman agreed, and all seemed to be going well.

As eager as Marguerite was to present her witness to the authorities, she was stymied by delays. To her frustration, no automobiles were available, and the few trains that ran from the small village were unreliable. After several postponements and a long wait, Meta Filip became suspicious. She agreed to go as far as Düsseldorf but refused to travel any farther. Marguerite returned alone to Coblenz.

In a lighter moment on her way back, she watched a group of British WACS searching German women who were smuggling food out of the British zone. "There was one immensely fat woman," Marguerite observed, "who became quite sylphlike after a string of hams had been removed from under her petticoat."

Although she had not produced Robert Minor, Marguerite had snared enough information to convict him. But before he could be brought to trial, he was released. Under pressure from influential friends of his father, including the investigative journalist Lincoln Steffens, the American government let him go free.

Marguerite felt the whole affair had turned into a fiasco. "He was a young newspaperman with a brilliant future as a cartoonist," she said. He was "an idealist and a radical," yet she believed he might have become more moderate over time "if a sense of injustice" at the government's zealous pursuit "had not driven him to take a definite stand in politics." Years later he ran as the Communist Party candidate for U.S. president.

Just as she thought that Minor might have tempered his radical feelings, she believed there were ample possibilities that a moderate, democratic German republic could have developed from its beginnings in Weimar. But rather than offering to help the Social Democrats rebuild their economy and restore their dignity, the Entente demanded heavy reparations and diminished the Germans, who turned to militant nationalism instead.

.   .   .

The announcement of the terms of the treaty had caused weeks of controversy within Germany. The Allies had warned that if the Germans did not accept the treaty, they would resume the war. The demands had torn apart the new government: some members wanted to reject the treaty with a loud and angry "No"; other members were more fearful of the consequences. If Germany refused to sign, they cautioned, Allied tanks would roll down the streets, and Allied planes would drop bombs on the cities.

On the night of her return to Berlin, hours before the official peace signing took place, Marguerite sat in a café on the busy Friedrichstrasse looking at a leaflet a passerby had dropped in her lap. The flyer called for the men of Germany to resume the war against the Allies: "Remember—Save your Honor—the World is Waiting!" it said. It was signed, "The Women of Germany."

For many people, the treaty felt like disaster. The parliamentarian Count Kessler wrote in his diary, "I have been indescribably depressed as though the sap has dried up in me." Yet other Germans were more pragmatic. Marguerite's hotel housekeeper Johanna saw the pamphlet and said, "*Gott Bewahre*. Honor is a fine thing but I prefer my bacon."

The day the agreement was signed was "a day of national mourning," Marguerite said. The Germans felt their country had been sliced in two, their colonies seized, and their children forced to pay reparations for generations to come.

And yet, for those who could afford it, life went on as it always had. At a dinner party hosted by a prominent businessman in his elegant home the night before the treaty was signed, Marguerite observed the well-dressed guests. It was hard to take her eyes off one woman wearing a recent gift from her husband; the exquisite pearl necklace around her neck had cost him several hundred thousand marks.

Chatting with leading men from industry, banking, government, and the press, she heard their blunt complaints and their overwhelming disappointment in President Wilson. "He violated every one of his promises to Germany," one said. "He was a tool of the French Premier Clemenceau," another added. "The terms will lead to bankruptcy and ruin," they insisted. "*Alles kaput.*" All is ruined.

With that, one industrialist boasted that he was spending ten million marks to enlarge his plant and increase his business. Another mentioned that he and his wife were leaving soon for a weeklong vacation in Switzerland. Her host steered Marguerite to a painting hanging on his wall. The sixteenth-century oil was likely done by Raphael, he confided; he had bought it the week before and paid 350,000 marks.

At the splendid table laid with fine china and crystal and adorned with hothouse flowers, the guests dined on eight different courses accompanied by three different wines. Afterward, sitting down to a round of poker, they smiled at their wins and shrugged off their losses.

. . .

The signing of the Versailles peace treaty marked the end of Marguerite's work in Germany. She had expected to be away from home for eight weeks and had remained instead for eight months. She had missed Christmas and her son's birthday and had learned of her father's death while she was in Paris. She had often worked late into the night "picking up facts and fitting them into an intricate picture puzzle." She had written lengthy newspaper stories and made voluminous, detailed secret reports.

Her undercover work demonstrated her ability to insinuate herself with serpentine ease into every level of society, and it proved her keen understanding of the political, economic, and social conditions of the country. She returned to America "with a very interesting report on what she had seen of the Bolshevik uprising in Germany," said Ralph Van Deman.

Her articles about the Germans were featured prominently in the *Baltimore Sun*. "She was able to get an insight into their after-the-war life that perhaps no other correspondent could get," wrote her editor in an introduction to her series.

Her name was more well recognized than ever before at home. Unbeknownst to her, she had also come to the attention of authorities in more distant places. In less than a year Mrs. Marguerite Harrison would pay a high price for her activities.

Those who have been away for any length of time are often surprised to discover that life goes on without them. The daily rituals take place whether they are there or not: meals are cooked, school attended, work done, holidays celebrated, deaths mourned.

So it was when Marguerite came home. Her son, Tom, had been accepted at Princeton and was looking forward to his freshman year at the prestigious college. Her mother-in-law, Mary Ames, had looked after the boy with generous love and good care. Mary's husband, Joseph Ames, had continued his work as an aeronautics physicist at Johns Hopkins in Baltimore and as an adviser to the American military in Washington. Marguerite's two loyal servants had managed her house and watched over her tenants. Her domestic affairs were in order, and she was eager to return to her old job. But her first priority was to settle her father's estate.

Her father was her idol, her role model, the man whose approval she always sought. She cherished him and said that, as a child, "He was the only one for whom I felt any great affection. I loved him with a passionate devotion." Unlike her mother, who was cold and distant, from the time she was born her father enveloped her with love. He stimulated her intellect, stirred her love of literature, including Shakespeare, Dickens, and Keats, boosted her zeal for travel and buoyed her knowledge of ships, encouraged her love of history, and intensified her interest in world affairs. Most important, he bolstered her belief in herself.

Before she left for Europe, she had informed him of her assignment, and he had written to her in Paris praising her patriotic efforts. The news of his death, days after his letter arrived, had stunned her. Just as she had done when her husband died, she went numb; no sobs, no tears, just numb. "I could not feel, I dared not think," she said. She filled her time with work.

Bernard Baker had been a major figure, not only in her life but in the life of the country. The *Sun* called him "the foremost man in the shipping business in Baltimore." The list of his achievements included the presidencies of banks and institutions, maritime adviser to the U.S. Congress, and membership on the United States Shipping Board. He had loaned his steamships to serve as hospitals during two wars and had worked for years to establish an American merchant marine. As a philanthropist, he was a generous supporter of health care and education.

He had created the Atlantic Transport Line in 1881, and less than a decade later, he reached the status of a Gilded Age tycoon. One of the richest men in the state, he confirmed his position with a monumental Georgian house like one he had seen in England. In an accidental meeting with the British architect who designed the original, the perfectionistic American said he wanted to reproduce the details correctly. Since neither man had any paper, the shipping magnate held out his arm and asked the architect to sketch the details on his shirt cuff.

Ingleside was a show house. With forty-nine rooms and nine bathrooms, it boasted four rooms more than J. P. Morgan's mansion in New York. Set high on over two hundred acres in Catonsville, ten miles west of Baltimore, the fieldstone mansion was surrounded by broad terraces and verandas and enhanced with thick white pillars. It featured a vast ballroom, oak-paneled dining room and library, intricately carved mantels, parquet floors, and a sweeping four-story staircase. Marguerite and her sister, estranged for many years, later sold it together for $150,000.

When her husband died in 1915, he left behind debts of seventy thousand dollars. To pay her regular expenses at the time, she took eyebrow-raising steps for a woman, even more scandalous for a socialite: she rented rooms to boarders, ran a decorating shop, and secured a job at the *Sun*. She had no legal responsibility to pay off Tom's debts; her inheritance from her father would allow her to live comfortably. Instead, she used the money to relieve the moral obligation she felt to pay the debts. Her expenses were still high, however, and she was happy to go back to work in the newsroom.

Disillusioned by the outcome of the war and Wilson's submission to the demands of the Entente and by the damage done through heavy reparations, the ill-conceived results of self-determination, and the failed notion of the League of Nations, she turned away from foreign affairs.

But she discovered that America had changed dramatically: priorities were upside down; values had reversed course. She was appalled that two million Black men had fought for their country overseas, yet they were not allowed to vote. Worse, when they came home, they struggled to find jobs.

At the same time, the Prohibition Act, banning the sale of alcohol anywhere in the country, had been passed: "forced on the people by a determined, fanatical minority, and its passage seemed to be the signal for the outbreak of an epidemic of narrowmindedness and intolerance." The extremists' bigotry was evidenced in the increasing power of the Ku Klux Klan, a brutal faction that terrorized Blacks and attacked Jews, Catholics, and foreigners.

Instead of covering national affairs, Marguerite slid easily into her former role as music and theater critic and reported on local news as well. Yet she soon found that covering ladies' luncheons and regional meetings were a far cry from the thrill of working as a special correspondent and espionage agent in Germany.

Since the time of her husband's death, she had felt no thrills in her personal life either. "I still felt afraid to form close ties. I did not even want to love my little son and I dared not risk being made to suffer again by the unexpected blow, such as I had experienced."

She contacted Marlborough Churchill: MI had paid her high compliments on her work and noted she had "rendered exceptionally good services." He was pleased to have her back. The main question was where to assign her. She was in demand by intelligence officials for posts around the world. General Churchill wanted her to go to Mexico; Colonel Van Deman wanted her in Japan. The station chief in The Hague wanted her to stay in Europe. "She is exceptionally qualified to work in such capitals as Vienna, Prague, and Warsaw and serve Berlin as its chief agent in all contiguous capitals. . . . She can take care of the outside of the spider's web," he wrote, adding, "she is exceedingly well equipped for it."

She had a different idea. From her days as a student at St. Timothy's, history had been her favorite subject. She had learned then that no country stands in isolation and that political events are interrelated. The war had proven this to be true. Now she saw that "the whole world was in a state of flux and change." Things had fallen apart; the center could not hold.

Walter Rathenau had told her the consequences of war were more social than political. The Russian Revolution had turned into a social experiment of its own. Was it possible, she wondered, that Bolshevism could provide some answers to the great unrest in the world? Was Communism the Second Coming? "I was not a Marxist or even a Socialist," she said. But "ever since the October revolution I had followed the course of events in Russia with breathless interest." Moscow was on her mind.

Part Two

Agent B

The spirit of Russia swirled through her dreams. It lured her to the vast steppes sweeping east from Ukraine to Kazakhstan, to the pastel palaces of St. Petersburg, and to the dazzling, spiraled domes of St. Basil's in Moscow. She had viewed the grasslands and graceful buildings at the Paris Exposition in 1900 where, from a plush seat in an exhibition car of the new Trans-Siberian Express, she watched in awe as scenes of the empire rolled by. Ever since, she had longed to visit Russia.

She embraced its soul in the novels of Tolstoy and Turgenev, the plays of Chekhov, and the poetry of Pushkin. She had studied Russian history and devoured Russian literature: she could understand Anna Karenina's passion and Levin's painful wrestling with life; she shared Turgenev's disgust with the cruel treatment of peasants, recognized Chekhov's wilting aristocrat, Madame Ranevsky, and the burgeoning bourgeois, Mr. Lopakhin, and appreciated Pushkin's Muse of Freedom. Even more, she was transported by Rachmaninoff's piano concertos, Rimsky-Korsakov's exotic *Scheherazade,* and the operas of Tchaikovsky and Mussorgsky.

She recognized the genius of Peter and the greatness of Catherine, respected the strength of Russia's armies and the scope of its empire, and felt empathy for its suffering workers and serfs. "I had always been a champion of Causes," she said. She knew that change was coming; it was inevitable. Despite all that, along with the rest of the world, she did not envision the enormity of the upheaval that would follow.

The grueling costs, human and economic, of the Great War, exacerbated by widespread famine and a feeble czar, unleashed a fury that brought on two tumultuous revolutions in less than a year. The first, led by Alexander Kerensky in February 1917, forced Czar Nicholas II to abdicate his throne, and spread honey on the hopes of the West. "The most absolute monarchy of modern times is to be succeeded by one of the most liberal democracies of modern times," the *Baltimore Sun* declared. Within a week the United States officially recognized the new government.

But the Germans wanted the Russian government to end the war between them. With that goal in mind, they smuggled the exiled, antiwar Vladimir Lenin onto a sealed train and sent him back to St. Petersburg. In October, Lenin led a Bolshevik Revolution that not only deposed Kerensky, murdered the czar, and scorned the bourgeois world, he duped the Allies by signing the Brest-Litovsk peace treaty with the Central Powers, and tossed cabbage on the honey.

Except for a few known leftist sympathizers like John Reed and Robert Minor, the Bolsheviks were suspicious of Western reporters and refused them entry. Washington, along with the European capitals, cut off relations with the new Soviet government and established a boycott, forbidding food, machinery, industrial parts, or equipment to be shipped to the Communist state.

No Western diplomats remained in Russia, leaving American officials with little knowledge of events behind the "Red curtain." Rumors were rife that the Bolsheviks had thrown their country into chaos and that a reign of terror had seized the public and sent it into shock.

In the offices of American diplomats and the military, in Congress and at cocktail parties, questions bubbled in the air: Who was really in control in Russia? Who was in charge of key posts and important departments? How large and how strong was the Soviet army? How weak was their economy? What was the condition of their industries? Was their farm production sustainable and was their distribution efficient? What was the morale of the people?

Should the United States continue to isolate the Communists and expect the movement to self-destruct? Or should it supply them with food and trust they would see the light and return to capitalist ways? No one knew for certain what lay beyond Poland's eastern borders.

America was gripped with fear that the Bolshies were exporting their revolution and plotting to overthrow the United States government. Washington faced major decisions, most notably, how best to bring the Bolsheviks down. Should it interfere and take aggressive steps? Or should it offer help and hope it would lead to reconciliation and a return to moderation? But the United States had little basis for analyzing options or reaching conclusions. To Marguerite, frustrated by watching events unfold from the sidelines, this was an opportunity to engage in vital world affairs and contribute firsthand information to her own government.

She had asked herself "if this new movement called Bolshevism was destined to remold society." What significance did it have for the world? Why did men fear it? she wondered.

Convinced that she could provide some answers, Marlborough Churchill challenged her to the task. With a salary of four hundred dollars a month, the code name "Agent B," a packet of cypher tables, secret codes, and the cover of newspaper correspondent for the *Sun*, she was ordered to leave at once.

Friends and family knew nothing of her undercover work. She assured them all that as soon as she arrived she would present her press credentials to the Kremlin, settle into the quotidian routine, and inform her readers of life under Communism. Except for her father-in-law, brother-in-law, and editor, she made no mention of her espionage assignment for MI or that she had counterintelligence orders to sniff out any saboteurs working to undermine America.

Her plans were to sail on the White Star Line with her seventeen-year-old son. She would stop in London, where she was to receive her credentials from the Associated Press, and then take Tommy to a Swiss boarding school, make her way to Moscow, and return to pick up her boy a few months later.

Always confident, Marguerite approached the Russian commercial office at 110 West Fortieth Street in New York and asked for a visa. She smiled at the man behind the desk in the Martens Bureau, named for Ludwig Martens, the Bolshevik diplomat who founded the unofficial embassy. She showed him her credentials as a foreign correspondent, pointing out she would be representing not one, but two outlets, the *Baltimore Sun* and the Associated Press. He offered a cool reception.

She had been in Germany as a reporter and witnessed the Spartacists' revolution. She admired the articles by John Reed, and now she wished to show the world the great results of the Bolshevik Revolution. Ludwig Martens listened politely. Despite her charms the man remained unconvinced.

Her sympathies lay with the Bolsheviks, she could assure him. She recognized the suffering of the masses, knew the hardships of the factory workers and the peasants, spoke passionately of Russian writers, and had read the words of Lenin and Trotsky. Her goal was to tell the Soviet story in a frank and honest way. The man thanked her for coming, but, he stated firmly, he could not approve a visa. Russia was not ready to welcome capitalist correspondents, was all he would say.

The United States and Russia were not at war, she told herself, the work itself was not dangerous, and it would not take long to carry out. Nonetheless, she knew that if she ignored the visa refusal and proceeded on her trip, she risked being imprisoned or expelled from the country. She relished the challenge.

.   .   .

In October 1919, Marguerite strapped a belt of a thousand dollars in gold coins around her corseted waist, stepped into a smart French suit, wrapped herself in an ankle-length fur-lined coat, and with her diamond brooch and strand of pearls tucked in with her wardrobe, she set off from New York, ready for the Russian winter she would soon face.

On board the SS *Adriatic* with her son, she settled into her stateroom and explored the ship. There was plenty for both of them to do on the weeklong crossing. The *Adriatic* was the only one of the White Star Line's fleet to have both an indoor swimming pool and a Turkish bath. Of course, there were the card rooms and dining rooms and decks for reading and lounging. She had fond memories of transatlantic voyages from her girlhood that she could share with her son.

Her father had taught her more about life at sea than most adult travelers would ever know. As a child, she could box the compass with ease, knew how to take solar observations, and understood the triple expansion engines. On deck, she loved to watch the flying fish, dolphins, and whales her father pointed out in the distance, or go below with him to the cargo hold, where a large supply of cattle was headed for the stockyards in England. "I loved to pet their sleek heads and hear them snuffle against my dress," she said. But she felt sad at the end of each trip when they moaned, and she was sure they knew they were being led to slaughter.

Standing next to her father when they reached Land's End, she waited impatiently for the captain to call out from behind his binoculars, "Land ahead, sir." When high winds nearly knocked her to her feet, her father threw his arms around her for protection, and once he guarded her from bits of an iceberg that flew across the deck. Whatever else happened, he sheltered her from nature's storms and from her mother's stormy temperament. Her father was gone now, as was Tommy's father, but the memories of both her beloved men remained.

Tom had been "a wonderful athlete and a keen sportsman," she recalled, one of the top riders at the hunt club, a fan of fox hunting, and a devotee of duck hunting. Accompanied by their young son, they spent almost every weekend from September to January at their farmhouse on the Eastern Shore. The couple who looked after the place had everything ready when they arrived by train on Friday nights.

Waking early and warming themselves over a hearty breakfast of bacon and eggs, she and Tom pulled on their thick flannels, heavy sweaters, and high rubber boots and set off in a rowboat to the leeward side of the cove. Their guns loaded, they crouched behind a clutch of cedar trees lining the riverbanks and watched the horizon for the canvasbacks. From behind his binoculars, Tom whispered, "Here they come, Mardie," and swiftly downed three ducks in a row. She too raised her gun, pulled the trigger, wounded the canvasback, and shot again to finish the job. It was a glorious way to spend the day, and they never thought about the cruelty to the animals.

Back at the house, their son's cheeks round and red as apples, they watched him play outdoors, throwing spent cartridges to their retriever dogs. When the fishing season started, Tom showed him how to hold the line, and when the hunting season came around, the father held the rifle for the small boy. They were precious times, "and the three of us were inseparable playmates and comrades," she said. Then, once again. she stiffened against the memories that brought back so much pain.

.   .   .

On the promenade deck she encountered a serious-minded man with wire-rimmed spectacles firmly perched on his nose. He introduced himself as Mr. Julius Hecker, a Russian-born American living in Lausanne, who had just spent two months in New York delivering lectures at "liberal institutions." Eager to hear more, she flashed a smile and gave him her full attention. She mentioned that she was bringing her son to Lausanne to attend the Auckenthaler School. He lived with his family on Rue du Leman, Mr. Hecker said, although on this trip he was going to Berne to do some work.

He was a Moscow-style missionary spreading the dogma of the Bolshevik religion. His job, he confided, was to introduce Bolshevism "in homeopathic doses" to the American public. When that succeeded, "it would be followed up with stuff that had more of a punch." A revolution in America is "inevitable," the man declared. She listened with great interest and indicated her sympathy for the cause.

There were several professors in New York, he revealed, whom he had converted to the Bolshevik doctrine. She could convert many more. He gave her suggestions on how to spread Bolshevist propaganda when she returned home.

She told him how she wanted to go to Moscow but had been turned down for a visa. If only they had known one another before she left, he sighed; he could have obtained full credentials for her from the Martens Bureau.

"I took a Kodak picture of him," she wrote, signing her code name, "B," at the end of her counterintelligence report. Only a few days out at sea and she was already using her cypher book to cable names and information.

She had other important news as well. On her stopover in New York before she boarded the ship, she met with Walter Pettit, a

Columbia University professor who had been sent by MI to survey the situation in Russia. He indicated that he knew she was sympathetic to the new Russian regime. How he had come to this conclusion he did not say. He told her that the American consul in Stockholm "is one of us," she cabled, "but said he has to keep it in the dark." She had found one mole at the Department of State and another one advising Military Intelligence.

.   .   .

As soon as the ship docked in Southampton, she strode down the gangway and headed for London, only to find that after months hiding out in the countryside, many people were eager to join with others in town. Hotel rooms were in high demand and the scarcity left her and Tommy nearly stranded, but years of family travel abroad had helped her spin a web of contacts. She thumbed through her trusty address book and secured a friend's spacious flat in Queen Anne's Mansions near St. James's Park. There was always a way, she knew.

The war had left its wounds on the British capital. Like everywhere else in the cold and hungry city, her quarters were frigid, and the ice box was empty. Nevertheless, pubs and jazz clubs were packed, and the frenzied dancers shimmying to ragtime reminded her of Berlin. She only had time to visit a few friends, including American-born Lady Astor, newly elected to Parliament. More importantly, she needed to confirm her status, arranged by Marlborough Churchill, as a correspondent for the Associated Press. The powerful news organization was more influential than her Baltimore paper and would provide her with better cover.

Armed with her new credentials, she was off with Tommy to Lausanne, traveling via Brussels through Luxembourg and France, on trains slowed and scarred from the war. What had once been a four-hour trip took eighteen hours to complete.

Tourists had vanished from Switzerland, and the many who had been spies had flown off like blackbirds after they ate the pie. But exiled royals were calling the neutral country their home, and she took advantage of their eagerness to tell their tales.

In a meeting with Prince Christian of Hesse, with whom she

shared mutual friends, he declared he wanted his country to become a republic, and at dinner with Prince Constantine of Greece, whose wife was the Kaiser's sister, Marguerite learned he wanted his country to return to monarchy. It was the same all over Europe: four empires demolished; five kingdoms overthrown; old systems upended; new systems in confusion; a yearning for the past, a hunger for the future. The only certainty was doubt.

In between interviews, she spent time in Berne with the American ambassador and followed his suggestion to pay a visit to Mr. Hecker: Washington wanted to keep an eye on him. Calling on the Bolshevik, she reaffirmed her support, and with their friendship intact, he assured her he would do his best to keep in touch with her son.

The rest of her time in Berne she struggled to book passage to Warsaw on the highly sought-after Diplomatic Express. Almost incidentally, she managed a few hours with Tommy at his boarding school in Lausanne and with a rushed goodbye, cheerily promised "to try to be back by Easter."

On the way to Poland, from the window of the Express she watched the train squeeze through tight Carpathian passes and glide by crystal-clear lakes. On the first leg, to Vienna, passengers spilled from already overflowing compartments, and when night fell, she had no choice but to lie on a table or sleep on the grimy floor. She chose the floor, and spreading out her blanket, she said goodnight to the porters nearby.

When the train pulled in at the Austrian capital, she stepped out and took a walk on the Prater, the usually busy main street. Only a few ragged souls braved the freezing air. A young girl carrying a backpack stuffed with provisions made her way along the snow-covered street. Marguerite approached her and explained that she was an American and was curious about postwar conditions. Although food was plentiful in the countryside, the young woman said, little of it made its way to the city. With no milk, no sugar, only half a loaf of bread, and a few potatoes a week, thousands of people were dying. For those still struggling to survive, homes and workplaces were dark and cold, and jobs were shriveling up as quickly as the people. There was a severe shortage of coal, and a copious supply of gloom.

Back on the Diplomatic Express, Marguerite found a compartment and relaxed in her plush seat. But as they neared the border of Czechoslovakia, she was shaken: soldiers marched on board, seized her passport, and told her she was under arrest. Her crime? she asked in German, fearful they had discovered her mission. She had neglected to request a visa, a guard answered; she would have to turn back.

Calmed by knowing that her secret remained safe, but discouraged by the threat of a lengthy delay, she turned on her charm, but her pleas of innocence were met by the border guard's frown. And then, keeping a cool facade, she suggested, perhaps she could pay a fine? A smile crossed the man's face. A few francs for his pocket and she was back in her compartment. A bit of a setback and a shock to her system; nonetheless, she was on her way to Poland.

CHAPTER 8

Into the Unknown

Crossing into a new country roused her sense of discovery. "To me, the passage of any frontier is a dramatic moment. The landscape on both sides of the invisible border looks much the same, but you cross it—presto!—you are among people of another race, speaking another language, with different aims, ideals and ambitions." The experience gave her a rush.

She thrilled at the thought of entering Poland, now an independent nation re-created after a century and a half of being divided among German, Russian, and Austrian regimes. She expected to see a country in celebration. What she found was a people in confusion. "Cold, dirt, patriotism," she said. "All three were there in abundance."

Dressed in filthy rags, hovering in cramped dark houses, or shivering in the frigid air, the Poles had little to celebrate. Yet, despite the bitter cold and the threadbare clothes on the tired people, she felt their pride in the new flags flying and in the old Polish music playing everywhere.

Before the war, Warsaw was a cosmopolitan city: its proud buildings boasted gothic, baroque, and renaissance architecture, its busy streets buzzed with electric trams and gas lights, its stores offered well-dressed shoppers elegant clothes and a wide range of products and foods, and its tree-lined parks offered moments of calm.

Now, nothing functioned as it should. Her room at the once-stylish Bristol Hotel was small and seedy. The lamps refused to work, the worn carpet was nearly bald, the yellowed curtains were coated in dust, and the mattress was filled with lumps. Like her hotel, the whole country was *popsuta*—broken. From lights to toilets to factories, Poland was *popsuta*.

Broken too were her plans to travel at once to Russia. A period of mass killings and executions had seized hold again in Moscow, and coded instructions from Washington to the military attaché in Warsaw made the situation clear: "Do not let Mrs. Harrison enter territory under Bolshevist control until further notice." She would have to wait. The delay dragged on for six weeks. With her rare aptitude for languages, she already spoke French and German like a native, and Italian and Spanish almost as well, but her Russian was meager; the postponement would give her a chance to improve it.

She also used the time to interview Polish officials, from the solid, steady chief of state, General Pilsudski to the poised blond-haired, blue-eyed female leader of the Polish Women's Legion, and she met with old acquaintances and Western diplomats. With the eastern part of Poland still at war with the Bolsheviks, she was able to gather intelligence about the Soviet military, including troop sizes and equipment supplies, which she reported to the American political attaché in Warsaw. She gave information to the Poles as well: it would cost her dearly later on.

On the lighter side, she celebrated Christmas, her second one without her son, with a cousin from Baltimore doing volunteer work in Warsaw, and dressed in her fancy frock, she rang in the New Year of 1920 with Mr. Hallyday, an officer of the American Red Cross, and his friends. She attended dances such as the Red Cross Ball at the fashionable Hotel Adlon and did the foxtrot with a blue-eyed American flyer fighting with a Polish squadron.

At a ball held at the Bristol Hotel, she waltzed with Polish aristocrats and said, "*dobry wieczor*," (good evening) to the new prime minister, Paderewski. She had met the world-famous pianist in Baltimore long before the country was reborn and had noted in her review that he brought tears to the eyes of the audience when he played the Polish national hymn. Sadly, she learned that, although he stirred audiences with his music, his actions as a political leader had been disappointing, and he was under fire for his failures.

Before she left New York, she had obtained credentials from

Dorothy Schiff, publisher of the *New York Post,* to file stories for the paper on daily life in Poland. Traveling around the country she wrote human-interest pieces that appealed to the many New Yorkers with ties to Poland and Eastern Europe.

Warsaw's Jewish population, which made up 40 percent of the total population, was thriving, but in other cities such as Bialystok and Vilna, she shuddered at the shocking poverty and maltreatment of the Jews. Refugees from Russia, they had fled the czar's pogroms only to face the same kind of ruthless attacks in their new homeland. The hungry Poles turned them into scapegoats; they blamed the Jews for their lack of food, accused them of being Bolsheviks or Communist sympathizers, and barred them from employment.

"My own impression," she said, "was that the Poles were entirely responsible for the pogroms." Their actions were unjustifiable, and yet she found their motives understandable. "Compelled to assimilate another alien people, friction was inevitable," she observed. Extremist nationalism was rearing its ugly head. Yet when she informed MI of the ugly events, Van Deman denied their existence. "As a matter of fact, there have been no Jewish pogroms in Poland," he told Marlborough Churchill.

At the end of December, she sent a letter to a nameless "Dear Friend" in Switzerland and told him she had organized her plans going forward, saying she expected to have "a very wonderful experience." She wished him a Happy New Year and added, "I hope you have seen something of my boy."

She included an article she had written on the Polish situation, noting that "the misery that exists is inconceivable." Starvation and illness were rampant and unemployment sky high. The Poles were desperate for peace with Russia, she said. She asked the friend to forward the piece to the *Liberator,* a socialist magazine that published articles by John Reed and cartoons by Robert Minor. The mysterious letter was to Julius Hecker; she did not say that, if published, she hoped the account would shore up her bona fides with the Bolsheviks.

It was the middle of January when she received approval from MI to continue her trip to Russia. Armed with letters of introduction from friends to their friends and relatives in Moscow, she left Warsaw eager to see what lay ahead, though not without some trepidation; she knew she was on her way to a snow-covered trek toward hostile soil. The daily language lessons in Russian had improved her ability to converse, but not enough to deal with the complexities of travel; to ease her way she befriended a Jewish American woman, a physician who wished to return to Russia, the land of her birth.

Together they set out, the short, plump Dr. Karlin carrying little but the clothes on her back, and the tall, shapely Marguerite balancing a sleeping bag filled with a blanket, pillow, several pairs of shoes, long felt boots, towels, a collapsible rubber washbasin, chocolates, and five or six cartons of cigarettes to use for barter in case there was not enough food; a suitcase filled with a tailored suit, several blouses, one woolen dress and one silk dinner dress, a felt hat, and underwear; and a canvas shoulder bag stashed with cosmetics, hair curlers, cakes of soap, and medicines for diarrhea and illnesses such as malaria and tuberculosis. Of course, she also carried her secret codes, her typewriter, and her Kodak.

Excited by the prospect of the adventure, she danced around officials in Warsaw, expecting their quick permission for the trip. But each step along the way to the border required permission from the provincial officers, some of whom refused to take a chance and sent her to plead her case at army outposts. With a wink of her eye or a clever word to an officer or a slight lift of her skirts as she climbed onto troop trucks, she charmed her way through each challenge, but delay after delay lengthened the wintry journey, and obstacles arose again and again.

At Minsk, in the impoverished Pale of Settlement, she waited several days for the Polish general in charge, only to see him shake his head at her request. Without doubt, he stated, she would be caught on the Russian side and shot. But first, he warned, the Russians would force her to give them information on Polish positions and the size of their forces. He refused to grant her permission.

The next best place to try was Vilna. Leaving her interpreter, Dr. Karlin, in Minsk, she traveled by train for twenty-four hours squashed among army prisoners in a fourth-class car. After several days in the distant town, with the help of a friendly officer, she was granted permission for the journey onward. But on her last night in Vilna, she was forced to fight off a drunken Lothario who pushed his way into her hotel room. She pushed back, and with her fists and her knee, she knocked him into the hallway. "He fell over with an awful thud, his saber rattling on the stone floor," she said. In the morning she returned to Minsk.

Clambering onto crude sleighs, mounting troop transports, and trampling by foot, she and the doctor marched east. Before they reached the frontier, they rode by sleigh along a heavily pitted road, tossed from side to side as the rough path curved sharply through a thick forest. To avoid falling into the ditches along the way, they stopped, filled the trenches with spruce boughs, and rode across to the other side.

At the border, a nervous Polish lieutenant led her through a maze of barbed-wire fence, trying hard to dissuade her and warning that she would be shot at once if she stepped onto Russian turf. She shrugged in defiance, and standing at the edge of the unknown, she headed off toward the eerie passage of No Man's Land. The doctor followed close behind her.

Against a bitter wind and temperatures well below zero, she wrapped her doubts in her long fur coat, and with a fur cap covering her head and fur-lined gloves warming her hands, she trudged in her *valenki*, the felt boots worn by Russians, through the deadly silence, crunching over miles of snow-blanketed wheat fields. Like Tolstoy's Prince Andrei, she knew that one step beyond that line lay the unknown. And what was there? Who was there? Beyond this field, no one knew. She would like to know, was afraid to know, wanted so much to cross it. Sooner or later she would have to cross it.

She was aware that once she reached the Russian side, she would have no one to turn to for help: no American diplomats had stayed in the country, no foreign embassies remained to represent her; she had no way to send a message out, and no one she knew to receive a message inside. She would be at the mercy of a dangerous adversary.

Small outposts of the Red Army stood in the distance. Kindly peasants took her in to comfortable quarters, but her heart beat fast when she heard the thump of boots and three men appeared at the cabin, rifles slung over their shoulders. One of them, wearing a coarse khaki uniform, his astrakhan cap ablaze with the five-pointed Soviet star, stepped forward. She cringed, not knowing whether the first Soviet officer she faced would shoot her or take her prisoner.

"I have come from America," she said in Russian, adding that she wanted "to learn the truth about the Soviet government." Stunned by the presence of the only American woman he had ever seen, the soldier gave her a quizzical welcome.

CHAPTER 9

A Clever Woman

Moscow felt as distant as the moon; time seemed an eternity as she lingered at the Russian Army posts, waiting for permission to continue on to the new capital. After two weeks, Marguerite boarded a train, found a place on a crowded boxcar, and slept on a shelf of hay; three days later, on February 24, 1920, she reached Moscow's Alexandrovsky station, where trains steamed to and from Warsaw, Berlin, and Paris. Without credentials to enter Russia, and knowing that she had to inform the authorities, she asked the interpreter to phone the foreign office and announce her arrival. She was ordered not to move.

At the station's newsstand she bought a copy of the Communist-sanctioned *Pravda,* one of the only newspapers it sold, and realized at once from the tone of the government mouthpiece that the kindly army people she had stayed with after she crossed the Polish border were a far cry from the worldly-wise officials and bureaucrats in Moscow. Reality sunk in. The blanket of calm in the provinces no longer served to protect her. Unsettled by the iron-fisted attitude of the revolutionary regime, she felt an attack of nerves. What had she gotten herself into? She had flirted with danger and survived this far, but what would become of her now?

She waited half an hour before a tense, wiry man approached. "Good morning," he said crisply, and introduced himself as Rosenberg, head of the Western Section of the foreign office. Dark-haired, stoop shouldered, and unsmiling, he spoke in fluent English and went at once to the heart of the matter: how did she get to Russia and why she was here? Her entry was illegal, and the consequences could be dangerous, he snapped. She had come from enemy territory: Russia and Poland were still at war. She could be deported, or even worse, imprisoned. "Hand over your passport and all your papers," he said. His brusque words did nothing to soothe her concerns.

Affecting innocence, she explained that the Russian army officers she met at the border had given their approval; her arrival was unorthodox perhaps, but, she assured the official, it was not illegal. Still, she had no choice but to do as he said. She surrendered the passport and documents, but brazenly managed to keep the letters and introductions buried inside her bag.

The foreign office, he told her, would decide her fate. With that, she was driven through festive Moscow streets, where adequately dressed people pulled sleds piled with goods, public buildings flew red flags or showed off banners in honor of the second anniversary of the Soviet army, and huge posters celebrated the proletariat. The car stopped at an official guesthouse, and she entered an atmosphere not quite as joyful: after her bags were searched and her Kodak camera and film were seized, she was ordered to report to the ministry in the morning. Too tired to dwell on the fact that she was under house arrest, she lay down on the thick mattress, the first she had slept on in weeks, and fell asleep.

In the morning she was driven by car to the Metropole, the once grand hotel where the Bolsheviks had fought some of their battles and which they now used as temporary quarters for the People's Commissariat of Foreign Affairs. There was no time for her to view what was left of the grand ballroom with its stained-glass ceiling and marble pool, or the mosaics designs in the dining room, or the art deco furnishings in the guest rooms.

Instead, she entered through the employees' entrance, climbed the dark flight of stairs to the foreign office, and contemplated her future: she had been told by General Churchill that, at worst, she would be ejected from the country; at best, but unlikely, she would be allowed to stay. How long she might remain was another question. A few days? A week?

She had come with an open mind, she promised the man who quizzed her. The old regime had been a disaster, she knew, and agreed that only "a complete social upheaval" could sweep it away. Her sympathies, she assured him, were with the Bolsheviks. She gained permission to stay for two weeks and radioed home that she was safe.

Seemingly beguiled by her charms, the foreign ministry made every comfort available to her. Ensconced at Number 10 Horitonevsky, a government guesthouse near the once posh Kuznetsky Most street, she was in the grand home of Herr Roerich, a rich German merchant who had fled with the Revolution. The velvet-draped room number 4, furnished with a brass bed and box-spring mattress, a large table, comfortable armchairs, and a voluminous couch, was spacious enough to work, entertain friends, and provide temporary sleeping space for Dr. Karlin.

Joining a few foreigners sympathetic to the Soviets, she took her meals in a dining room paneled in oak at a table covered in crisp white damask and laid with silver cutlery that disappeared over time. Her tablemates included Michael Farbman of the *Chicago Daily News*, Korean and Swedish Communists, Russian foreign office representatives, and a cultured if unctuous host who, she soon learned, worked for the Cheka, the secret police.

The midday dinner of soup, kasha, and coarse black bread was not elaborate, nor did it resemble the delicacies of Russian literature. The thin soup made with bits of meat and noodles was a far cry from Tolstoy's turtle soup and sturgeon; the dry buckwheat grains could hardly compare with Chekhov's buttery *blini* topped with caviar and sour cream; the coarse black bread was an insult to Gogol's housewife's poppyseed *piroshki;* and the ersatz tea was a splash in the face of the wine and vodka enjoyed by the fictional characters. Yet the meal at the Horitonevsky was far better than the meager rations available to most.

Along with the adequate food served at the table, comfortable lodgings cleaned by a maid, a hot bath in a tiled bathroom every Wednesday, a billiards room, a garden, and twenty-five cigarettes every other day, she received rare access to officials in high positions and was soon collecting exactly the kind of information Churchill had sent her to find.

.   .   .

Her request to interview the head of the foreign office was answered on the second day of her stay. Told to meet with Georgy Chicherin at midnight, she appeared at his office at the appointed time, but she was kept in the waiting room until two a.m. To her surprise, the commissar who worked while others slept was not the "masterful-looking" person she expected, but a gentle, pale asthmatic, a well-bred distant relative of the poet Alexander Pushkin.

Seated at a large desk in a cold, drafty office, a muffler wound around his neck, Chicherin was a small, delicate man with tired greenish-blue eyes, light-brown hair, and a blond beard and pointed moustache. He laced his fingers together and in perfect English asked politely how she managed to fool the foreign office and enter the country illegally. And then in a stern voice he warned her of her tenuous status. She nodded and said she understood.

A good reporter, she promptly engaged him in friendly conversation, expressed her admiration for Russian writers, and found he was intelligent and well informed on the subject. But he was also adept at debate and swiftly moved the discussion away from poetry to current political prose. Deeply knowledgeable about foreign affairs, he spoke about the situation with Poland and declared he was eager to make peace. As for America, he told her, he was disappointed in President Wilson's inability to fulfill his promise of real self-determination for all nationalities wanting their own states. "Look at Russia," he said smugly. "We have done a much better job." They had given sovereignty to Estonia and would soon add Latvia and Lithuania to the list.

At the same time, he was glad the Americans had recently established Prohibition. "Why?" she asked in surprise, knowing how Russians eagerly tossed down their vodka. He gave his answer with conviction: "Because Prohibition will further the cause of the World Revolution." He went on. "Deprive the workmen of their meeting places in bars and saloons and they will flock to political meetings." It would spread the popularity of Communism, he explained. She filed her story. From the viewpoint of her editors, her trip was already a success.

With help from the influential and sometimes insolent Mr. Rosenberg, the man in charge of all visitors' arrangements at the foreign office, her calendar soon filled with appointments. She had interviews with Krasin, the Commissar of Foreign Trade, who was formerly the Russian representative of Siemens Electric Company in Berlin and spoke with her in German, and with Radek, the bespectacled, brilliant head of Western propaganda, who spoke in fluent English and told her that war with Poland was essential.

Meetings soon followed with the commissars of communication, education, health, agriculture, and economics. Each was trying to bring innovative concepts to archaic institutions, admirable ideas that she found uplifting, but with the lack of means to carry them out, their execution was flailing toward disaster. The public health system was important and one of the "most efficient" agencies, but a shortage of physicians and supplies kept it far from its goals. The public school system, she noted, "is magnificent in theory"; it offered free education from kindergarten to the highest levels of university. But with many children lacking proper clothing or shoes, and many schools closed because they lacked fuel for lighting or heat, the majority of students, whether in primary school or doing graduate work, could not attend classes. Left at home while their parents went to work, hundreds of children roamed the streets, begging, stealing, and behaving in ways that Marguerite found "appalling."

To help improve the situation, the government created group homes for thousands of youngsters ages three to sixteen. Installed in the seized mansions of the bourgeoisie, they were taught by the Montessori method and instilled with Communist ideals. In one grand house, Marguerite saw a five-year-old girl and asked her about the doll she was carrying.

"What a pretty doll," she said. "Is it yours?"

"Oh no," the child answered, "she isn't my dolly, she's our dolly."

It was a far cry from Marguerite's own childhood, when she kept her doll, Eunice, close to her side. On trips to Europe, Eunice traveled with her own trunk filled with a proper wardrobe for lunches, teas, and dinners; she was taken to museums, rode on donkeys, and always sat next to Marguerite at mealtime. Most importantly, she was her closest confidante, the one to whom Marguerite told her most intimate secrets.

.   .   .

The commissar of economics had a major plan to electrify the entire country. It was, she said, a "nice dream, but in fact there was a shortage of fuel, raw material and labor, so almost all factories, except for essential industries, were closed." As for the commissar of agriculture, he planned to organize rural farms into communes, but without agricultural implements, farm machinery, or even the seeds, there was not the slightest hint of success.

She made visits to railroads, factories, hospitals, and schools and, except for the homes for children, found them all disappointing. In contrast, she spent time with two of the most important Soviet women, the short, stout secretary of the Comintern, Angelica Balabanova, and the delicate, blond commissar of the Women's Department, Alexandra Kollontai, and found them both formidable. She arranged for an interview with Kollontai, was informed the official was recuperating from an illness, and was told to call on her in her suite at the Hotel National. The luxurious hotel that once welcomed diplomats and business barons was now home to Vladimir Lenin and other high-ranking Soviet leaders.

The woman who appeared hardly fit the image of the tough Communist official: instead, she was "wearing an exquisite boudoir gown of green velvet trimmed with sable; her little feet were encased in velvet slippers of the same shade, and she was altogether chic and charming."

The pretty daughter of a general in the czar's army, Madame Kollontai was as brutal on women's and children's issues as her father had been on the battlefield. "She considered family life absolutely subversive," Marguerite said, and believed that from birth, "children should be regarded as the property of the State." She saw the relationship between the sexes as "mainly for the purpose of reproducing the race," and insisted that the only restraints should be the "law of eugenics." She did not mention her lover, Alexander Shliapikov, the former commissar of labor, who would become leader of the Workers' Opposition.

The meeting at the Hotel National was an hour's walk from the Horitonevsky; other interviews similarly took place miles away from the guesthouse. The electric trams, crowded when in operation, were out of service until the April thaws, and the *izvozchiks*, the cabbies, charged fares that smacked of profiteering. Instead, Marguerite read-ied herself each morning for a long walk through the snow-covered streets.

Slipping into a clean blouse, she buttoned up her wool suit, envel-oped herself in her fur-lined coat, and pulled on her fleece boots. Braced against the brutal cold, she walked everywhere, tramping in the middle of the street, avoiding the sidewalks filled with mounds of snow and slush, and strode past men and women hunched in their heavy coats, dragging sleighs laden with hefty piles of wood, pota-toes, and other necessities.

Trudging down the Tverskaya, once the main shopping street, where some goods were still displayed in the windows, or the Myas-nitskaya, where the seized offices of Westinghouse were boarded up, or through poor neighborhoods where well-stocked stores once sold their wares to the workers, she faced the silent storefronts shuttered and sealed by the Soviets.

In their place the government offered stores where people waited for days on long lines to purchase a single hat or a pot. In contrast, big open markets, long a feature of Moscow life, stretched for blocks, and although they were technically illegal, most of the time the Bolsheviks turned a blind eye and allowed anyone who had anything for sale to offer it in the Russian souk.

Back at the Horitonevsky, she made friends with Frank McCul-lagh, an English journalist who, unbeknownst to the Bolsheviks, had fought as a captain for the British in Siberia, was taken prisoner, and escaped. He made his way to Moscow, and using the *Manchester Guardian* as his cover, was gathering intelligence for the British gov-ernment. Soulmates, she and McCullagh attended foreign office brief-ings and visited forbidden places together.

Another guest was an owlish-looking, Russian-born "quiet little man" who had lived in America for thirty years. He introduced her to some of his friends and wrote in his diary that Mrs. Harrison was "very clever." She found him to be an "exceedingly sweet-tempered person." She smiled as she thought of what her friends back home would say of her gentle new acquaintance: he was the notorious anar-chist Alexander Berkman.

"Knowing him as I do I cannot imagine him trying to blow up Mr. Frick or anyone else with bombs," she said. And yet, in 1892 while Marguerite studied history and the roots of revolution at the elite St. Timothy's school, and while her mother hosted society dinners and her father raised his status as a shipping magnate by sending grain to the Russian czar, the mild-mannered Sasha Berkman tried to assassinate the millionaire industrialist Henry Frick. The anarchist shot Frick twice—once in the shoulder, once in the neck—and then drew out a dagger and struck his legs; somehow, his target survived.

Sentenced to twenty-two years in prison, Berkman was deported in 1919 and shipped off to Russia, where, as a youth, he had been a victim of the czar's pogroms. Returning to the land of his birth, he was ready to give his life "a thousand times to the service of the Social Revolution," he said, and rejoiced on the day he stepped on Russian soil. The event stirred him profoundly: "It was the most sublime day of my life," he wrote in his diary.

Berkman arrived in Russia passionate to support the Revolution, but he was taken aback by the devastation he found in St. Petersburg. The population of the former capital, now called the more Russified "Petrograd," had not only sunk to half a million from three million, but those who stayed faced famine, starvation, and disease. Rats roamed the streets, vermin crawled through the buildings; boards covered the storefronts; the streets were empty, and, he noted, everything was silent.

.   .   .

The historic first session of the Moscow Soviet took place at the famed Moscow Opera House on March 6, 1920. On her arrival, Marguerite found the building, once known as the Great Imperial Theatre, cordoned off and the Red Army cavalry standing on guard outside. She made her way to the entrance, showed her invitation, and entered the elaborately carved and gilded theater where armed guards were stationed all along the corridors.

The entire building had the feel of a theatrical set. Red flags flew everywhere, giant banners hanging in rows on the stage proclaimed in several languages, PROLETARIAT OF THE WORLD, UNITE, and huge triple portraits of Lenin, Trotsky, and Karl Marx swagged the stage, the balconies, and the wedding-cake boxes.

The ruling Communist powerhouse thronged the hall. Members of the Soviet sat in the orchestra seats, and from the imperial box above, the people's commissars and Central Committee members looked down on them. Army brass, union leaders, foreign diplomats, and invited members of the press settled into the best boxes; the proletariat were assigned to lesser seats.

When everyone was settled, the orchestra conductor raised his baton, and as the solemn strains of the Communist anthem began, the audience stood; in one thundering voice, four thousand people roared "The Internationale."

"Arise ye workers from your slumber!" the crowd bellowed, "Arise ye prisoners of want." Marguerite had memorized the lyrics of this refrain of the French Revolution and sang along loudly with the others: "For reason in revolt now thunders!" "So comrades, come rally! And the last fight let us face. The Internationale unites the human race."

The music came to an end, the crowd sat down, and the opening speaker reached the podium. The sight of Vladimir Lenin, "a short, thickset unimposing little man," with pale face and pale hair, left her feeling disappointed. Sporting a small goatee and wearing rough English tweeds, "he looked like a prosperous middle-class businessman."

There was no hint of a bourgeois man once he began to speak. His piercing gray-blue eyes and forceful personality projected steely strength, and though he lacked eloquence, his crystal-clear language fascinated all who heard him. Standing before the enormous crowd, his thumbs thrust in his vest pockets, his face turning first this way and then that, he made each person feel as though he was speaking directly to them. "His tremendous sincerity, utter self-confidence and quiet power," mesmerized the audience. "He was absolutely sure of himself," she noted. His oft-quoted observation that a lie told often enough becomes the truth was well known.

Nonetheless, he spoke the truth about the disastrous state of the food supply and transport systems. Millions of tons of fish, raw foods, sugar, and fats left by the German army in Ukraine and tons of Russian grain in Siberia were all abandoned because no transportation was available to bring goods to the cities.

A year earlier, in March 1919, the *Baltimore Sun* reported that Bolshevik forces had gained control of Ukraine. "The Ukraine is the grainary of Russia, and Odessa before the war was the greatest grain shipping port of the Ukraine. If the Bolsheviks can control the great agricultural region of the Ukraine, they might be able to relieve the shortage in Moscow and the North," the paper said.

Lenin acknowledged that the railroads were in shambles; thousands of freight cars were broken and deserted, and nearly a thousand engines wrecked, yet no replacement parts existed in the country. He blamed the American and English embargoes that prevented machinery and parts from being imported without which repairs could not be made.

He went on to warn his comrades that "gigantic sacrifices were demanded of us" and called on the members to lead the way. Hunger and suffering prevailed; it was the mission of the masses "to restore a ruined country and a ruined economy."

To great applause, Lenin predicted victory against the capitalists everywhere. Perceptive workers in every country, he said, "are aligning themselves with the Communist International. Therein lies the full guarantee that the victory of the Communist International, throughout the world, in the not very distant future, is assured."

The crowd cheered, the musicians started up again, and the audience rose and raised their voices once more in "The Internationale." The pattern was repeated: speaker after speaker addressed the audience, and at the beginning and end of each speech, the orchestra played, the crowd stood, and their voices rang out. "We were continually bobbing up and down," Marguerite said.

Two days later, she attended a conference celebrating International Women's Day. Looking around at the audience of women laborers, she could not help but notice the sea of brightly colored scarves. As always, almost every woman had covered her head with the familiar floral-patterned babushkas. "I have often wondered if Russian women sleep in their shawls," she remarked.

Her new friend Angelica Balabanova, the key speaker at the conference, electrified the huge crowd. Though physically unimpressive, "her eyes shone with profundity, compassion and goodness," one woman remarked. Raising the hopes and the pride of the audience, Balabanova told the audience that the Russian female worker, "once confined to being a washerwoman and nothing else, could now be anything she pleases."

.   .   .

Whether Marguerite spent time with laborers or labor leaders, her ability to connect and empathize gave her a distinct advantage over most of her male counterparts and gave her the insights that MI needed. Her orders were to assess who was in charge, what their personalities were like, their background, their knowledge, who was on their staffs, how they operated, what they were achieving, and where they were failing. And when a high-risk opportunity arose to find out more, she did not hesitate to take the chance. Her friend McCullagh called her "plucky."

The week of the Soviet meetings, she and McCullagh learned that a special exhibition had been organized by the Rosta, the official Soviet propaganda organization, for high-ranking members of the Communist Party. The secret presentation was on display above the ramparts and behind the crenellated brick walls of the Kremlin.

Heavily guarded and solidly built in stone, the Kremlin was a fortressed city surrounded by red walls and filled with white and yellow palaces, gold-domed churches, red and green towers, and dark dungeons. Although it was nearly impossible to penetrate the area, she had recently been inside to interview Karl Radek, commissar of the Rosta, and planned to use his card, which she had conveniently forgotten to turn in, to try and secure permission to enter the grounds.

Approaching the high Kremlin gate, she showed the card and announced to the young woman behind the desk that she had an appointment with the chief of propaganda. As the receptionist reached for the phone to call his office, Marguerite counted on the fact that the telephone lines were weak and often not in working order. If the phone call went through and the official on the other end denied she had an appointment, Marguerite would claim she had some follow-up questions to her interview. If the Rosta chief still refused to see her, she and McCullagh would be ordered to leave the Kremlin at once.

Fortune smiled on them: discouraged by the phone situation, the impatient young woman signed the permission, and the pair were soon inside the grounds. As they walked along the path of the vast building in search of the Rosta exhibition, Marguerite spotted a broad-shouldered man of average height wearing an army uniform and Sam Browne belt. She saw his curly brown hair, dark moustache, and beard, his penetrating eyes, his high forehead and pointy chin, and recognized him at once: she had seen him deliver his speech at the opening Soviet session. Standing at the podium of the Opera House, with his military bearing and his hands behind his back, she remembered he had spoken compellingly in "short, terse, pithy sentences interspersed with real flashes of humor."

"That's Trotsky," she told her friend and ran to catch up with the Soviet leader in charge of the Red Army.

"*Tovarich* (Comrade) Trotsky," she called out, taking him by surprise. Would he be so kind as to give her a short interview? It was a daring move since interviews required formal written requests and received formal written answers. Comrade Trotsky seemed astonished at her audacious approach, but he was a journalist and knew the importance of spreading the Communists' word. He had spent years in Europe and months in New York writing for socialist papers and continued to keep his hand in matters of the Soviet press. He stopped and nodded.

Apologizing for her Russian, Marguerite asked if he preferred to converse in English, German, or French. He would speak in French, Trotsky replied, cordially praising her Russian as better than his English. Almost at once she threw her questions at him, asking about his plans for the army, and though he refused to address the subject, his hard mouth formed itself into a "whimsical smile," and she "suddenly realized this grim-visaged man could be very charming."

They stood and talked for several minutes, discussing the Russian military and the Russian economy, until he turned the interview around; he questioned her about conditions in America and asked her impressions of Soviet Russia. A few minutes later Trotsky declared he was late for an appointment and politely dismissed her.

"It has been a great pleasure to have a little chat with a bourgeois who has braved the discomforts of life in Russia at the present time, in order to obtain firsthand material about our proletarian dictatorship," he said with great formality. She thanked him and offered to shake his hand. "Au revoir, and a pleasant visit, madame," he said; and then the driving force of the proletariat revolution took her hand and kissed it.

.   .   .

Pleased to have talked even briefly to one of the three most powerful leaders of the Communist government, she continued her walk with McCullagh around the Kremlin, determined to find the Rosta presentation. As they came upon a special room at the Department of Justice, they saw signs for the exhibit. The notices clearly advised them to keep away, but they ignored the warnings and surreptitiously slipped in. They discovered a treasure chest of information.

Maps showed the up-to-date telegraph lines that crossed the country sending out the Rosta's news reports to every small town and city in Russia; charts covering the walls showed Communist propaganda centers and their results in foreign countries around the world; massive lists of names and numbers revealed the complex organization of the Communist Party. With no guards to stop them, the two spies stayed for hours, reading the text in Russian, memorizing some of the material, brazenly making notes on the rest, knowing that if they were seen they would be reported to the Cheka. They had taken the risk of being arrested or worse, but the wealth of material was worth it.

The exhibit, like her meetings and interviews, reinforced her belief that the Bolsheviks were "securely in the saddle" and would be strengthened by foreign intervention. She cautioned those inclined to overthrow the new Soviet government that interference from the outside would only intensify nationalistic feelings inside Russia.

CHAPTER 10

Safe Dreams

Art provided an escape.

As often as she could, she slipped away to galleries and museums, particularly the Tretyakov, the celebrated museum lined with early Russian paintings and icons, and the Museum of Modern Western Art, the former home of Sergei Shchukin. His collection of works by Monet, Degas, Renoir, and Gauguin covered the walls from floor to ceiling.

In the evenings, Moscow's theaters and halls sprang to life, their rows filled with citizens from every stratum of society, their stages showcasing Russians who had performed in Europe and America and were recognized as some of the greatest artists in the world. "It was February 1920 and Moscow was cold, hungry and at war with half the world. It had not lost its love for or appreciation of the drama."

Privileged to purchase seats in the best boxes, she attended concerts, ballets, the opera, and dramatic offerings, often with Comrade Axionov, the smooth-tongued Cheka minder from the Horitonevsky guesthouse. Although most of her colleagues saw him as an oily creature who coiled himself around his victims, she chose to view him as a charmingly erudite man who opened the door to a world of arts and intellect. A poet, translator, and expert on art and the theater, the bald-headed, red-bearded courtier made "an amusing companion," she said.

Well connected to the revolutionary literary community, *tovarich* Axionov took her to the poets' club, Domino, on Tverskaya Street, where over ices, coffee, and cakes at the Poets' Cafe, he introduced her to some of its leading members. In a country where poets were worshipped as cultural idols, she heard the Futurist Vladimir Mayakovsky, deemed by Stalin "the best and most talented poet of our Soviet epoch," recite his militaristic "Left," along with his passionate rhymes of unrequited love.

At least one evening a week she attended the Bolshoi Opera and watched Serge Koussevitzky, who would later become director of the Boston Symphony, conduct the Moscow Symphony Orchestra. She listened to Feodor Chaliapin, whom Toscanini called the greatest bass he ever conducted, sing *Faust* and other operas. At the Conservatory, she was dazzled when she learned that the members of the chamber music quartet each played a Stradivarius given to them by the government. "If anything could have induced me to become a Communist it would have been this fact," she said. "I have never heard anything more luscious than the ensemble." To someone like her, who had once considered becoming a professional pianist, this was a heavenly feast.

On one winter evening she joined a group of residents around the guesthouse samovar and supped on thick black bread and ersatz tea before they all headed off to the theaters. Despite the February chill and the paltry amount of food, Moscow offered a full supply of music and drama.

Together they set off for the half-hour walk, tramping along the hard-packed snow in the middle of the street, avoiding the icy piles falling from the roofs and the mounds piling up on the sidewalks, gaining groups of people as they trekked along. Some had tickets for Tchaikovsky's *Pique Dame* at the Bolshoi Opera; some were going to hear Chaliapin sing Mephistopheles in *Faust;* a few were headed for a comedy of manners at the Little Theatre; a few to see a Russian version of *Measure for Measure;* others to the Gabima for the Jewish theater.

It was opening night at the Art Theatre, where she had tickets for Lord Byron's play *Cain.* In spite of the cold, audience members were ordered to check their outer layers; handing over her fur coat in the shabby unheated hall, amidst the Bolshevik bigwigs and their party colleagues, she saw a sprinkling of aristocratic and bourgeois ladies in sables, velvets, and jewels.

On other occasions at the same theater, which was headed by

Stanislavski, she saw Pushkin's drama *Boris Godunov;* Chekhov's comedies; and plays by Shakespeare and Oscar Wilde. The *Sun*'s former drama critic drank it all in like a giddy girl at a party. Confidentially, the great actor Stanislavski told her he longed to be performing in America. "It is the dream of my life," he said. Two years later he showed off his famed method on a European tour.

After the theater, she took her place at the Metropole, where, with a handful of male correspondents, she sat in on the late-night foreign office press briefings and heard the day-old news delivered in French. She also made nightly visits to the Rosta, the Soviet propaganda agency whose secret exhibit she had seen, and where she was able to read the up-to-date news in Russian. The reports, which contained everything from distant strikes and minor uprisings to the firm hold of the Bolsheviks around the country, gave her an in-depth picture for MI.

Like everyone in Moscow, she read the two most important papers, *Izvestia* ("News") and *Pravda* ("Truth"), and noted a favorite saying of many Bolsheviks: "There is no truth in the News and no news in the Truth."

She worked long past midnight in the small, frayed room at the Metropole assigned to foreign correspondents. Seated in one of the old French gilt chairs, sharing black-market tea and sugar with journalists from the *Chicago Daily News*, the *Chicago Tribune*, the *London Daily Herald*, the *London Express*, and the French paper *Le Journal*, she wrote her newspaper stories, submitted them to the Soviet censors, and then, hoping they would not be waylaid, she radiogrammed them to the AP.

She considered her articles to be objective and fair. If the censors blackened out some lines, so be it. It was a small price to pay for the access she gained and the insights she would pass on to MI either by coded messages or in person after she left the country.

A glance at her watch often showed it was two or three in the morning when, alone and unafraid, she made the half-hour walk in the dark from the foreign office to her guesthouse. She felt no fear of mugging or murder: Moscow claimed its place as one of the safest cities in the world. If there was danger, and there was, it came from the secret police, who spied on all and held everyone under suspicion.

On some nights when she and her colleagues were hungry, they walked together to the Horitonevsky, where she cooked them scrambled eggs on a small kerosene stove in her room. Sipping tea or enjoying a rare cup of cocoa, they smoked cigarettes and talked excitedly for hours.

In typical Soviet style, it had taken her five days and a tangle of red tape to buy the saucepan for her stove. On the first day, she submitted her identity papers and "bourgeois press" credentials and received a purchase order in exchange. The next day, she turned in the purchase order for an order to go to a showroom store and choose the pan she wanted; she then traded that order for a purchase coupon for a store in her neighborhood. When she figured out what day the pan would be available, she walked there early in the morning, before the store opened, to be sure that a pan would still be available. In the end, she said triumphantly, she received a saucepan that was "good and cheap" and only cost her three rubles. If she had saved the time and bought the pan in the open market, she would have paid almost three thousand rubles.

As her guests ate the food and drank their tea, the conversation flowed, and her comfortable room was transformed into a salon. The discussion turned into meaty debate, and the best talks took place when a few of her Russian friends joined the group, arguing into the early morning about politics, art, theater, philosophy, and religion.

Talking and shouting through air thickened with cigarette smoke, they disagreed about who was right: Trotsky, who favored a small Soviet government and wanted peace with Poland, or his bitter rival, Stalin, who urged a tight rein on the government and saw victory over the Poles as the key to conquering Germany, France, and the rest of Europe. They argued over which was better: Stanislavski's Art Theater and its emphasis on realism, or the breakaway Kamerny Theater, which produced symbolistic plays with stage settings that Marguerite called "bizarre and somewhat bewildering."

They quarreled about the lush, modern paintings of Monet and Renoir hanging in the Shchukin Museum, comparing them with the constructivist propaganda works of Malevich and Rodchenko, the red and black posters plastered around the city that Marguerite preferred. She had only disdain for new works shown in the galleries and meant to "represent the Spirit of the Revolution." "Cubists, futurists, expressionists, utilitarianists, and many others of which I never even mastered the names, had apparently entered into a race to see which could produce the most bizarre effects."

She spoke of the "amazing conglomerations of the colors of the spectrum, applied in cubes, half-moons, circles, and streaks." One group of artists worked only in black and white, others used dark varnish to paint wiggly lines on black backgrounds. "They seemed to me either utterly childish or monstrously decadent," she said with disgust.

The conversation moved from artistic styles to more philosophical musings: Should propaganda be considered art? Could art express ideology or was it about impressions and emotions? What was the role of religion? How powerful was the Church? Was it superior to the government or was it subsumed by it? Or, was Communism the new faith?

Marguerite reveled in the discourse. She may have been an eighth-generation American and the patrician daughter of a Gilded Age tycoon who had been presented with a silver tea set by the czar, but she felt "very much at home," she said, among the Russian people, no matter if they were Communists or monarchists. The unflappable newswoman who suppressed her feelings and admitted she "felt afraid to form close ties," even with her young son, found the Russians' exuberance irresistible: "I loved their generosity; their Oriental sense of hospitality, their sensitivity to beauty, their indifference to material discomfort, and above all, their delight in purely impersonal debates on every subject under the sun."

It thrilled her when she was advised she could continue her stay for another month, far longer than any of the other visiting journalists. Apparently, she had shown interest in all the right activities of the government, from health care and education to women and industry. It was true that once in a while she tested the limits, slipping out of the clutches of the foreign office; nonetheless, the foreign office seemed pleased with her stories.

She shrugged off the news when she heard she had to leave her guesthouse to make room for the arrival of an English Labour delegation. Told she was being moved to the Savoy Hotel, she pushed away fears of its reputation for housing suspicious foreigners and for turning a blind eye to their arrests. She was sure her position was safe.

Cut off from communication with the West, she was unaware that MI in Washington had sent an urgent message to Warsaw warning that she was in danger: "her clandestine status was suspected by the Russian Bolshevik Colony in Switzerland when she passed through that country," the American attaché said. Apparently, Mr. Hecker had been hard at work.

.   .   .

She was taken by surprise when at four a.m. on an April morning, crossing the Strastnoy Boulevard on the short walk to the Savoy from the foreign office, she was approached by a soldier. As he fell into step beside her, she heard him ask, "*Vasha familia?*" "Garrison," she replied, pronouncing her family name the Russian way. "Christian name?" he wanted to know. "Margharita Bernardovna," she answered. "You are arrested," he said, and with a smile he showed her papers with the orders. With that, he led her around the corner to the most feared place in Moscow.

She shuddered at the sight of the Lubyanka prison number two, the special section of the prison used by the infamous Cheka, the All-Russia Extraordinary Commission, where solitary confinement, torture, or execution, or combinations of the three, awaited suspects accused of espionage. The massive building that loomed before her, once the home of a Russian insurance company, boasted a motto over its entrance: "It is prudent to insure your life."

In a dingy outer room, she was questioned briefly by a man in a leather jacket and boots, then taken elsewhere to be stripped, searched, and fingerprinted by a female warden who led her through the corridors upstairs. They stopped at a tiny room that contained only a bed made of thin boards on trestles, a small table, and a wastebasket used as a toilet. The window was covered over in whitewash; the heavy door had a peephole controlled from outside. She looked around and saw there was no one else in the cell. The heavy door closed with a thud.

"Curiously enough, I was not panic-stricken," she later said. Months of living in countries where arrests were common and life was cheap had hardened her to danger. "If you are among people who place little value on human life you unconsciously absorb something of their point of view." Besides, she had taught herself years before not to feel her emotions.

She knew that she had crossed the red line more than once when she eluded the foreign office and went off on her own without a minder, or when she had exchanged money on the black market and used it to buy food in the illegal souks, or when she developed friendships with people opposed to the government, but she felt certain that friends in the foreign office would come to her rescue.

Exhausted, she dropped down on the bare planks in the cell, covered herself in her fur-lined coat, and slept. But the sound of the peephole opening and a searchlight shining into the room woke her every half hour.

In the morning, a hand reached in and gave her a broom to sweep the small space. A few minutes later a slovenly woman brought her moldy bread and weak tea. She waited, but no one else came. At noon she ate a bowl of thin soup and bits of kasha and waited some more. "I began to grow restless," she said. "The suspense was trying."

Later that afternoon, when a soldier appeared and beckoned her to follow, she walked behind him through a maze of hallways, up and down steep stairs, arriving at last at a comfortable office furnished with bookcases and leather chairs. She glanced around and saw a lean man with burning, fanatical eyes stretched out on a sofa in front of a glowing fire; he was Menjinsky, head of the special section of Cheka. A second man, short and blond, sat opposite.

Behind a large desk a slender man in his thirties, his dark hair parted in the center, his face clean-shaven with a neat moustache, introduced himself as Mogilevsky, Chief Commissar of the Foreign Department of the All-Russian Extraordinary Commission, the Cheka. She recognized his name and knew that he dealt with espionage cases and counterrevolutionaries. The three men bowed courteously, and as she bowed back, Mogilevsky motioned for her to take a seat.

She had expected to confront a brutish figure, but instead she faced an elegant man with a quiet composure and the sleek look of a puma. Speaking in fluent French, he quickly came to the point: "We have been watching you for some time, Citizeness Garrison. We are fully aware of the nature of your visit. We know that you are here as a representative of the American Secret Service."

Stunned by what he said, she was even more astonished by what followed. It felt as though Mogilevsky was pouncing on her with his words: "You acted in a similar capacity in Germany last year. We have reports from both America and Germany to prove this." With that he showed her detailed accounts, and as she digested the information and saw the reports, she knew it was too late. But she refused to give in so easily. "That's all very well," she countered, "but what if I deny it? What you have told me is circumstantial. What is your proof?"

Mogilevsky smiled, opened a leather case, and drew out a paper that shocked her. He was showing her a copy of a coded document with a handwritten note at the bottom that she had typed and transmitted to Washington: it was the memo she had sent from the *Adriatic* about Julius Hecker. As soon as she saw the government watermarks she knew that this was authentic. There was a leak in Military Intelligence, and her report had been stolen; a mole had slipped in and infiltrated the American agency. The game was up: without a doubt, the Russians would deport her.

Deport her? Twirling his fingers, the interrogator shook his head. "No, my dear lady, you know too much for that." He gave her a crooked smile. "Your fate will depend entirely on your own attitude." She could be shot for acting as a Polish spy, he suggested, but there were things she could do that would be more helpful to the Soviets. She waited silently for him to continue.

"We want information about foreigners," he said. "For instance, what do you know about your friend, Mr. McCullagh?"

"Know?" she asked, feigning surprise. She knew he worked for British intelligence. "Only what everybody knows," she replied. "He is one of the most famous British war correspondents."

"Has he ever been in the Intelligence Service?" Mogilevsky asked. "Certainly not," she answered coolly.

The Cheka official questioned her at length, but she refused to succumb to his cross-examination, knowing that her friend had probably been arrested too. Finally, the interrogation stopped, Mogilevsky pressed a bell, and an aide brought them cigarettes and glasses of tea.

As suddenly as it had begun, the conversation changed, sounding less like an inquisition and more like the cosmopolitan talk in a drawing room. Well mannered and cultured, the men asked for her impressions of Moscow and engaged her in a discussion of dance, music, theater, and art. Under great strain, her stomach in knots, she tried to appear relaxed as she sat tall in her chair, legs crossed at the ankles, sipping her tea and chatting about symphony concerts and constructivist art. But what she desperately wanted to know was, what would happen next? Would they hand her a lifeline or throw her a hangman's rope?

She felt great relief when Mogilevsky announced, "We are prepared to give you your liberty, Citiziness Garrison." But before she could relax, he continued: Her release could only take place "under certain conditions."

"What are they?" she asked. "First," he cautioned, "you will make no attempt to leave Moscow," and added that her stay would be "indefinite." Secondly, she was to report to him twice a week and supply him with information about the foreigners, particularly the British and Americans, she encountered. "Your freedom will depend on how useful you are to us," he warned.

He was offering her a Faustian choice: she would be kept in prison and charged with being a spy for the Poles, or she would be released in Moscow and become an agent for the Russians. His words soured in her stomach.

"I sat back in the chair grasping the arms tightly, my brain racing madly in an effort to make a decision," she recalled. Should she accept the offer or turn it down? She felt "like a drowning person who sees all his past life in a second." Images of her son waiting in Switzerland, of her friends and her life back in Baltimore floated in her mind. "In that moment I renounced everything . . . that made up my existence. It was finished—and I felt as if I had already died and been born into a new nightmare world."

No doubt, espionage against the Soviets would lead to her execution; espionage for the Soviets might only postpone her death. Yet, who knew what might come next? Calmly, she answered Mogilevsky: "I accept your proposition." She signed an agreement to spy for the Cheka with a salary of 42,500 rubles.

CHAPTER 11

Nightmare

Her Russian friends called it *koshmar,* a nightmare. Drenched in fog, laden with a sense of doom, she was sleepwalking through a bad dream. She never knew whose eyes were watching her, whose footsteps were shadowing her, whose ears were listening at her walls, whose hands were rifling through her belongings.

Released from the Lubyanka, she set out at once to inform MI of her situation. It was important, she knew, to relay as much information as she could as quickly as she could. Within a few days her remarkable ability for recall enabled her to put together a coded report of her imprisonment along with a five-page assessment of the Soviet government that included the secret Rosta information she had discovered at the Kremlin.

She alerted those who thought the Bolshevik government was a weak or easy target to the realities of Russian politics. Her confidential analysis began: "General political situation is absolutely controlled by Communist party. All of their meetings are packed and independent political activity is impossible."

Her freedom had a deadline, but she had no knowledge of the date. She hurriedly arranged meetings with foreign businessmen and correspondents traveling to Riga or Berlin and gave them messages verbally or in typed memos, squeezing her words inside matchbooks or writing them with invisible ink on foreign bank notes. She alerted them about Americans imprisoned by the Cheka and informed MI of foreign visitors and European correspondents in Moscow; only those deemed sympathetic to the government were given permission to be there.

Sending the messages was a daring move on her part; perhaps too daring, warned the American ambassador in London. "I trust that Mrs. Harrison realizes the danger she runs in sending such communications and the [Riga] Consul has been sufficiently impressed with the absolute need of secrecy. Otherwise," he wrote chillingly, "she will not last long."

Her memo had included intelligence on foreign Bolsheviks plotting to enter the United States. As the attaché at the American legation in Finland explained in a memo to the Department of State, the Soviets were "organizing with great energy the extension of Bolshevism to other countries. They have formed a bureau for that purpose," and its representatives were working in at least eight countries, including the United States.

The Bolsheviks had developed a sophisticated system for penetrating foreign borders. Delegates from England and other countries invited to attend meetings in Russia were often informed that their passports had been lost, but the Cheka simply kept them. They either altered the documents for their own emissaries or produced others based on the ones they stole. They had "the most up-to-date machinery" and "the best experts engaged at the work," the attaché said. Furthermore, they had a department dedicated to discovering messages written with invisible ink, and another for forging the foreign money they sent abroad.

At the same time that Marguerite sent her lengthy memo, the ambassador in London dispatched a "Confidential and Urgent" letter to MI in Washington stating that Mrs. Harrison had been put under arrest and was likely to be expelled from Russia. Added to the pile on General Churchill's desk was a letter from her father-in-law: "We have not heard from Mrs. Marguerite Harrison for nearly three months," wrote Joseph Ames worriedly. "Would you be good enough to have someone in your office write me about what is known of her?"

The response to Dr. Ames came from Colonel Coxe, the acting chief while Churchill was ill and in the hospital. Coxe, who first met Marguerite at his office in Paris in November 1918 and had read the reports she sent from Berlin, held great faith in her abilities: "Our latest information concerning her, dated April 15th, is to the effect that she has aroused the suspicions of the Soviet Government of Russia as not being a true Bolshevist and that that Government is undecided whether to expel her from Russia or allow her to remain in that country."

He ended his letter with a touch of humor: "I feel certain that Mrs. Harrison will be able to convince the Soviet officials that it is to the interest of the Soviet Government to allow her to remain. I would not be at all surprised to hear that she had been given an important position under the Soviet Government with Lenin and Trotsky depending upon her for guidance."

.   .   .

Despite Coxe's confidence, a phone call to her room that same day left Marguerite feeling shaky. "Bonjour madame," the man said softly. "I would like to see you this afternoon. Meet me in the Alexandrovsky Gardens at four o'clock." There was no need for him to state his name; she recognized the voice immediately. Mogilevsky wanted her to report to him with information.

The Cheka official was sitting on a bench in the gardens outside the Kremlin walls when she arrived. "Any news?" he asked; he had a habit of twirling his moustache. He had ordered her to keep watch over the foreign guests at the Savoy, including an Afghan who invited her to tea. Tall and dark with deep brown eyes, the Afghan asked her if she had a husband. When she answered "no," he asked if she had found a man in Moscow. When she answered "no" again, he responded:

"You are young and you look healthy. I got plenty wives in Afghanistan, but here it is very lonely." Coming a little closer, he eyed her more intensely; "I don't want Russian woman," he said. "I always wanted English woman. We marry now, what you say? We stay married while I'm here or I take you back to Afghanistan. Fine country. You be first wife." She would think it over, she replied, and quickly slipped away.

Mogilevsky demanded more serious news. Among the foreigners she had met were a Czech Communist, some Swedish businessmen, a delegation of German workers, two activist Hindus from India, and a former Austrian officer. Considering the information to be harmless, she offered up some tidbits on each, and while answering her examiner was arduous, she seemed to satisfy his demands. To her relief, he moved on to other subjects and talked about the revolution that he, like so many of his colleagues, was certain would take place in America and England. Thankfully, he made no mention of the reports she secreted out.

The meetings in the park, sometimes weekly, often more frequent, continued, and although they carried a whiff of seduction, she knew the head of Cheka was deadly serious. Seated on a bench or strolling along the paths, he interrogated her for hours, demanding reports on recent acquaintances, probing deeper and deeper into the activities of people she knew, particularly British and American correspondents.

Aware she was being used as a trap, she had spread the word and warned friends and colleagues who were not sympathetic to the socialist ideology to keep away from her. But Mogilevsky's questions were difficult to sidestep: Who did she see? Where did she see them? Why did she meet them? What did they say? Why did they say it? Who else was there? Where else did they go? What did they want? What were their opinions?

"It was a tremendous tax on my ingenuity to furnish him with information which would satisfy him and at the same time do no one any harm," she said. The long sessions left her feeling "quite limp." Mrs. Harrison could try to be clever and play a game of defiance, but Mogilevsky was toying with her life.

Oddly, she admired the ardent Communist who worked twenty-four hours a day for the Cheka. "He was ruthless," she conceded, but "not cruel or bloodthirsty." As they engaged in rounds of coy debate, she found something intriguing about her Grand Inquisitor. They discussed their beliefs, shared similar literary interests, respected each other's intellects, and compared their backgrounds: she the socially prominent Protestant daughter of an international business mogul; he the son of a Jewish merchant from a small village who found inspiration in Bolshevik ideas. Despite the vast gulf between them, "There gradually grew up between Mogilevsky and myself a curious sort of camaraderie," she said. "I took a certain enjoyment in our verbal duels. His was a keen alert mind and he was a stimulating and resourceful enemy."

Along with the challenging sessions, she continued to attend the midnight press briefings at the foreign office and wrote her stories for the AP. Moreover, with the type of bold behavior Coxe admired, she never stopped smuggling out reports, either verbally or written, to MI.

She breathed a sigh of relief when, at the beginning of May, she received permission to return to the Horitonevsky from the Savoy; nonetheless, her fate seemed sealed. Unlike the British, who were offering aid to the Russians in exchange for release of their citizens, the Americans did not seem to be negotiating aid deals with the Russians. Although as a British citizen, Frank McCullagh had been allowed to leave, she had no way to escape. She often heard it said in Moscow that "everyone has sat in prison, will sit in prison, or is sitting in prison." Therefore, "it made little difference what I did or where I went. Eventually I would go back to Lubyanka." Her words revealed a sense of yearning for an end to the unease.

Whatever her movements, she could feel the eyes of the Cheka and sense the shadowy figures stalking her. The diversionary tactics she had learned were put to good use. She knew how to surprise her pursuers by stopping short, how to disappear into a doorway, or veer off suddenly into a side street. But the strain was enormous. In a covert message to the American consul in Finland, she asked him to contact the AP and send instructions for her to return home. She never received an answer.

She had learned from the deaths of her husband and her father that the best way to stay calm was to keep busy, "so busy that I would have no time to think during the day." But in bed in the dark, the calm disappeared, and her mind raced from one harrowing scenario to the next. "It was only at night when sleep would not come that I yielded to despair."

.   .   .

At the Horitonevsky guesthouse, the cast of characters kept changing, but she was pleased that Alexander Berkman remained and was now assigned by Mogilevsky to the room next to hers. His frequent visitor was his friend and political partner Emma Goldman, who had just come from Petrograd and was living at the National Hotel. As leading figures of their party, they played an important role for Americans coming to Moscow. Mogilevsky may have been curious, but their influence was too great to do them harm.

Emma Goldman, small and thickset with intense dark eyes, had been deported with Berkman and arrived in the old capital filled with hope. But she quickly became disillusioned. The sound of gunshots in the night filled her with fear, and when her good friend, the journalist Jack Reed, confirmed that five hundred counterrevolutionaries had recently been lined up against a wall and executed, she called it "wholesale slaughter," and said, "I never thought the revolution would signify callous indifference to human life." Dismayed "by the labyrinth of Soviet Russia," she found herself "stumbling over the many obstacles, vainly groping for the Revolutionary light."

Passionate in her beliefs, she felt as strongly about free love as she did about free speech and had enjoyed a romance with Sasha Berkman years before in New York. Keenly intelligent, she had founded *Mother Earth*, a well-regarded anarchist journal, hired Berkman as its editor, and published the work of John Reed, Louise Bryant, Margaret Sanger, Eugene O'Neill, Leo Tolstoy, Robert Minor, and Man Ray. A provocative speaker who drew large crowds, she fought hard against America's effort to join the World War and helped drive the anticonscription movement, leading to her exile.

Marguerite found her to be "a sympathetic soul," honest and good-natured. The two women became friendly, caring for Berkman, who was ill. They administered medicines for his stomach problems, feeding him the soft foods they cooked over Marguerite's kerosene stove, changing his hot water bottle, and chatting for hours in his room. Emma's wit, her perceptive insights on leading Bolsheviks, and her scornful comments on their business methods delighted Marguerite.

Berkman's disappointment with the czarist tactics of the Soviets was growing daily. Looking out from behind his owlish horn-rimmed glasses, he talked of his concerns over their ruthless methods. His years in U.S. prisons had left him deeply scarred, and now the cruelty of the Cheka and the brutality of the Red Army crushed his belief in the Soviet system. He too was appalled by the numbers of executions and the tortures taking place and was even more dismayed by the lack of freedom of speech and the loss of human dignity. What had become of his sweet dreams? What had become of his youth?

He had thought that Communism was a step on the path to anarchy which he considered "ideally altruistic" and had hoped that anarchism would blossom into individualism. Out of that, he was certain, would come a socially responsible society. It was an idealistic view seen through a darkening lens. Nonetheless, he still imagined some rays of light.

While Berkman felt at home in Soviet Russia, Marguerite noted that Goldman felt "like a round peg in a square hole." Uncomfortable in the country she had fled as a child, uneasy with the language, unsympathetic to the Communists, she was desperately homesick for America. And while Marguerite thought her time in Russia had not lessened her beliefs as an anarchist, she did think her experience with the Bolsheviks made her "a much better American."

The anarchists had been an influential group in Russia for more than fifty years, promoting ideas like equality for women, communes for the serfs, and free education for all. But their opposition to Bolshevik methods put them at odds with the government. They were strongly in favor of the individual and strongly opposed to the dictatorship imposed after the Revolution.

Marguerite attended meetings at the anarchists' "Universalist" club on the Tverskaya, where the Cheka bloated the room with its spies. "There was at least one Chekist to every anarchist or impartial listener," she said. Like the Mensheviks, the Populist Socialists, and other opposition groups, they were permitted to run their own club but constantly persecuted by the secret police. Although Berkman and Goldman were treated with respect, many others in the party were repeatedly put in prison. Then again, arrests were hardly surprising. "Everyone spends time in prison," Russians repeated in disgust.

Marguerite had promised MI to keep an open mind, to be objective in her thinking and impartial in her reports. Eager to hear many points of view, she went to a range of political meetings, attended an array of church services, visited the few shops still open, and stopped at the stalls in the markets to chat with the vendors.

At the sprawling Sukharevka, she found rows of stands offering everything from highly prized Chinese porcelains, ball gowns, and Oriental rugs sold off by aristocratic families to plain cloth and tools stolen by government workers. In some sections, dealers offered expensive shoes, cosmetics, and food, while in other areas they peddled gramophones, records, or cheap pens. Added to the scene, ragged children with sunken eyes tugged at shoppers' hems, begging for a kopek or something, anything, to eat.

Often the police raided the souk, hauling off traders, forcing them to give up their illegal wares to Cheka officials who kept the goods for themselves. Marguerite found the frequent *bladas* on the Sukharevka "very exciting," and after being caught in several raids, she learned to recognize the silent warning system among the professional dealers, many of whom paid off the police with protection money.

First came the whispers, nods, and winks, and then the hushed bundling up of their wares as they dismantled their stands and rushed to the exits seconds before the troops arrived. A short time later the dealers returned; once again they opened their tables, spread out their goods, and went on with business as usual.

Marguerite favored the areas that sold French soaps, cigarettes, and food, especially fresh produce, eggs, meat, butter, and sugar; she willingly paid one dollar for a loaf of white bread, or four times the cost of black bread; two and a half dollars for a pound of butter or sugar; six dollars for tea. Wherever she went, she felt the eyes of the Cheka on her.

Rarely did she take her meals at the guesthouse, where the conversation was muffled with fear, and the dinners featured sparse, dismal food. Rather, as the snow puddled and finally melted away, she enjoyed the offerings at the Sukharevka's outdoor restaurants. Like the Russians she met there who could still afford the steep prices, she relished the tasty white bread and butter, the meat *kotleta, pierogi,* and sweet Russian pastries.

Other times she ate with friends in their modest homes or at illicit restaurants where an introduction was necessary. Her escorts included a friendly foreign office official who often took her to the home of a government worker; the man provided tasty conversation while his wife served thick vegetable soup, good meat and chicken, pastries, and real coffee.

On other occasions she went with theater acquaintances to the homes of actors, and more than once she was taken out by the small delegation of the Jewish Joint Distribution Committee. They not only brought her to restaurants that served specialties such as gefilte fish and roast duck with apples and onions, they also helped her out with personal needs. The warm summer weather called for lightweight clothes, but her one silk dress had been stolen from her room at the Savoy, and the only suit she had was made of heavy wool. Judge Harry Fisher gave her two of his silk shirts that she cut and sewed to fit her, and before the committee left with her coded messages to MI tucked inside their bags, another colleague gave her his toothpaste and soap.

She had met a number of Jewish people through Dr. Karlin and frequently visited their homes. She liked their company, found their conversations stimulating, and enjoyed their good food. Many Jews held important positions, but contrary to stories she heard before she arrived in Russia, she reported, they did not hold the majority of high-level positions.

They had eagerly supported the Revolution and at first fared well; indeed, she said, "for the first time in history, the Russian Jew was a free citizen." Many Jews had been merchants or small businessmen, but because they were not trade union members, they did not enjoy Communist Party privileges. When the government shut down the shops and seized their businesses, they turned to black-market trade, which led to arrests and long prison sentences. Most would have favored a coup, but they realized that a counterrevolution would have brought back the pogroms.

For Marguerite, dining with friends, whether in private homes or restaurants, offered an opportunity to speak with people from all types of backgrounds. Invited to visit the executor of Tolstoy's estate, she met the famed author's youngest daughter, Alexandra. An outspoken woman who loudly protested the lack of free speech, Madame Tolstoya spent years in and out of prison but never refrained from expressing her disgust with the Bolsheviks. Not long after they met, Marguerite heard her deliver an impassioned defense at her own trial.

Wandering into various shops, the American entered one that served mushrooms, the most basic and beloved of Russian foods, and *varenets*, the traditional sweet baked yogurt. Speaking with the amiable owner, a former colonel in the czar's army, she was invited to join his family for their five p.m. meal. In their modest apartment, she saw the former bourgeois couple, educated and refined, suffering the degradation and deprivations of Bolshevik life.

The colonel's wife, employed in education, and his daughter, a dance student who worked as an office clerk, spent six days a week at their jobs and then waited on line for hours to purchase their meager rations of food, clothing, and household necessities. They worked, cooked, cleaned, and did the laundry, and yet, Marguerite said admiringly, they maintained an air of elegance in their stylish clothes and at their well-dressed table.

Over a typical dinner of potato soup, black bread and butter, kasha, and raisin tea, they shared their stories and introduced her to their friends. Most intriguing was their guest General Alexei Brusilov: a genuine hero of the Great War, he had shattered the Austrian army on the Eastern Front and was well respected by the Allies for his brilliant leadership.

The general was as distinguished in his looks as he was in his military skills. Small and slim, with a high forehead, smoothed-back white hair, and sweeping waxed moustache, he had the sly look of a fox, spoke fluent French and German, and was a legendary figure to every Russian.

Invited to his home on Mansurovsky Pereoulok, close to the Kremlin and the Cathedral of Christ the Savior, where he faithfully attended church, Marguerite walked past creamy stone buildings of baroque and Italianate design. Although most of the bourgeoisie were forced to surrender their homes to the workers and lived with their families crammed four to a room, he was allowed to maintain his spacious apartment with his wife in the smart Ostozhenka neighborhood. The elegant Nadia Brusilov, thirteen years younger, was an intelligent writer adored by her husband.

The Brusilovs' flat flowed with constant visitors, from artists and writers to army officers, who often arrived bearing fresh fruits and other scarce foods. Presiding over tea in the drawing room, or dinner at the table, the couple led their guests through a range of topics. Nadia came from a family of strong women: her mother was a well-known novelist; her late aunt, the mysterious Madame Blavatsky, led the Theosophists in America; her sister, Vera, living in Brooklyn, was married to Charles Johnston, a founder of the movement. Nadia herself wrote on military affairs, but she peppered Marguerite, who became a frequent guest, with questions about life in America.

Most of the attention, however, focused on General Brusilov. Over dinners as special as fresh fish or sorrel soup topped with sour cream, gifts sent by admiring old soldiers, the retired warrior spoke about the motherland. A loyal Russian to the core, he had shifted his support from a constitutional monarchy to Kerensky, but he stopped short, full of forebodings now over the Bolsheviks. Hardly an admirer of the Communists, he was, nonetheless, a strong nationalist and stood firmly against outside interference. Asked about his support for the Bolsheviks in 1917 at the time of the October Revolution, he answered that he had been concerned about British and French intervention: "In the moment of peril, I offered myself to collaborate in order to save Russia from foreigners. I am a soldier."

In May 1920, when the Poles attacked the Russian border, he volunteered to help the Bolshevik military and served as an adviser to the general staff of the Red Army, allowing the government to use his fame to garner support for his country. And yet, he was clearly against the Communists and their methods. Why was he giving aid to their government? he was asked.

"We got ourselves into this mess through our indifference, selfishness and corruption," he told Marguerite. "It is up to us to get ourselves out." She heard him repeat those words many times and took them as a warning to the Americans who wanted to interfere and overthrow the regime. Yet, his loyalty was suspect, and his name was often raised by the Cheka when Marguerite was interrogated.

His son had disappeared in the war, and his daughter-in-law, Anna Ivanova, who came from a rich and prominent family, was allotted only two rooms of her grandmother's large house. The circle of friends she entertained in the small space included wives of professors and military men imprisoned by the Bolsheviks. Marguerite often accompanied her to the open market, where the younger woman sold off family heirlooms and used the money to buy food and medicines for those in prison.

.   .   .

Every country had its share of men incarcerated by the Cheka. Russian prisoners received packages of necessities from their families and friends, but for the rest, their only hope lay with representatives of the Red Cross. One of those who aided in the effort was the Norwegian explorer and diplomat Fridtjof Nansen, who had come to Moscow for the International Red Cross. His special mission involved repatriating hundreds of thousands of war prisoners, many of whom were held in Russia. He was staying at the Horitonevsky when Marguerite met him.

He had no one to help him, and for a short time she served as his secretary, noting the names and locations of American soldiers in custody, information that was important to MI. At the end of tedious days, they relaxed in her room, drinking tea. The cruelty and corruption, greed and ignorance of the czars' reign had made the revolution unavoidable, the diplomat told her. But he was taken aback by the brutality and exploitation by the Soviets. Nonetheless, she admired his ability to keep an impartial view, to focus on the humanitarian rather than the political situation.

The Reverend Frank North also helped prisoners, both British and American, through the British Red Cross. The Americans would not acknowledge that any of their citizens were spies, but officials in Washington wanted to know who had been arrested, how they were being treated, and what condition they were in. MI instructed Marguerite to make contact with the reverend, and she volunteered to serve as his assistant, typing lists of names and helping him supply the prisoner's needs. She knew that everything she did and everyone she saw was under suspicion by the Cheka.

When the British government agreed to give food aid to Russia in exchange for the release of prisoners, Reverend North was able to shepherd a small flock of his countrymen out of Moscow. Before he left, Marguerite stopped by his office to say goodbye. A week later, when the clergyman and his group reached the Russian border, every man and woman was stripped naked and searched; the Soviets were certain Marguerite had slipped them secret material for Washington.

CHAPTER 12

Shock

Nothing quite matched the secret report Marguerite obtained at the end of May. It came from Royal Keeley, an American technical consultant hired by the Bolsheviks to analyze Soviet industry. She had met him briefly when she first crossed the border into Russia; now he wanted to meet in Moscow. They agreed on a covert rendezvous as soon as possible.

Keeley had traveled for almost a year as a management expert doing research work for the Bolshevik government, covering the length and breadth of the country, compiling material on every aspect of Soviet industry. He had been sympathetic to the Communists when he arrived and was treated initially with the courtesies afforded an imperial guest. He was provided with secretaries, a private train with his own sleeping and dining cars, accommodations in the finest hotels, and plentiful meals with good food available only to a handful of high officials. Assigned by top Russian leaders to "go to all the factories, see the actual conditions of every factory, and study the psychology of the working force," he was told to deliver his far-ranging report directly to Vladimir Lenin.

His account, Marguerite said, was "most remarkable." His detailed observations on farming, factories, food supplies, and transportation were damning to the Soviet government. They revealed the run-down equipment, the wrecked trucks, abandoned railroad cars and ruined engines, the lack of fuel, the shortage of food and extensive famines, and the massive unemployment that were devastating the country.

The Russian population consisted of more than 120 million people, yet only a handful reigned at the top. "Everything is in the hands of Government," he said later, with "unscrupulous, unprincipled bandits" controlling "all labor, fuel, food, clothing, and raw material."

The entire country, he reported, was bound in red tape. Every individual was "loaded down with documents—an official passport, a compulsory labor book, permits for food and food cards, permits for a place to live, permits to ride on the street cars." Five or six cards were required just to buy a railway ticket, and each one had to be "signed, countersigned, and red stamped," all of which took as long as two weeks.

As a result of the Bolsheviks' insistence on total control, machines were standing idle and factory production was "painfully low." Unskilled, ignorant workers were assigned to jobs they were incapable of performing, educated people were ordered to draw up plans for projects that would never be carried out, and workers had lost all sense of morale.

The disparaging report enraged Lenin. Instead of praising the consultant for his honest observations and sending him home with gratitude, the Communist leader refused to let him out of the country. As Keeley was about to make his exit from Russia, Lenin rescinded his visa and ordered him to remain in Moscow. Worried about his tenuous state, and certain he was headed for prison, he wanted Marguerite's help.

At their clandestine meeting Keeley told her he was determined to have his report reach officials in Washington and noted that he had added material not included in his original account. "No monarchy was more autocratic than Soviet Russia," he stated. "Freedom of speech is unknown. Freedom of the press is a joke." As a socialist, Keeley still believed that "Bolshevik Russia is visionary," but he deemed it "impractical." In the end, he said, "Bolshevism cannot work."

He had managed to make three copies of his report: one he gave to a man planning to go to Georgia, another to a man who promised to relay it to Poland; the third copy he handed to Marguerite. She took the document and slipped it into her bag. Her challenge was to find a trusted courier willing to smuggle the report out of the country.

Moscow was a cosmopolitan city with visitors from every continent. While the Communist government used its right hand to put an authoritarian chokehold on the people, suppressing free speech and freedom of the press, limiting movements and monitoring friendships, it reached out with its liberal left hand to welcome idealists, official and unofficial, from countries around the world. She had met Turkish nationalists, Persian peacemakers, Chinese dealmakers; Czecho-Slovak, Hungarian, and Austrian negotiators; Italian, British, and German labor leaders; French, Indian, Irish, Mexican, and Korean trade unionists; and other assorted delegates to the Third International, as the Communist international organization was known.

The Savoy Hotel was the official residence for most of the peace delegations including the Letts, as Latvians were called, who she knew were favorably disposed to America. With their diplomatic status she believed they would provide the safest means to deliver Keeley's report. But only visitors with special permission from the Extraordinary Commission were allowed to call on the Letts. Giving them the papers could cost her imprisonment or even her life: she was willing to take the risk.

Hoping to find her Latvian friend, she stopped by his hotel one afternoon. The soldier on duty presented her with the registry book that every visitor was compelled to sign, and that she knew was sent daily to the Cheka headquarters. She scrawled her name and address on the page, described her work as a journalist, and listed someone from a different delegation as the reason for her visit. As required, she surrendered her identity documents to the guard, who would hold them until she was ready to leave.

She walked confidently into the Savoy, appearing to look for her friend, and strolled through the extravagant public rooms. The famed hotel, with its marble floors, wood-paneled walls, and ornate ceilings, embodied the decadent czarist past, but the peeling paint and shabby conditions served as instant reminders of the Bolshevik present. Eluding any Cheka agents trailing behind her, she hunted discreetly for the servants' stairs and stole up the back steps.

The Latvians had been given their own floor, complete with their own dining room and kitchen, but not knowing if her friend was there, she was hugely relieved when she found him. "Luck was with me," she said. The delegate agreed to make arrangements to deliver the report to the American consulate in Riga. He would send the document by diplomatic courier, but, he cautioned, there was no guarantee it would be safe. "I must warn you," he said, "even the diplomatic mail is sometimes searched." Reassuringly he added, "You have a good chance." With those words, she descended stealthily down the backstairs, regained her identity papers, and strode out of the hotel.

A while later, to her great relief she learned that her packet arrived safely in Riga. A highlight of her work in Russia, the information proved to be some of the most important intelligence she delivered to MI. It "more than compensated me for all I had suffered and all the risks I had run since I had undertaken to double-cross the Cheka," she said. Shortly after they met, Royal Keeley was arrested and sent to prison. As for the other two copies, neither one reached its destination.

. . .

Within days, after another of the long interrogation sessions with Mogilevsky, the Cheka commissar gave her instructions: "I want you to meet the members of the British Labour Delegation," he said, "and draw them out on their opinions." During their six-week visit, the foreign office had arranged for the group to make a tour down the Volga River. A coterie of foreign journalists, among them her former colleagues in Berlin, George Young and Arno Dosch-Fleurot, would accompany the Labourites, and "you will of course be included," he said.

The delegation, most leaning to the left but a few to the right, had come primarily to confirm the wonders of the Revolution. But no one, not even professed Bolsheviks, was above suspicion by the Soviet government; all visitors were watched and assessed. Her assignment was to discern those who were committed followers and those who were feigning support.

Marguerite knew that whatever she said to Mogilevsky would not harm the delegates; the Soviets would not risk the economic relief aid they were about to receive from the British. In addition, the Labour group's diplomatic immunity assured them they would not be punished for anti-Soviet ideas. What's more, the trip gave her the opportunity to relay messages through her British counterparts.

The journey offered as much a glimpse into the czar's old realm as an evaluation of the new Communist state. On the luxurious private train that took them east to Nizhny Novgorod, the well-lit sleeping and dining cars offered comfortable beds, crisp linens, and plentiful meals. At their destination point, they were feted at a banquet where *zakuski,* the traditional Russian hors d'oeuvres, were served, and caviar, the great Russian delicacy, was in full supply. Eager to try the moist black grains, Marguerite took a bite of the salty roe; it was her first and last, she claimed.

Excited to see the great Russian experiment, the next day the group boarded the *Belinsky,* a lavish paddleboat steamer furnished with comfortable cabins and good food, although vodka, a mainstay of Russian life, was not available except for those who brought their own. At several towns along the river, the delegates were treated like marionettes in the hands of the Bolshevik masters: welcomed by brass bands, cheered by large crowds, they were put on display as proof that the workers of the world were coming to the side of the Communists.

But it did not take long before some of the visitors recognized the charade; resentment rose each time they reached a village and were trotted out to dance on the Soviets' stage. When the group was invited to ask questions, the accompanying interpreters made certain that the guests heard only the government's point of view.

Although a few delegates maintained almost total faith in the Bolshevik experiment, other guests, including Bertrand Russell who had come to write a newspaper series, were "profoundly shocked" by the ruthlessness and imperialist goals of the Communist dictatorship. As a Fabian socialist, he believed in a democratic form of socialism brought about by reform, not revolution, and later wrote that he was "overwhelmed by a sense of horror" on the trip. "Cruelty, poverty, suspicion, persecution formed the very air we breathed."

Aloof and aristocratic, Russell was a "congenial" soulmate, Marguerite said. "We naturally drifted together as we had much the same background and intellectually had a great deal in common not withstanding our divergent political views."

He sometimes joined her as she, the only Russian speaker among the foreigners, ventured off to talk with the local villagers. She listened to the peasants, who were less interested in Soviet affairs and more concerned with farming problems, food shortages, and the famine they warned was coming soon.

She expected to see men who were tall and blond, singing of slaving to fell the stout birch trees. Instead, she saw dreary little towns, no river traffic, and no bearded Volga boatmen pulling hard on the oars of the riverboat.

Marguerite's situation did not escape the brilliant Russell, who called her "charming," and remarked on her "skillful nursing" when one of the British delegates took seriously ill. He noted that during the entire trip, the Cheka minder Axionov "watched her every movement and listened to her every word." He even shared a compartment with her on the train and crept behind her on the boat to listen to her conversations. She was "in obvious terror and longing to escape from Russia," Bertrand Russell said.

.   .   .

On the day she returned to Moscow, she reported at once to Mogilevsky for the mandatory debriefing, informing him about each of the delegates: what they said, why they said it, what they knew, how they knew it, what they thought of Russia, what they wanted, what their real interests were. She gave fulsome reports on some, but her refusal to befriend Leslie Haden-Guest, a Conservative member, earned her a verbal slap in the face.

She had steeled herself for the grilling by Mogilevsky, but she was taken aback by another encounter later that day. At the foreign office, where she went to write her story for the AP, Mr. Rosenberg, the head of the Western section, stopped her in the hallway.

"Ah, Mrs. Harrison, you are just the person I wanted to see," Rosenberg declared. "We have received an application from a woman colleague of yours who wishes to come to Russia as correspondent for the *New York World*. I wonder if you can tell me anything about her."

Marguerite paused. "What is her name?" she asked. "Is she an American?"

"No," he replied, "an Englishwoman. Her name is Mrs. Stan Harding."

The very name made her heart pound violently; the mistakes she had made in Berlin were careening into her future. The Cheka had all the information on Marguerite Harrison's work in Germany, and they knew her connection to Stan Harding. If the woman came to Russia, she would quickly find herself at risk; worse, she would imperil Marguerite. The situation, she told herself, was "a pretty mess." Stan Harding stirred trouble like a witch stirs her brew.

Trying to be nonchalant, Marguerite answered: "Why, yes I know her. We worked together in Berlin, but I don't think it would be advisable for you to give her a permit."

"But why?" Rosenberg asked. "The *World* is a liberal paper, is it not?"

"Yes, but you want a more serious person than Mrs. Harding," she said. "I do not think she is the type of journalist you would welcome in Russia." Rosenberg murmured "Hmm," and walked away.

Resolved to prevent disaster, Marguerite contacted a few of the foreign correspondents on the Volga trip who were preparing to leave for Riga. "Please warn Mrs. Harding not to come," she begged. But would her words convince Stan Harding to stay away or would she take them up as a challenge? Marguerite could only hope her warning would have the right effect.

CHAPTER 13

A Brave Front

The rare sound of an automobile drew Marguerite to the window. Below, the sight she had feared came into full view: In front of a black Cheka car standing outside were Mogilevsky and Mrs. Harding, striding like two good friends to the doorway of the Horitonevsky. She knew that Mogilevsky had accompanied the journalist from Petrograd, and she had been told by him that Mrs. Harding would be staying in her room, yet it was unsettling to hear the knock on her door. The British woman was standing before her, glowing with joy. "My dear," Stan Harding exclaimed as soon as Mogilevsky bowed and left, "I am going to get us both out of this mess."

The remark "terrified me beyond words," Marguerite recalled. Had Stan Harding come on a whim to try and save her, unaware of the seriousness of the situation for both of them, or was she on a secret assignment for the British government? In either case, she was putting their lives in danger.

Steering away from the subject, Marguerite offered her a cup of tea and asked about her travels. Surprisingly, Mogilevksy returned before long, ordered the British woman to pack up her belongings, and told her he was taking her to the foreign office to put her papers in order. Startled, the newcomer followed him out of the guesthouse to the waiting car. As they rode toward the Hotel Metropole, the car reached the front of the Lubyanka, and the cunning Mogilevsky turned to Mrs. Harding: "Madame," he said, "I have to tell you that you are arrested."

.   .   .

A phone call a few weeks later ordered Marguerite to the Cheka office at Lubyanka. It seemed she was following in Stan Harding's trail. "I suppose this means that you have decided to lock me up at once," she said to Mogilevsky when she arrived.

"No, my dear lady," he replied with a smirk. "Not yet. I only require a small service of you. You will leave this office in a moment and in the corridor you will meet Mrs. Harding. I merely want you to pass her without speaking to her."

Given little choice, Marguerite did as she was told. In the hallway she saw Stan Harding walking toward her, her head held high, a soldier at her side. As they came closer, she looked straight into Marguerite's eyes, and, her face glowering with rage, she left no doubt she felt betrayed. There was nothing Marguerite could do to convince her otherwise. Days later, acting as she did for other prisoners, Marguerite brought parcels of food and cigarettes to Stan Harding. But no amount of tea or tobacco could calm the woman's fury.

.   .   .

Volunteers for the Red Cross had been looking after the large group of British and French soldiers and the handful of American civilians held in prison, providing them with direly needed food and medicines. After the British concluded the relief agreement that allowed Reverend North and their civilian subjects to leave the country, there was no one to care for the American political prisoners.

The French agreed to attend to some of the British soldiers, but they lacked the funds to supply the American citizens too. Instead, Marguerite spent a good part of her days raising money, or using her dollars from home, which she exchanged on the black market to purchase food and medicines for the men. At times she also bought illegal rubles as a favor for foreign socialists who refused to accept the official government rate. Twice a week, on Mondays and Thursdays, with a helper in tow she shopped at the Sukharevka for bread, coffee, tea, sugar, and tobacco along with meat, eggs, potatoes, beans, and vegetables that she cooked on her small stove.

As she described it, a typical weekly parcel for each man included: "three pounds of black bread, a sixth of a pound of tea and coffee, a quarter of a pound of sugar, half a pound of butter or bacon, a small amount of cooked meat or sausage, a few hard-boiled eggs or boiled potatoes, an earthenware bowl of baked beans, baked apples or boiled vegetables, and once a month a cake of soap." Wrapping a package for each prisoner, on Tuesdays and Fridays she brought the *peradacha* to the prisons where the eight Americans were held and asked for a signed receipt in return. The receipts contained more than signatures: coded notes and invisible messages were sometimes written with soapy water or urine.

Among the prisoners was Royal Keeley, the industrial expert who had given her the secret report on conditions in Soviet Russia; Albert Boni, the publisher of Boni and Liveright and the Modern Library, who was writing a series for the *New York Sun;* Mr. Flick, an aptly named filmmaker, and Xenophon Kalamatiano, a businessman charged with helping British and French agents in an attempt to assassinate Vladimir Lenin.

At Kalamatiano's arrest the year before, his captors discovered that the cane he always clutched held an inner tube; when they opened it they found a cypher code, secret reports, a pile of rubles, the names of the thirty Russian spies in his network, and payment receipts from his agents. Although his co-conspirators had managed to leave the country, Kalamatiano had no such luck: with the concrete evidence he was a spy, the Cheka kept him under tight control.

Unbeknownst to Marguerite, another American was also imprisoned in Moscow. Frank Moser, a flyer with the Polish army whose plane had been shot down a year earlier in Siberia, was arrested by the Russians and put in a work camp with Polish prisoners of war. Recently he was transferred to a British camp. That was all she knew until she received a smuggled note.

Writing on a smidgen of cigarette paper, he explained that he had given a false identity: he was actually one of the American volunteers who had fought with the Kosciuszko Brigade against the Bolsheviks. Do you remember me? he asked. His real name was Merian Cooper; she had met him in Warsaw, and they had danced together at a Red Cross ball.

Now he was ill and starving, and in desperate need of blankets, pillow, food, clothing, toothpaste, soap, and—"for God's sake, if you can," he begged—"a pipe and tobacco." With the Poles and Russians still entrenched in war, she knew they would both pay dearly if his real identity was known, but she took the chance and brought her acquaintance his weekly packages. A few years later, they would have their own adventure together.

In addition to the gratifying yet constant work for the prisoners, she maintained her regular schedule attending the midnight briefings at the foreign office and wiring her articles for the AP. And always, she tried to keep away from friends and circumvent the questions at the arduous interrogations by the Cheka. Her attempts led to contentious moments with her inquisitor. Although she sometimes revealed too much and was accused by a few acquaintances of causing their arrest, Mogilevksy found her answers inadequate. His patience was growing thin. Unless she changed her ways and took her work "seriously," he warned, she would find herself back in prison.

Under the daunting pressure, she felt cut off from friends and ached to go home. The feelings intensified as summer waned and many foreign businessmen and correspondents left Russia. Even Sasha Berkman and Emma Goldman had departed, traveling around the country, collecting material for a new museum on the history of the Revolution. Those who stayed behind offered her few ways to convey messages or receive instructions from the West; more alarming, it was becoming even more difficult to know who could be trusted. Some of the messages she wrote on Danish and German banknotes were landing in the wrong hands.

By early fall, as the days were growing shorter and colder, the guesthouse lacked heat, food was becoming more scarce, and the government was threatening to close down the illegal markets; each trip to the Sukharevka might be her last. Darkness fell over her like a shroud.

Henry Brailsford, a left-wing British journalist who had stayed at her guesthouse, returned to London from Moscow and wrote to Dr. Ames, "she is painfully anxious and unhappy." He noted: "She is, formally or informally, kept as a hostage under surveillance." Although

Marguerite Harrison, Turkey 1919. Sitting cross-legged on the ground, enjoying a meal with villagers in the Taurus Mountains.

(ABOVE) Marguerite Harrison, Moscow 1921. She made the hat and outfit from men's shirts given to her by an American vistor to Russia.

(TOP LEFT) Marlborough Churchill, head of the Military Intelligence Division and in charge of Marguerite's espionage activities immediately after the Great War.

(CENTER LEFT) Walter Rathenau, Berlin 1920. He was a leading industrialist and intellectual who became foreign minister in the early days of the Weimar Republic.

(LOWER LEFT) Käthe Kollwitz, Berlin. A major artist, she lost a son in combat and wrote in her diaries of the painful aftermath of the war.

Berlin 1919. Street fighting between the Freikorps and the socialists.

Ralph Van Deman, called the father of military intelligence.

Stan Harding. She sought thrills that put people in harm's way.

(ABOVE) The anarchists Alexander Berkman and Emma Goldman. Marguerite said Goldman's experience with the Bolsheviks made her "a much better American."

(RIGHT) John Reed and his wife, Louise Bryant. The leftist journalists became disillusioned by Bolshevik brutality. "John was a real American," his wife said after he died in Moscow in 1920.

(BELOW) Lubyanka 1920. Over the entrance to the dreaded prison were the words "It is prudent to insure your life."

Solomon Mogilevsky. Marguerite called her Cheka interrogator "a stimulating and resourceful enemy."

Marguerite Harrison, 1920, at the Polish/Russian border. She was accused by the Bolshevik government of being a spy for the Poles.

Gertrude Bell, 1902. She was the chief British spy in Baghdad during the Great War and a close confidante of King Faisal of Iraq.

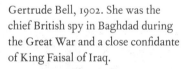

Marguerite Harrison, Turkey 1923. Wearing her pith helmet and safari jacket during the filming of the silent movie *Grass*.

Marguerite Harrison, Turkey 1924. Setting off from the Syrian/Iraqi border on a "Bedouin airplane."

Merian Cooper. Wartime flyer and filmmaker who was always grateful to Marguerite for saving his life in prison.

Ernest Schoedsack. He had a cheerful air but no patience for women on a film shoot.

Marguerite Harrison, Iran 1924. With Bakhtiari tribesmen on the migration across the Zardeh Kuh.

Iran 1924. The Bakhtiari regal barge on the icy Karun River.

Arthur Blake. British actor
who changed Marguerite's
life.

Marguerite Harrison, 1924,
fashionably dressed in her
astrakhan hat and coat and
her diamond brooch.

she was "anxious to return home," she had been "refused repeatedly, and was finally told that she would be allowed to leave Russia only in exchange for someone of real importance, e.g. in return for the release of Eugene Debs."

Debs, a labor leader involved in the deadly workers' strike in 1894 against the Pullman railroad car company, was a committed Bolshevik and founder of the International Workers of the World. A well-known orator, he had been arrested under the Sedition Act and given a ten-year sentence for protesting America's involvement in the war. Officials in Washington had no interest in releasing him, but as Brailsford pointed out, officials in Moscow had no interest in releasing Marguerite, except in exchange for Debs.

The Cheka sessions became more frequent and more intense, the questions repeated over and over. The ruble was decreasing in value, and the Communists were desperate to control the exchange rate of their money. Ordered to give detailed reports on foreign missions and black-market trading, she yielded.

The Chinese Military Mission, she said, made enormous speculations in Moscow. Arriving with a trainload of flour, rice, and tea, they sold small amounts of white flour for fifty-five thousand rubles and charged similar amounts for other items. The Austrians brought large quantities of their old rubles, hoping to trade them on the black market to pay for a prisoner exchange. They were angry when the head of their mission sold the money at the official rate. Some foreigners were selling tea at twenty thousand rubles a pound, or like the Estonians, bought valuable items cheaply in Russia and sold them privately in exchange for a 10 percent commission.

She revealed the negative remarks of German and Estonian correspondents toward the Bolshevik methods, putting her colleagues at risk. And she informed the Cheka of the activities of Claire Sheridan, a British sculptress and niece of Winston Churchill who was invited to Moscow to create a bust of Lenin: "She did not have a reputation for being very intelligent," Marguerite said.

She was also asked about Washington Vanderlip, an American businessman who had come to Russia with an offer to develop coal, oil, and fisheries in Siberia for a sixty-year lease worth some $3 billion. The entrepreneur had made a purchase of feathers and plumes for 175,000 rubles and was also trying to buy diamonds and furs that he would sell when he left the country. For hours on end, the Cheka examiner asked questions, often repeating the same ones again and again. Marguerite squirmed, but in the end, she succumbed. The sessions made her depressed.

Setting her further on edge, State Department officials in Washington had recently informed the Foreign Office in Moscow that as long as the Russian government refused to permit its citizens to choose their leaders, the United States refused to establish trade relations. Making matters worse, the Americans had arrested a large number of Communists.

The chances that she would be allowed to leave the country were growing ever slimmer: the more prolonged her stay, the more information she had about the dictatorship and the less inclined the Bolsheviks were to let her go. The Cheka rope was tightening around her even as she still managed to slip away. How much longer could she evade the noose?

In the past, something had always come along to save her; now she was anxious about what felt like the unavoidable end. She was no longer flirting with danger; she was dancing with death.

At night she lay in bed listening for the sound of a Cheka car, fearing her arrest, terrified at the thought of solitary confinement. She was desperate to leave the country, but as the military attaché in Berne noted in a secret report to the Director of MI: "Things look bad for 'B.'"

Her mood did not improve when she attended the trial of Alexandra Tolstoya. The esteemed author's daughter had won a high award for her bravery as a Red Cross nurse during the World War. Now, along with twenty-eight others, she was accused of supporting the Tactical Center, an organization that favored free speech, free press, and free political activity. The trial of the members, charged with conspiracy against the Soviet government, went on for four days. Marguerite joined the large audience of friends, family, and strangers in the auditorium of the Moscow Technical School where the grim event proceeded in the August heat.

In a "brilliant speech," Marguerite observed, Tolstoya declared she had helped the group because, like her father, she was a pacifist. Furthermore, she believed in the rights of the individual and the rule of the majority, and she was firmly opposed to the current dictatorship run by a minority. "She then added with a fine gesture that they might do what they pleased with her body, that she would always be free morally and spiritually, no matter how long she might be kept in prison," wrote Marguerite. At the end, Alexandra Tolstoya was sentenced to three years in prison, but with the help of the powerful women's commissar Madame Kollantai, she was released after twelve months.

.   .   .

It was around the same time that the tall, handsome American Marguerite saw at the foreign office introduced himself. John Reed, the radical journalist and author of *Ten Days That Shook the World*, had been in Finland where, under pressure from the U.S. government, he was held in prison for three months, kept in solitary confinement in a cold, damp cell, and fed a diet of raw fish. Upon his release he returned to Russia, but the experience had exacerbated a chronic kidney ailment, and he struck Marguerite as looking very ill and dejected.

A founder of the Communist Labor Party of America, he had come to Moscow for the World Congress meetings of the Third International. Now the Bolsheviks were ordering him to travel to the Caucasus, where they were holding an Oriental Conference. Although he felt gravely weak and begged not to go, the officials bullied him and insisted he leave soon for the long train trip to Baku.

During her talks with John Reed, he disparaged Lenin's dictatorial ways. Although he still held Communism in high esteem, he was disgusted by the rough methods and frustrated at his own inability to change the situation.

Marguerite was convinced his radical beliefs had been brought about by his "spirit of bravado" and what he had felt was "unfair treatment" at home. Indeed, he told her he wanted to go home and face the charges of sedition against him. "He struck me as an intensely honest, rather fair-minded person," she noted, and bade him good wishes for his trip to Baku.

While he was away, his free-spirited wife, Louise Bryant, arrived in Moscow. "I liked Mrs. Reed very much," Marguerite said. They had both started their careers as society reporters, went on to become foreign correspondents, and were interested in fashion as well as revolution. The chic, attractive journalist had come from New York sporting the latest styles with narrow skirts and straight lines. "She was the only fashionable looking woman I had seen for such a long time that I was quite dazzled by her," Marguerite declared. Even so, the Cheka man who followed her reported that Mrs. Harrison argued with Mrs. Reed over her Communist ways.

Days after Louise's arrival, on September 15, Jack Reed returned from the Caucasus, shouting with joy when he saw her, a splash of sun shining on a coal mine. Jack's rakish look was long gone, and he seemed older and sadder than his wife remembered. An outbreak of typhoid had struck him on the trip, making him even frailer than before he left for Baku. Yet, filled with excitement, he summoned his strength and brought her to meet Lenin and Trotsky. He took her to the opera to see *Prince Igor,* to the Bolshoi ballet, and to museums and galleries, but after a week he was too feverish, too sick to continue. Taken to the hospital, he lay gravely ill for twenty days while his wife stayed at his side. On October 17, John Reed died. He was thirty-three years old.

Louise Bryant was staying at the Hotel Delovoy, close to the Kremlin and convenient to the meetings of the Third International. The official hotel for delegates was forbidden to Marguerite, who was suspected of probing for information about the people and workings inside the Communist Party. Despite the ban, two days after John Reed's death, accompanied by her friend Mrs. Skala, who represented the Czech Red Cross, Marguerite skirted the Cheka and went to see her acquaintance.

The widow was distraught. "He was consumed with a desire to go home," Louise said, certain that her husband would have received far better treatment in New York. The Bolshevik doctors' methods, the nurses' incompetence, and the food he was given were all far below

American standards. What riled her even more was that the Soviets had claimed his body and put his corpse on display in a silver coffin in Red Square. "John was a real American," Louise Bryant repeated again and again. "I know he would have wanted to be buried on American soil."

CHAPTER 14

Orders

They came for Mrs. Harrison late the following night. She was alerted by the rumble of the car engine and the knock on the door. "*Zakhodi* (come in)," she called out. She had returned from work at two a.m. and was still wearing her khaki suit and pongee blouse when the Cheka operatives appeared in her room. "I suppose you have come to arrest me," she said calmly, almost relieved as she looked at the well-dressed woman and two young men with rifles and tall Cheka caps. She had presumed for weeks that they would come, and their arrival loosened the bindings of anxious expectation.

They showed her their Cheka orders for her arrest, one dated October 20, 1920, the other written in red ink to search her room, and she watched in silence as they began to comb through her belongings. They investigated the brass bed and the mattress, the big couch, and the plump easy chairs; they inspected behind the drapes and the radiator, and around the rest of the room. They seized her books and papers of every kind and scrutinized blank pages for invisible ink; they collected and counted her money, a million and a half rubles to be used for prisoners' packages; they examined her suitcases, linings and all, and went inch by inch through her fur-lined coat. The woman searched her body and clothes, running hands through Marguerite's hair, inside her pockets and her corset, and along her stockings, but did not, Marguerite noted with relief, order her to undress.

Their hunt completed, they packed up some of her possessions—including her wedding ring, gold watch, a sapphire earring, her identity cards, a sewing pillow with needles and thread, and her Kodak camera and film—and gave her permission to take her bed roll and one bag. She filled them with soap, toothpaste, and other toiletries and cosmetics, a change of underwear and pajamas, a second pongee blouse, a steamer rug, cigarettes, and chocolate, and she hid some pencils inside the case. After they gave her a receipt to sign, they locked and sealed her room and drove her off in an English car to the dreaded Lubyanka.

She recognized the squalid room where they brought her, the same filthy room where she had been held six months before, and she took a seat at the end of a long row of men. She waited for an hour until someone handed her a lengthy form to complete, and then, left alone with six soldiers, she stood helpless as one of them searched her body while the others gawked and laughed. Enraged, she tried to stop them by saying she was an American, which only made them laugh more. A lot of good that will do you, they scoffed.

When they had finished their fun, she was led through a maze of stairs and hallways to a small room where she was officially searched again, this time by a female guard. Only then was she taken to a dingy cell, room 39, where three women were confined; one lay on a bed of boards and straw, two others were curled on the floor, all pretending to be asleep.

It was six a.m. and she was exhausted, but as soon as the guard left, they plied her with questions: Why was she there? What had she done? Where was she from? Who did she know? For the rest of the day they shared their stories. One was the girlfriend of a Hungarian prisoner of war and was arrested for trying to help him escape; the second woman worked at the foreign office, and the third, whom she recognized, was a friend of the foreign correspondent for the *Chicago Daily News*. The last two had been arrested that day, and although they claimed they did not know why, Marguerite suspected they had engaged in illegal trade.

At nightfall, she spread her bedroll on the floor, and with a sense of relief that the event she feared had already happened, she fell into a deep sleep. The next day she was taken to be photographed and given a new identity: Prisoner 2961.

She spent two more days in the room with the women before a soldier appeared, called out her name, and ordered her to come with him for a *Na dopros*. She was in luck, one woman said. People sometimes waited weeks for a hearing.

Once again, she followed the soldier up and down a web of stairs and halls until they arrived at the office of Solomon Mogilevsky. Told to take a seat on a leather armchair, she was surprised to see a beautifully bound copy of Rabelais resting on his desk. He had a weakness for old French literature, he confessed. She too admired Rabelais and Voltaire, she said, and tried to engage him in a discussion of Renaissance writers and freedom of the individual. But his steely mind was focused on her efforts against the Bolsheviks.

"I hardly need to tell you why you are here," he said.

"I can guess the reason," she replied calmly. "We have been playing a game and I have lost."

The game, he averred, was more dangerous than she realized. "You were convicted of espionage," he reminded her, and in exchange for her release, she had promised to work for the Soviets. Not only had she failed to take the work seriously, but she continued sending reports to the American government while at the same time she withheld information useful to the Russians. "Do you know that you deserve the death penalty?"

"I realized that long ago," she answered brazenly, looking him straight in the eye. Nevertheless, she pointed out, she had been fair and objective in her reports. "I do not believe in Communism, but I think that it is an interesting social experiment which deserves a trial."

For three hours he grilled her, boring down on her relationships with foreign correspondents and foreign businessmen, demanding to know more about her Russian friends, especially General Brusilov, quizzing her about the prisoners for whom she provided packages. Finally, after a string of "I don't know"s, he let her go. She returned to room 39.

Not long after, a guard appeared. "Pack your clothes," he ordered.

"Where am I going?" she asked.

"You'll see when you get there."

Her heart sank when he refused to allow her to take her fur coat. "You won't need that," he said. She knew she was headed for a sinister place.

He led her down the hallway and opened the door of a dingy cell.

She stepped inside, saw the plank bed and wooden headrest, the small pine table, and the *parashka*, the tin waste can; she heard the door slam and the key turn in the lock. This was the moment that frightened her most; she was panic-stricken, with nothing to do, cut off, alone, in solitary confinement.

Looking at the frayed papered walls covered with writing in various languages, she read the words of men waiting to die. One prisoner had scrawled, "*Rira bien qui rira le dernier.*" Sadly, there was little doubt who had the last laugh. With her knowledge of German, she made out the words of a Dutchman who swore that if he died in prison, "it will be as a loyal Communist." A Russian prisoner had listed the dates of his *dopros* starting on May 5. On July 15 he wrote in Cyrillic: "Now I've told everything. This is the end." She panicked at the thought: she too was waiting for the end.

Despite her terror, she developed a remarkable disengagement from her situation: "I had good cause to know that my position was very serious, but at the same time I figured it out that unless the United States actually went to war with Russia it was unlikely that I would be shot." If she could keep her health, both physically and mentally, she told herself, she could play out the waiting game. She observed coolly, "I had no reason either to complain of my arrest or to expect early liberation. It was simply the fortune of war."

A small, whitewashed window blocked out most of the daylight, and a guard in the hallway controlled the electric bulb in her small, dark cell. Her watch had been taken, and the only way to guess the time was from the actions of the sentry: the clicking of the peephole—"an instrument of terror"—when he swung it open, the switching on of the light every thirty minutes, and the turn of the key when he brought her meals. In the morning he came with weak tea made of dried carrot, and a piece of black bread; in the afternoons it was kasha, along with a morsel of foul-smelling herring and a fish eye staring through watery soup.

From the hall she heard the frantic calls of prisoners desperate to use the bathroom, which was allowed only once a day, and the harrowing screams of those being taken to other places or to be shot by a rifle squad in the courtyard. When the small peephole in the door budged open, she saw the eye of the guard watching as she dressed and undressed and peering at her while she sat on the waste can that was the toilet. When her food was brought, she saw only the arm and hand that delivered it. Depression engulfed her. She was Prisoner 2961: meaningless; a single figure among thousands of others trapped by the Revolution.

"What man matters in times like these?" she asked herself. "We are in the midst of a conflict of forces, not of individuals." And then, "little by little I learned to detach myself utterly from the world which seemed irretrievably lost and to find a new world of my own bounded physically by four walls, but spiritually limitless."

She had no one to talk to and nothing to do but brace herself against the agony of isolation. She soon realized the only thing she could do to keep from going mad was to stay busy in her present life. She made herself a strict schedule and concentrated on her daily routine: each morning after she swept her nine-foot-square cell, she searched for bedbugs and vermin and broomed them out; folded up her bed roll; sponged her body in cold water; and put on the only clothes she had, her khaki skirt and pongee blouse. Once she was dressed, she spread out a handkerchief on the table, ate her coarse black bread, and drank the ersatz tea. Afterward, she exercised in the cramped space, walking back and forth five hundred times.

The rest of the day she played solitaire with a pack of cards she made out of toothpaste and cigarette boxes, writing the numbers with the stub of a pencil she had hidden; it worked until the guard caught wind of it and seized them. She made straws from burned matches and played pick up sticks; she sang songs, recited poems, tested her memory with questions on languages and history. In the evening she repeated the short walk five hundred times back and forth in the cell.

The activities made the hours pass, and yet the time crawled on. Except for one heartening moment when an unsmiling guard gave her twice her ration of cigarettes, she had no one to connect with, no one to talk to but herself. Desperate after seven days of feeling tortured by the silence and afraid of losing her mind, she asked for pencil and paper and sent a letter begging Mogilevsky to see her. "I have an important communication for you," she wrote. He was the only person she thought would respond to her appeal. Two hours later she was granted a meeting. "What is it you have to tell me?" he asked.

"I can't stand being alone any longer," she conceded and pleaded to be removed from solitary confinement. But when the Chekist asked her some questions, she refused to give any direct answers. "You are impossible," he said in disgust and sent for his assistant, who grilled her for hours.

She tried to protect her friends, but it taxed her acuity to evade responding when he repeated his questions again and again. When had she last seen General Brusilov? he wanted to know. In September the general had signed an appeal with Lenin and Trotsky urging White Army officers to join the Red Army and defend the state against outside interference. But what was his real attitude toward the Soviet government, the Cheka wanted to know. What about his wife? His daughter-in-law?

Finally, she had no choice but to answer: She had spoken to Brusilov about a month ago, she replied. "He said that his name as well as other generals' names were used by the Bolsheviks," though he did not know anything about current military affairs. What he wanted was to publish his memoirs and notes, "but he did not do so because it was impossible to write openly about his attitude to the Soviet government."

As for his wife, "She is very disappointed with the fact that he works with the Soviet government." She added that his daughter-in-law worked for the Red Cross. Though her testimony may have been problematic, she left no doubt about the family's loyalty and spelled it out clearly: "No one is involved in counterrevolutionary activities."

Asked about Alexander Berkman, she answered, "Naturally, he sees Communism as a step towards anarchy, an ideal state," and related that he wanted to use youth education as a means "against the Soviet government." She was more protective of Emma Goldman, who, she noted, "is not yet prejudiced against the Soviet government."

In the second lengthy session Mogilevsky's aide informed her that if she was lucky, and if the Americans freed one of the men they had arrested for counterespionage, she and others might be released. He tried to persuade her to write a letter asking for the return of the Soviet spy, but she refused. In the interim, she was granted permission to move into another cell. This time she found herself with seven other women crammed into a room shaped like a tapered coffin. The promise of a prisoner exchange faded into the funereal air.

. . .

Except for Marguerite, who was the only American woman in the entire Lubyanka prison, the inmates in her new Cheka cell were all Slavs, most of them round-faced with pale skin and light-brown hair, but as different from one another as caviar from herring. A few had been rich and aristocratic, their fitted leather dressing cases peeking out from under their beds; others were poor and illiterate and stored their meager belongings in kerchiefs; some, with bags made of canvas, came from the bourgeoisie. Many claimed innocence and did not know what crimes they had committed; a few were certain they would be executed.

All faced the same challenges: how does one endure the real and imagined tortures, the menacing illnesses, the appalling filth, the horrid food, the monotony, the loneliness, the interminable wait for an unpredictable end? She observed that those from the upper and lower classes adapted most readily, while the bourgeois clung to their old ways.

She could tell at once the highborn background of a cellmate who welcomed her in impeccable French. Like all the others, she wore the clothes she had come in, but in her case, it was an expensive Parisian suit. "I see that you are a foreigner," she said to Marguerite, adding graciously, "This is very poor hospitality to offer you in Russia." The countess and the socialite became fast friends. Elena Sologub came from a prominent family whose house had been used by Tolstoy as the home of Pierre in *War and Peace;* it was a place Marguerite had wanted to visit when she arrived in Moscow. The countess had been taken from the one room where she was still allowed to reside and arrested, accused of friendship with a White Russian whom she did not know. Such were the mysteries of the Cheka.

The others in the cell included three women who worked in the War Office and were charged with witnessing a plot against the government; two wives whose husbands had been arrested; and one hapless sixteen-year-old who had repeated someone's words that there would be a counterrevolution.

Marguerite quickly attuned herself to the rhythm of prison life. Her day began when the guard arrived with a huge kettle and she scurried to find at least one or two tin cups, filling them with enough hot water to last throughout the day. Shortly afterward another guard brought in the rations of black bread, sometimes edible, sometimes the consistency of mud and the color of dirty putty, that made up her breakfast. Often, before she and the others were finished, the guard escorted them to the washroom, where they washed themselves with cold water, two at a time at a metal trough.

Much of her morning was spent hunting for the typhus-bearing lice, fleas, bedbugs, and other disease-ridden vermin that crawled through her bed and her clothes and nested in her hair. Like every woman she was required to help clean up the cell, and once or twice a week, on the orders of the "*starosta*," the group's chosen mayor, she performed her duties: she swept out the room and neatened it up; gave out the daily rations and returned the emptied wooden soup bowls to the guard; and cleaned out the *parashka*, the metal waste can, of urine, feces, and menstrual blood. Along with these tasks, once a week she got down on her hands and knees and scrubbed the floor, and once a month, wearing, as always, her khaki suit, she cleaned the three hall toilets that were used by more than a hundred people a day. It was interesting to read the new messages the men had scrawled on the walls.

Twice a day she did the Swedish gymnastics popular in the United States, stretching her arms up, back, and to the side; rising on tiptoes and bending her knees; lifting heavy objects; and doing other exercises for balance, strength, and flexibility, performing them so intently that one woman thought it was the American way to pray.

She washed her body, her blouse, and her underwear with the warm tea she saved in the morning and repaired her well-worn garments with the needle and thread she received as a volunteer mending the vermin-ridden clothes of the male prisoners. The work also allowed her to use precious scissors, otherwise forbidden: "I never realized to how many uses one pair of scissors could be put." She needed them for cutting her nails and hair, mending her shoes, opening tins of food, and slicing the meat or sausage that came in her weekly *peradacha*.

The packages were sent by her friend Mr. Skala, who, along with his wife, an American of Czech descent, ran the Czechoslovak Red Cross. Fellow residents of the Horitonevsky, they had taken over Marguerite's work looking after the needs of American prisoners. After Marguerite gained permission to receive supplies from them, she sent Mrs. Skala a long request:

"If you can get in my room, I would ask the following things— cigarettes, a plate, cup and saucer, towels and soap, tube of green soap, pillow and shawl, blankets for my bed—a glass jar, books. Also, my clean clothes from the wardrobe and pajamas. For the *peradacha*, I would like a hundred cigarettes a week, eggs, butter, potatoes, honey, vegetables, beans or a little meat. I also need thread and needles and some hairpins."

The note never reached the Skalas and was kept instead by the Cheka. None of her own belongings from the guesthouse made it to the prison, but her plea for a pair of shoes was answered. Her old pair were tattered and worn through, and she was relieved to unwrap the package, only to find a pair of men's shoes several sizes too big; nevertheless they were a solid improvement for her feet.

. . .

Books and magazines, writing, talking loudly, or singing were all forbidden, but some nights after the guard switched off the light in the cell, the roommates sang in hushed voices to entertain each other in the dark. Marguerite dug out her secreted pencil and made notes of the words to an old Russian song; other times she noted names and information she had gathered.

During the long days of doubt and dreary musings, Du Maurier's *Peter Ibbetson* and his dream life floated through her mind. Peter's motto, "Through hardship to the stars," gave her comfort and support; she even penciled his words *per aspera ad astra* and cross-stitched them with her needle and thread on a piece of an old sack. When the Cheka found them, they were certain it was a secret message.

In her free time, when she and her cellmates weren't heatedly discussing politics, religion, family, or any of the many other subjects the Russians loved to debate, they played cards with miniature decks created from the tips of cigarettes and numbered with burnt matches. Seated at the pine table they marked with squares, they played chess and checkers with pieces shaped from stale bread; played dominoes with bits of paper; and engaged in fortune-telling sessions in search of favorable news. All of this was forbidden, they knew; still, they were taken by surprise when a guard rushed into their room. "You're playing cards," he said accusingly.

"Certainly not," Marguerite replied in Russian. "We haven't any cards in this room."

"What have you got in your hand?" he demanded.

She opened her clenched fist slightly and dismissed the idea: "Only a little waste paper," she said, adding, "how's the weather this evening?"

The fellow burst out laughing and left.

At other times, eager for any signs of life beyond their cell, the women flouted the rules and took turns looking out the peephole into the busy hallway: she liked to see General Klembovsky, whose wife she knew, when he was let out from solitary confinement for a walk in the hall. More daringly, the women tapped on the pipes or the walls, sending coded messages to the men in the cell next door.

Contact with another human being, however contentious, felt like a gift. To Marguerite, even interrogations were a welcome relief from the monotony, but it was hell when she was cross-examined: threats of a trial and execution for espionage were too much to bear and shattered her hopes of protecting friends and acquaintances.

.   .   .

Even as the women took these risks, they were well aware that the threat of punishment hovered over them. No diversions could erase their fears of being sent to a tiny cell in the pitch-black basement or being led to the courtyard and shot. The reminders were constant, and it was hard to hide from the shrieks of hysteria by a prisoner being taken away. Once, she recalled, she heard the screams of a man who had completely lost his nerve. He "struggled all the way down the hall with his captors, yelling piteously all the while, 'Oh, God, I won't go, I won't go.'"

The only variation in the daily routine was the rare arrival of a holiday, when they were given butter, sugar, fifty cigarettes, and coffee made from roasted breadcrumbs, powdered acorns, or roasted barley and cowpeas. At Easter, they celebrated with brightly painted Easter eggs and a special meal shared from their *peradachas*. The weeks leading up to Christmas were more painful, and in her wretched state she sadly recalled her times of joy. "Try as I might to obliterate them, home memories came crowding back." Reminiscences of family times were flooded with the fragrance of pine trees, the music of Handel's *Messiah*, the jolly image of Santa Claus. This was the fourth Christmas she was away from her son, Tommy. But she had made the choice herself: the lure of adventure tugged harder than the pull of her boy.

Just before Christmas, on a semiannual trek to the public baths, she marched with her cellmates through streets thick with snow. Passing Trubnaya Square, where holiday trees were being sold, they gathered loose branches scattered on the ground and brought them back to their cell. After they tied them together and placed them in a bottle, they set to work on decorations: they used the red cardboard from a carton of cigarettes and red paper from a can of condensed milk and made stars that they attached to the tips of the limbs; they used the silver wrapper from a bar of soap, rolled it into tiny balls, and strung it along the branches; and they topped it all with one inmate's thin gold necklace and an image of the Virgin Mary.

At midnight on Christmas Eve, the women sat down to a feast of tinned corned beef, salt herrings, rice pudding, black bread, butter, and sugar shared from their *peradachas*. They were of various nationalities: Pani, an innocent Polish woman arrested for a phone call she received; Elizaveta, a pretty German married to a Russian, who did not know why either of them had been arrested; Anna, an affectionate Russian spy and prostitute who embraced Marguerite when the American gave her a tin of red nail salve that she rouged on her cheeks; Maria, a Lithuanian, who had naively delivered a letter to a Polish priest; Vera, a Lettish Communist who had worked as a Cheka spy and turned agent provocateur; Olga, a Russian who had not officially declared her cache of family silver.

As each woman spoke of her Christmas the year before, Marguerite recalled her own holiday celebrations with cousins in Warsaw. At the end, they took turns singing Christmas carols, and her voice rang out with "Oh, Little Town of Bethlehem."

The most moving part of the evening was a short speech by Elizaveta. As terrible as it was to be away from home and family, she told them, this was not an altogether unhappy Christmas. They had all been taught the message of goodwill to men, and thrown together by fate in the worst circumstances of mental anxiety and physical hardship, they had learned to live together in peace and comradeship. She expressed her hope that wherever they were the following year they would recall their Christmas in Lubyanka and send a silent message of good cheer to their old cellmates. Her words touched them all: a long silence followed, and then two of the women burst into loud sobs. A little while later, after the guard turned off the light, Marguerite played the role of American Santa and tucked small gifts of chocolate under each of their pillows.

.   .   .

The cast of characters in her cell changed with the political winds; the latest arrival often came with a stream of news from the outside world. The Cheka inmates, whether nationalists, socialists, or nihilists, Russians, Poles, Finns, Letts, Lithuanians, Estonians, Ukrainians, or Jews, were all involved in one way or another with political affairs and brought information that kept Marguerite up to date on events. To her distress, there had been no movement toward negotiations with Washington and no indication that American relief was possible. She clung to the hope that there would be an exchange of prisoners, but she had serious doubts that her government would make such a move.

Except for three letters, including one from her son and one from her father-in-law, Joseph Ames, it had been months since she heard from her family and friends. Letters had been sent and money wired, but none had reached her: instead, it had all been snatched by the Soviets. She could only hope that family and friends were working on her behalf.

In fact, Dr. Ames and Albert Ritchie, the governor of Maryland, along with Van Lear Black, publisher of the *Sun*, had been busy tracking down information. Forlorn in her cell, she was not aware that messages were being wired from Moscow and European capitals, that her imprisonment had been reported around the country, and that her face was pictured in newspapers from New York to California. Nor did she know that Dr. Ames had received word through the Martens Bureau from a highly placed Soviet official describing her situation.

Marguerite Harrison was "a professional spy employed by American Military Intelligence," he was informed by Moscow. Referring to her first arrest in April, the man wrote, "Confronted with overwhelming evidence she confessed and offered her services to the Russian Extraordinary Commission, revealing American and British spies as evidence of loyalty." She continued until October, when she was rearrested "as it became evident that, while she gave some valuable and correct information, she continued to sell herself to the enemies." Then came the ominous words: "She cannot be released."

The Russian continued with a sneer toward recent arrests of Russians in the United States: "She is in good health and is treated much better than America would treat a prisoner under similar circumstances." The letter was signed "Chicherin, Commissar for Foreign Affairs"

But in truth, Marguerite was ill, suffering from an overload of fetid air, poor food, and long confinement in the Lubyanka. She had developed a bad cough that only grew worse, aggravated, no doubt, by her constant smoking.

At Easter she and her new cellmates heard the cringe-making words "Pack your clothes" and concluded they had flouted the rules once too often. But instead of facing punishment in the dark cellar, they were led to a garret room where the window was sealed tight and the cold, damp air reeked from the putrid smells of an uncovered waste bucket and the stench of cheap fresh paint. After only one night in the space, the women's faces turned sickly green. Their health did not improve when more than once the plumbing broke, making the toilet off limits for twenty-four hours, and shutting down the hot water for washing or tea.

By the late spring Marguerite was aching and feverish, weak from insufficient food and suffering from severe bronchitis; she could do little more than lie on the wood planks that served as her bed. The attaché in Riga reported to Washington that visitors told him "she is a physical and nervous wreck but," he added, "they praise her pluck and morale."

It took weeks before the doctor agreed to send her to the Novinsky, a hospital prison for women. Frail and shaking, she followed the armed escort and nearly passed out as she hauled her heavy bags down four flights of stairs. At the bottom of the staircase, the door closed on the blackened world she had lived in for eight months.

Stepping out from the shadows onto the busy street, she felt blinded by the hot sun and deafened by the noise of streetcars, the traffic of cabs, and the crowds of people in Lubyanka Square. When she looked for the Cheka car to take her to her destination, the young soldier admitted that no travel arrangements had been made and, worse, he had no idea of the address. She told him to go back and find out, but he was afraid to ask his superiors.

As tempting as it might have seemed, she knew she could not escape, yet she faced a dilemma: desperate to get to the prison, she had no means to reach it. When a pedestrian passed by, she stopped him and asked if he knew the way to the Novinsky. Politely he provided the information and told her it was six *versts* away and too far to walk. The man tipped his hat and rushed off, fearful of being seen speaking to a prisoner.

They would have to walk, the soldier insisted. He refused to hail a cab, but she knew her wobbly legs would not carry her the four miles to the outskirts of Moscow. But neither of them had money, and after several cabs declined to take her, she stopped the one-legged driver of a droshky, pulled out some food from her bag, and bartered two cans of American corned beef for the ride.

Settled in their seats, the guard with his rifle securely between his knees, and she with shaky legs, a high fever, and a deep cough, smoked cigarettes and chatted while they rode to the grim complex that comprised the Novinksy. The long gray brick buildings served as holding pens for hundreds of women who were brought there each month, some transported onward to the infamous salt mines of Siberia, others shipped farther east in Asia, where few inmates survived the grueling labor camps.

CHAPTER 15

Do svidanya

"A wild shriek" pierced her ears—not a call for help, but a cry of joy that greeted Marguerite as she entered the prison. "Margharita Bernardovna! *Slava Bog*" ("Thank God"), shouted a group of women who had been in the Lubyanka. She had not seen them in months, and they seemed a vision in a feverish dream, brought to life by the warm kisses they planted on her cheeks. After they convinced the doctors she was a model of cleanliness and did not require the usual quarantine, she was allowed to stay in their large cell. To celebrate their reunion, they brought her hot tea and a bed.

The Novinksy was a "terrestrial paradise" compared to the hell of the Lubyanka. Inmates were allowed to use their free time as they wished; she spent much of her days outdoors, relishing the summer sunlight and fresh air in the large courtyard where she met up with friends or sat on a bench and read. Unlike the Cheka prison, the Novinksy offered a library with classic books in Russian, and novels and magazines in Russian, French, German, and English. Newspapers were brought every day to the socialists, and she was able to share her friends' papers. Except for the food, which she found to be worse than at her former compound, given her circumstances, this was the best she could hope for.

But after her cough deepened and her high fever persisted, her stay in the large cell ended. Diagnosed with tuberculosis, she was brought to the hospital and placed in a room with one woman arrested for espionage and an attendant who had been arrested first for smuggling, then for receiving stolen goods, and then for joining her brother-in-law to murder her sister, after which she married the husband. "She was lazy and an incorrigible thief," Marguerite said, but kindhearted and generous, "and I could not help being fond of her."

Two more big hospital rooms held thieves, street gang leaders, and prostitutes who traded stolen goods and services for rubles or bread and provided "sexual perversions" to the women in prison. "I realized the incalculable evil that may come from segregating the sexes and suppressing normal instincts in penal institutions," she said. She was convinced that nothing was being accomplished to help the criminals occupy useful places in society.

Although the hospital food, including tinned meat supplied by the British, was an improvement over her prison fare, by July she was aware that all of Russia was suffering from severe food shortages. The famine predicted by the farmers along the Volga had come true; millions of Soviet citizens were starving. It echoed a famine in 1892, when her father sent a ship filled with grain to help the struggling Russian people. In return the czar showed his gratitude with a gift to Bernard Baker.

When the royal present arrived in Baltimore, they pried open the wooden crate, removed the mounds of straw, and carefully drew out a silver-banded cloisonné tea service. A kaleidoscope of enamel bits made a magical pattern embedded in the teapot, creamer, and sugar bowl, and on the long-handled spoon, the tongs, and the cups and saucers. For twelve-year-old Marguerite it was a first taste of the mystery and wonder of the Russian empire, and, like the tea set itself, it stayed with her for the rest of her life. Now she sat locked in a Moscow prison drinking ersatz tea out of a tin cup.

In a sign that the Russians might be ready to accept a prisoner release as a quid pro quo for American food aid, she received a note and a *peradacha* from Royal Keeley. He informed her he had been freed from a labor camp and would try to see her. But the flicker of hope faded when the Soviets turned down his request for a visit and denied his plea for her release.

A week later she was taken by surprise when she was told an American had come to see her. Although they had never met, she recognized the man as Joseph France, a U.S. senator from Maryland. A

Republican sympathetic to the Russians, he had come to investigate the economic conditions and had agreed, at the request of her friend, Van Lear Black, publisher of the *Baltimore Sun,* to try and secure her freedom. He had been able to see Vladimir Lenin, Foreign Minister Georgy Chicherin, and the leading diplomat Maxim Litvinov, he told her, but they had made no promises; on the other hand, they had not flatly turned him down.

That night she was awakened by Cheka guards who forced her to submit to a search and to surrender any papers she possessed. "What does this mean?" she asked one young man, giving him the precious notes she had made.

"It means that you will be deported in the morning," he answered. But his black leather-coated partner fired a forbidding look and stopped him from revealing any more.

It did not take Marguerite long to pack her things the next day, but the goodbyes to her friends stretched on for hours. Going from room to room, she became aware of how strongly attached she felt to her fellow inmates. No matter how different their backgrounds, whether rich or poor, patrician or prostitute, educated or illiterate, Eastern Orthodox or Jewish, Communist or nihilist, "prison friendships are about the most real things in the world," she observed. "People know each other as they are, without hypocrisy or concealment, and if they grow to care for each other under such conditions the bond between them is very close, indeed." It was a strong declaration from a woman who prided herself on keeping her emotions under control.

When word came that the car had arrived to take her away, her friends gathered for an old Russian custom, a last minute of silence to wish her godspeed. Then, covered with hugs and kisses, and cries of *Vseyvo horoshevo!* ("Good luck") and *Do svidanya* ("Au revoir"), she was off, teary-eyed and on her way to the Lubyanka, not quite certain if she was actually being deported or being sent to another prison.

Mogilevsky was waiting. She learned from her nemesis that after a letter was sent by writer Maxim Gorky to the Americans, with some help from the Norwegian diplomat Fridtjof Nansen, Moscow and Washington had reached an agreement. Under the auspices of the American Relief Administration, led by Herbert Hoover, the United

States would send food aid to Russia, but only on condition that the Russians released their American prisoners first.

Senator France, she was told, had nothing to do with the agreement; his arrival in Moscow had been coincidental. But as a favor to the senator, who was pushing for recognition of the Soviet state, she was the first to be sent home; the rest of the Americans would leave in a few days.

During the course of the sixteen months she had been under Mogilevsky's control, he had been her captor and her protector, her Torquemada and her Lancelot. He bullied her with spies who listened to her conversations, read her communications, and shadowed her on the streets. He punished her with prison and solitary confinement, and he threatened her with endless incarceration and even execution. He intrigued her with his erudition, provoked her with his politics, beguiled her with his charm. In response, she had surrendered with sympathy and affection.

Her opponent continued the conversation now on a personal note: "You and I have been enemies, it is true," he said, "but it was all part of a big game. I hope you feel that I had nothing against you personally and also that sometime you may be able to come back to Russia under happier auspices."

"I feel exactly the same way, Citizen Mogilevsky," she replied, "and I hope that one day I will return to Russia under different conditions."

She was aware that their words had different meanings. His hope was that she would be converted to Bolshevism. Her hope was that Bolshevism would change. She knew that the old czarist system had to be removed, that the Revolution had been necessary, but she also believed that the majority of Russians deserved the right to choose rulers who represented them. Her dream was not that she would become a Communist, but that "the Communist dictatorship might be changed into something approaching real Socialism." It was a message she would carry home.

They shook hands and said goodbye, and he left. A while later, still wearing her grimy khaki suit and pongee blouse, with a toque hat she had made from the tail of one of the men's shirts, and men's shoes that were much too big, she was rushed by car to the Vindavsky station; with only a minute to spare before departure time, she caught up with Senator France and boarded the train for Riga. Slumber came as soon as she pulled the curtain in the lower berth of the sleeping compartment.

.   .   .

With a shortage of coal for fuel and the neglected state of the railroad ties, the train hemmed and hawed its way to Latvia. As they reached the frontier, she worried when her luggage was searched and her papers examined, and she heaved a sigh of relief when the guard stamped his approval. But from there the train refused to move; as minutes ticked away and she and the senator checked the time, she felt her panic grow. She had known several people, including Royal Keeley, who had been stopped and turned back just as they were about to cross the border.

Minutes turned into half hours, half hours into hours, until six hours later, after the sun rose, the train shuddered into the Riga station. Waiting for her were the American military attaché Worthington Hollyday and his wife: "I must have been a comical sight," she recalled, as she emerged with her face stained from washing with tea, her shabby clothes, and her clownish shoes.

At their apartment she enjoyed a panoply of comforts from a long-ago life: she soaked leisurely in a hot bath in a porcelain tub, changed into fresh silk clothes laid out for her on the thick, soft bed, and although her stomach had shrunk from the meager prison diet, she savored the good meal served on china plates, not in wooden bowls, and took pleasure in drinking from a real glass rather than a tin cup. In the morning, after she enjoyed the real coffee brought by the maid, and soaked again in the smooth tub, she was prepared to work.

She spent several hours dictating a report for MI, and then agreed to a few requests for interviews. She scanned through stacks of newspaper articles and learned that she had been a front-page story across the United States. She was the only American woman who had endured a stay in a Russian prison. She read through piles of telegrams and felt her heart beat a little faster when she saw the one from Tommy saying he was coming to London to meet her.

Later, walking outside on cobblestone streets filled with Art Nouveau buildings, she was confused by the noise and the traffic, and she felt uneasy stepping off the curb. She shopped for a new outfit, but the old khaki suit remained in her bag; it held too many memories to toss away. It took a few days for her to adjust to life outside of prison: "My mental detachment from the world had been so complete that I was somewhat like a nun suddenly turned out of her convent."

In spare moments she reflected on the year and a half she had spent in Russia. She had existed mainly on kasha and black bread and had been stifled and sickened in a prison cell. "From a material standpoint I had suffered," she said, "but I had gained from another point of view. I knew the heart of Russia." She had lived with Russian people inside and outside of prison: "I had gained a just perspective, and I felt that I understood all that is good and all that is bad and all that is historically inevitable in the great upheaval which is, in spite of everything, modernizing Russia."

She knew the pain the Russian people endured, but she also knew the strength and spirit they possessed. As much as the dictatorship tried to drown them out, they were buoyed by the *Duchovnaya Zhizn*, the spirit of the mind. "There is no place in the world where people live it more abundantly," she said.

Four days later, still accompanied by Senator France, she boarded the train for Berlin. The politician had left the American officials in Riga with a sour taste. He "accepts at face value the mass of misinformation given him by Bolshevik leaders," the U.S. Commissioner, civilian head of the American Occupation, wrote in a "Very Confidential" memo to the secretary of state. A few days after that, the commissioner in Berlin confirmed that the senator left Russia "even more favorably disposed towards the Bolsheviks than when he went in." On the other hand, he said, "Mrs. Harrison impressed me as a clear-headed and intelligent woman."

The first to greet her in Berlin was Merian Cooper. He had escaped from the prison camp and, with enormous gratitude for the help she had given him in Russia, had made plans to help her escape as well. Over a long dinner at the Adlon, she recalled how she had "suffered tortures of anxiety" when she was supplying him with food and other necessities," putting both their lives at great risk.

Her friend Dr. Hugh Young, who had come from Carlsbad on vacation with his wife, found her pale and thin, and "distinctly tea-colored." The last time he had seen her was in Paris; she had arrived at the end of 1918 for the peace talks, eager to tackle her new work as a spy. Now, she was undernourished and still carrying a touch of tuberculosis, yet her nerves seemed strong and she was starting to readjust to normal life. He took her shopping, and dressed in her smart new clothes, she dined at the American embassy, where the British and French ambassadors stayed well past midnight plying her with questions and paying close attention to her answers.

In Germany, where diplomatic relations had not yet been restored, she provided the U.S. Commissioner with a ten-page report on Russia, from foreign policies to domestic economics, from the state of its railroads to the reach of its political arm. With remarkable recall she was able to supply names, numbers, and details that others might easily have forgotten.

Once again she advised Washington to forestall the competition and open relations with Moscow. The British have already established business, she said, noting the "enormous amount of British canned goods coming into Russia," and that "the Germans were supplying Soviet hospitals with large quantities of drugs" including a vaccine against an outbreak of cholera.

As the daughter of an international businessman, she understood the power of commerce. The market potential for America was vast. The Russians had almost no raw materials or manufactured goods on hand, and no means of production. "There is practically no platinum, the gold mines are producing about 15% of pre-war production; the sugar industry will have to be built up from the beginning." The list went on: There was little flax, no rubber, no leather, no high-grade tools for factories. It would take some time before investments delivered a profit, but she was certain they would be substantial in the long term.

Russia was desperate for food. Outside the two major cities, Moscow and Petrograd, where the government provided enough to eat, more than thirty million people were starving or facing partial starvation. But she warned them not to hold out hopes for a revolt against the Bolsheviks. "The people are too thoroughly exhausted morally and physically to make an organized attempt."

The Communists controlled the region with a strong arm that reached through eighteen autonomous republics, from Europe to Asia, Ukraine to Siberia, Georgia, and Azerbaijan. In addition, she wrote, "They are developing their international propaganda on broader lines than ever." She finished the report only hours before she left for London.

The first person she met in England was her son, handsome and smartly dressed in a suit and straw hat. She had not seen Tommy in almost two years, and at nineteen he had changed from an adolescent into an adult. "I could hardly believe my eyes when I saw a tall young man open the door of our compartment and take me in his arms. We were both trembling with excitement, but there was nothing dramatic in our meeting."

"Hello mother," he said almost casually.

"Hello, Tommy dear," she replied. "Goodness, how you've grown." And then, pushing away their emotions, they embraced in silence.

.   .   .

The America she came back to had turned further inward; in spite of its emergence as a world power after the Great War, it had narrowed its focus to domestic affairs. Even more than before, she was "appalled" by the support for Prohibition, which flooded the country with underground crime and poisonous alcohol; she was "shocked beyond measure at the activities of the Ku Klux Klan" with its lynchings, cross burnings, and verbal attacks on Blacks, Catholics, and Jews; she was disappointed in the growing attitude of intolerance and "loathed the small-mindedness of the Harding regime."

She was an internationalist, and she felt trapped. Communism, she advised, was not a thing to be fought with blind fear and hatred, "but combatted with intelligent counterpropaganda at home." Conservatives, she said, accused her of being "a Bolshevik in disguise. Reds thought me bourgeois and counterrevolutionary."

Her aim was to see relations with Russia restored. Although she insisted her own sympathies were with the Social Revolutionaries, who favored a socialist democracy, she was convinced the Communists would control the Russian government for some time to come. Change would be evolutionary.

Regrettably, she noted, "the great powers of the world have done all that they possibly could to hinder this evolution by blockades, intervention and intrigue. They have never done the obvious thing," she said, "which is to leave them alone. By isolating Russia, they have brought about the very thing they have been trying to prevent, a prolongation of the Communist dictatorship."

Through a series published in the *Sun,* and in magazine articles and lectures she carried out her mission, explaining both the good and the bad in Bolshevism. She disliked its methods but admired its aspirations: the elevation of workers; the emancipation of women; the attention to children; the focus on education; the electrification of the nation; the importance of medicine and health care.

Despite this, she said, most Americans "lost their ability to see both sides of social and political problems; they could not see any good in Communism." Try as she might to induce her countrymen to look out the window and see the world, she found them staring in the mirror and looking back at themselves.

Her friends, who welcomed her warmly, were the same staid society matrons she had left behind, pursing their lips at foreign affairs, puzzled at her reluctance to return to the bridge table, the garden club, and the opening races at Pimlico; their biggest concerns were the problems they had with servants.

What's more, her onetime friend Stan Harding was on a rampage, publicly accusing Mrs. Harrison of being responsible for her stay in prison. Rumors started flying: some people thought Marguerite was a British agent; others were sure she was a Cheka spy. A few had heard she was Trotsky's mistress.

It thrilled her that soon after she arrived home, in a meeting with Marlborough Churchill in Washington, he told her that she had "given the Military Intelligence more information about Russia than any other agent." He applauded her reports for being "accurate, fair minded and impartial," and was joined in his praise by the army chief of staff.

A few days later, Secretary of Commerce Herbert Hoover invited her to a meeting on Russia that lasted nearly four hours. She talked about Russia again at lunch with William Hurley, in charge of counterintelligence at the State Department, and told him there were interesting contacts she could make in New York; she would stay in touch.

But the Military Intelligence Division had been downgraded, and with America no longer at war, the State Department took over a large part of its portfolio, liaising with the Bureau of Investigation at the Justice Department for counterintelligence work. In addition, MID's Cipher Bureau, headed by Herbert Yardley, was secretly moved to New York, where the Black Chamber, as it was called, went undercover as a commercial firm. Yet Marlborough Churchill sometimes rode the night train to attend clandestine meetings with Yardley.

Despite the high regard for her work, Marguerite was no longer needed by MID. She, however, still required an income. She was dismayed to learn that all of the twenty thousand dollars she had given to a brokerage firm before she left for Russia, had dissolved in a stock market slump in 1920. In addition, many of her antiques, furnishings, and heirlooms had disappeared, stolen by boarders convinced she would never return.

She resumed her former position at the *Sun*, writing theater and music reviews, but she found it dull. Only months after being lauded, she now felt blasé and longed for her work in the heat of revolution. Memories of Russia tugged at her heart.

"In spite of all that I had suffered, I still loved the country and the people," she said. She felt a kinship "deeper than sentiment, stronger than political prejudice," and "bound up with obscure memories of a distant past." She imagined that before the Middle Ages one of her ancestors had been part of a Mongol horde sweeping across Asia into Europe. With passionate intensity, she began to plot her way back.

Part Three

CHAPTER 16

Changes

On a blustery day in Washington in 1921, presidents, prime ministers, and premiers from Europe and Asia held on to their top hats and climbed the marble staircase of Memorial Hall to attend the first-ever conference on arms control, the Washington Naval Conference. High above the columned entry on D Street, where their flags flapped in the wind, Arthur Balfour of Britain, Aristide Briand of France, and Baron Kato of Japan, along with other leaders and deputies, the international diplomatic corps, the members of the House and Senate, and four hundred journalists from around the world, including Wickham Steed of the *London Times* and H. G. Wells of the *New York World*, settled into their seats for the Washington Conference on Limitation of Naval Armaments.

The Harding administration had invited the leaders to discuss events in Asia. The Far East was a hot pot, a Pacific stew boiling over with Japanese, Chinese, French, British, Russian, and American interests. The country causing the biggest tremors was Japan. Quiet deals were being made in shoji-screened rooms perfumed with joss sticks and stippled with silk-clad women pouring tea; above the hush, the roar of a coming war could be heard. America, wary of Japanese militarism, worried over the growing arms race between Japan, Britain, and the United States.

The American chargé d'affaires in China had spelled out his fears in a cable to the secretary of state: "The Japanese government and nation are drunk with ambition. They aspire to control the western

share of the Pacific Ocean and the resources of the hinterlands . . .
and they dream of the day when they can humble the United Sates and
are systematically preparing for it."

American ambassador Paul Reinsch wrote from China that unless
the U.S. government felt strong enough to stop the Japanese, "there
will come a sinister situation dominated by the unscrupulous methods
of the reactionary military regime" that he called "cynical of the principles of free government and human progress." If this force remains
unopposed, he warned, the Far East would confront "the greatest
engine of military oppression and dominance that the world has yet
seen."

Japan's postwar government was flexing its muscles, building a
powerhouse navy of battleships and cruisers to dominate the Pacific
and dreaming, too, of economic wealth dug from caves chunked with
coal, wells filled with oil, and waters teeming with fish in places named
Sakhalin, Vladivostok, Nikolaevsk, Mongolia, Manchuria, and Siberia. The yellow dragon was flaming its tongue at new territories and
new commercial markets.

To be sure, the British were increasing their tonnage and the
United States was strengthening its navy, determined to make it second to none. But while the Western Allies were ablaze with cravings
not unlike those of the Japanese, they held no desire for the economic
and human costs of another conflagration.

To calm the nerves, Washington had called for this naval meeting. Now, on Saturday, November 21, the distinguished audience in
the white-paneled hall awaited the opening remarks of the United
States secretary of state. Standing before them, tall and aristocratic,
partly bald and smartly bearded, with a handlebar moustache and eyes
that sparkled, Charles Evans Hughes declared: "The way to disarm is
to disarm." But no country wanted to disarm completely. Discussions
were difficult and progress slow.

For four months the ministers met publicly in the great hall and
privately in quiet rooms, and after the meetings, consulted with their
governments via thousands of cables whisked to their capitals across
the seas. While the emissaries conferred in English, French, Italian,
and Japanese, Washington intercepted their communications and
couriered them to New York. At the Black Chamber brownstone on

East Thirty-Seventh Street, cipher experts secretly worked to decrypt the missives.

During her years as a music and theater critic, Marguerite made trips to New York to interview performers for the *Sun*. Now she was there occasionally, giving talks on Russia. The frenetic city offered a change from the familiar routine of Baltimore. Indeed, the whole country was seeking change. The prosperity that comes with war had run its course.

At the start of 1920, the stock market tumbled, employment fell, and people trembled as a severe recession darkened the skies. Pushing away the clouds, singers crooned, "Look for the Silver Lining," and by summer of 1921 the sun glistened again. Americans started spending their dollars as though they were dimes, and vocalists asked, "Ain't We Got Fun?" On bandstands, radios, and gramophones, Ethel Waters sang, "There'll Be Some Changes Made," and millions of people sang with her: "There's a change in the weather and a change in the sea. . . . So from now on there'll be a change in me."

Toward the end of the year Marguerite changed too, giving up her home in Baltimore and moving to West Forty-Fifth Street in New York where she took an apartment at the Hotel Schuyler with her son. Tommy had refused to go to college and was working instead at the International Mercantile Marine Company, Bernard Baker's former business; she was lecturing on "Life in Russia" to ladies' clubs, labor groups, and liberal colleges.

Her name was well known from news stories about her imprisonment and release, and although she openly admitted she had entered Russia illegally, she never uttered a word about being a spy. Indeed, her well-received talks highlighted the good intentions of the Soviets and the better side of Russian life.

Emphasizing the necessity of the Revolution, she blithely waved off the brutality of the Bolsheviks, smoothed over the rough patches of hunger, isolation, illness, and mental torture during her stay in Lubyanka, and stressed the need for America to recognize the new Russian government. While some observers rolled their eyes and complained she showed too much sympathy for the Soviets, the State Department gave her a nod of consent; she was unearthing radicals who turned out to hear her.

With only her lecture fees and a stipend from the *Sun,* she conceded that her income did not cover expenses; nevertheless, she managed to pay her rent at the air-conditioned residential hotel that called itself "a home away from home." Her new home was in walking distance from the Black Chamber operating covertly ten blocks away. No matter the size of her income, her language gifts and analytical skills seemed to make her a logical addition. But the enigmatic Cipher Bureau kept no lists of employees and no records of its cash payments to the translators, analysts, cryptologists, and clerks who worked there. Only the head, Herbert Yardley, knew their identity; except for a few, their names, perhaps including hers, remain a mystery.

That was not the issue, however, when she alerted Mr. Hughes, head of counterintelligence at the State Department, that something important had come up. He informed his counterparts at the Justice Department and arranged for a bureau agent to see her and write up a report. The meeting took place on a damp, gray December day at her midtown hotel.

As she explained, her lecture agent had planned a multiple-city tour, but something else piqued her interest: she had received an invitation from David Dubrowsky, head of the American branch of the Russian Red Cross, to speak in several midwestern cities with the hope that she, along with Senator France, would raise funds for the organization and stir interest for recognition of the Soviet Government.

With many midwestern farmers eager to sell their grain to Russia, it was not a far-fetched idea. She was suspicious, however, when he readily offered to pay her substantial lecture rate of $150 per speech, and she found it even odder since charitable organizations expected their speakers to forgo any fees at all.

Dr. Dubrowsky was a familiar figure. He had often appeared in Moscow at Mogilevsky's office, looking comfortably at home, and she knew that he stayed in an apartment building used only by the Cheka. Moreover, she had received Russian Red Cross speaking invitations from three other Americans linked to the Cheka.

She would make the Midwest tour, she told her visitor, only if the Bureau wanted the information she might uncover, including Senator France's connections and Dr. Dubrowsky's endeavors. But her real goal, she added, was to develop deeper friendships with these and other radicals so that she might go back to Soviet Russia as an American spy. She would make her decision the next day, she informed him.

She heard promptly from Bureau of Investigation director William Burns and his aide J. Edgar Hoover: As "a person of some importance," they said, her presence on the tour would "do more harm" than any possible information she could uncover. A disheartening response to hear four days before Christmas; so much for her wish to return to Russia.

In January 1922, her book *Marooned in Moscow* came out to excellent reviews. The *Atlantic* called it "the most informing book upon Russia . . . that has yet been published"; the *Washington Herald* declared it "impartial and penetrating"; and the *New York Times* reviewer deemed her "plucky and lucky," and said, "I have not seen any book on contemporary Russia more interesting and valuable as this."

Her popularity as a speaker grew, her lecture schedule increased, and her itinerary expanded from New York and Washington to Buffalo, Rochester, Cleveland, and Chicago. And after years of self-imposed drought, her social life flourished. In New York, where maître d's at speakeasys like 21 and steakhouses like Delmonico's bowed to gentlemen in dinner jackets and ladies in beaded gowns, she dined on specialties like Mongol soup and foxtrotted to Benny Goodman's "When Buddha Smiles."

Businessmen, bankers, and lawyers, dazzled by her looks and daring, leaned across the table, lit her cigarettes, and gazed into her teasing eyes, aching to change their lives and take the kinds of risks that she did. "Many of them were in love with me, simply because I appealed to their sense of adventure," she said. "There was a prominent lawyer who longed to be an explorer, a well-known businessman who yearned to go to sea, a banker who wanted to be a cowboy."

But as much as she enjoyed their admiration, she felt little attachment to the men who pursued her. She lusted after greater adventures.

Marlborough Churchill appeared to help.

April 14, 1922
Dear Major Churchill,
Your letter was forwarded here from Baltimore and I

received it this morning. I am interested in hearing what you
have in mind.

   Marguerite E. Harrison
   57 W. 45th Street New York

April 26, 1922
My dear Mrs. Harrison:

   In reply to your letter of April 19, I shall greatly appreciate
it if you will meet me at the ladies' dining room of the
University Club at one o'clock, Monday, May first.

   I will arrange at the same time for the interview I
referred to.

   M. Churchill
   Major, General Staff Washington

As she lunched with Churchill at the exclusive male club down
the street from the White House, the talk in Washington touched on
events of the Naval Conference. Two months earlier, in a moment of
triumph and glee, the Cipher Bureau had broken the most important
of all the transmissions, the Japanese code. With Tokyo's secret negotiating positions in hand, Washington had agreed with the British, the
French, the Italians, and the Japanese, the key participants, to sign
pacts limiting the number and size of each country's warships; to end
Japanese occupation of parts of China and Siberia; to maintain China's
Open Door Policy of equal access for foreign commercial interests;
and to reduce Japan's influence in the region. Or so America hoped.

   The Far East region included Russia, China, and Japan, but
their borders were unfixed and their populations complex. Much was
unclear. Who were the inhabitants? Who was really in control? Territories long identified with one country had changed hands and now
were controlled by others. Parts were under the Russians, parts were
occupied by the Japanese, parts were held by the Chinese. How did
the local people view the occupiers? How strong was the military in
each area? The economy? How stable were the local governments?
Would the occupiers withdraw? Clouds of questions hung in the air.

   America's own interests ranged from vast oil deposits and coal
mines north of Japan in the Sakhalin Islands to control of the Trans-

Siberian Railway east of Vladivostok, to Japanese markets and trading rights in China. Yet, few Americans had visited the sprawling area since the end of the Great War. Information was almost as sparse as the Siberian steppes.

Robert Eichelberger had been a strategic adviser with the American Expeditionary Force, conducting intelligence operations in Siberia, Vladivostok, Japan, the Philippines, and China. He was an expert on the Japanese and was convinced when he left Tokyo that Japanese militarists were firmly set on "the conquest of all Asia." On his return to Washington, he worked for MID in the Far Eastern Section, serving as an adviser at the Naval Conference.

After the naval pacts were signed, he cautioned: "any agreement that made the Japanese so happy might possibly not be . . . in the interests of the United States." The day after Marguerite lunched with Major Churchill, she met with Major Eichelberger.

She was, admittedly, not an expert on Asia but was well aware of U.S. concerns with Japanese inroads in China and Siberia. And she wondered how much the Naval Conference agreements on limitations could be carried out without taking into consideration the Russian Bear.

To what extent had Red propaganda taken root among the Asian peoples? she wondered. How broad was the Bolshevik influence in Asia? How deep was Japan's penetration beyond its own borders? How strong were the Chinese? Would the Japanese and Chinese combine their interests against the Russians? Would the Bolsheviks take over the Far East?

A few weeks after her meetings with Majors Churchill and Eichelberger, she booked passage across the Pacific. While she was concluding her plans, Marlborough Churchill wrote a letter to military attachés in the Far East. The dispatch hinted at danger lurking in her exploits:

May 25, 1922
This is to advise you confidentially that Mrs. T.B. Harrison (Marguerite E. Harrison) will probably visit the Far East in the near future and may ask you for endorsements or letters setting forth the fact that she was [at] one time employed by the Military Intelligence Division.

. . . although it is a fact that Mrs. Harrison was employed
by the Military Intelligence Division during the war
and for a short time afterwards and did excellent work
for us, it has not been deemed expedient to give her any
letters in Washington, either in this office or in the State
Department. . . . if such letters were found in her possession,
they would militate against her in the eyes of Soviet
authorities. . . .

Mrs. Harrison is a woman of great refinement and excellent
education and thoroughly reliable as far as I know. There is
no reason why you should not extend to her such courtesies
as may be appropriate, but you should politely decline to give
her anything in writing in the way of endorsements or to
indicate to anyone except the American Consul that she was
ever in our service.

M. Churchill,
Major, General Staff Washington

The letter raised a number of questions: Did she plan to go to
Russia? Why would she be arrested by the Soviets if she was traveling
in Asia? Had Marlborough Churchill hired her in secret? She stated
later in her autobiography that since her arrest had revealed her identity, she could no longer work for her government as a spy; furthermore, Churchill never mentioned that she was once again working
for him. But intelligence officials cloak themselves in ambiguities and
shield their words with omissions. They do not often announce their
espionage agents, not even to others in their employ.

Her explanation of the trip conformed with her past objectives: "I
felt that I could do something really constructive by trying to interest
American audiences in international politics," she wrote in her book.
Indeed, in April she had written a front-page story for the *New York
Herald* about her old friend Walter Rathenau, currently the German
foreign minister, calling him "a savior" and "the real governing power
in Germany today."

To broaden interest in foreign affairs, she planned to deliver a new
series of lectures: "I wanted to present some new subject that was distinctly of the moment." But how was she paying for her travels? She

was hoping to write for a magazine, yet an assignment was unlikely to cover the high costs of such an extensive trip.

Her lecture agent even opposed the idea, arguing that audiences would not have enough interest in the Far East, and magazine editors did not take to it either. Nonetheless, she persuaded William Randolph Hearst, publisher of *Cosmopolitan* and *Hearst's International* to sign a contract. Saying farewell once again to her son, she boarded the Canadian Pacific sleeper to Vancouver; from there she set sail on the *Empress* liner to Japan. As she made her way across the Pacific, news crossed the Atlantic that right-wing Germans had murdered Walter Rathenau, foreign minister of the Weimar Republic. Some observers claimed it was because he was too liberal; Marguerite was certain he was killed for being a Jew.

The two-week voyage to Asia allowed her time to complete a series she had already promised to *Cosmopolitan:* "Unfinished Stories" were tales of women she had met in Russian prison. Upon her arrival in the Far East, she told friends, she planned to gather material for both *Cosmopolitan* and *Hearst's International*. When she returned home, she would be ready to deliver a new series of talks on the future of the Far East.

In America, an attitude of Western superiority had fired up strong anti-Asian sentiment. The Chinese Exclusion Law of 1882 had already blocked immigration, and recently published books ranted about the "Yellow Peril," accusing Asians of existential aggression against the West. The fictional Dr. Fu Manchu, subject of fourteen novels, the first one published in 1913, was described by its author, Sax Rohmer, as "the yellow peril incarnate in one man" and "the greatest genius which the powers of evil had put on earth for centuries."

But Marguerite did not believe that the renaissance of the Mongol peoples was a menace to civilization. "I could not see why the West should be 'supreme' in Asia," she stated. If Americans pictured Asia as an ancient land of evil, inferior people, she would present a more informed and comprehensive view. She spoke neither Japanese nor Chinese, nor was she familiar with their literature or knowledgeable about their cultures. She was off to untamed waters and undreamed-of shores.

CHAPTER 17

Dragons and Bears

Customs men wearing smart Western uniforms welcomed Marguerite to Yokohama, and a well-equipped electric train carried her swiftly to Tokyo, giving her the sense of a country speeding into modernity. But looking out the window, alongside the tracks she saw the feudal past rush by as barefoot peasants toiled knee deep in rice fields not far from their villages crowded with houses made with paper partitions and straw roofs. "They looked exactly like the figures I had seen in eighteenth century prints," she said.

The clash seemed even more jarring in the capital. As soon as she entered the city's busy Nihonbashi district, her taxi dodged ancient rickshaws and new electric trams, while on the sidewalk young couples walked arm in arm past ladies shuffling meekly behind their husbands. Men wearing *hakama* and *haori*, the traditional loose-fitting pants and wide-cut coat, spiffed up their outfits with straw hats and oxford shoes while wives in kimonos and wooden sandals carried their babies on their backs. The Mitsukoshi Department Store handed customers special cloths to cover their shoes and then whizzed them up on escalators to shop for Western clothes. The country was a model of cultural ambiguity.

The nineteenth-century Imperial Hotel exemplified the mix. Only a month before Marguerite arrived, an earthquake toppled the old wooden edifice while a new stone building designed by Frank Lloyd Wright was still under construction. Fortunate to be one of the first guests in a newly completed wing, she stayed for two months in the Mayan-inspired hotel, a mix of new and ancient Eastern and Western styles applauded for its soaring ceilings, broad balconies, and vertical windows streaming with light. She dined on French food in its restaurants, danced to jazz in its famous Peacock Room, and mused about the Far East at its reflecting pool.

Moving easily into her journalist's role for Hearst, she made her way to the press bureau of the Japanese foreign office, where an American, Mr. Moore, gave her letters of introduction to high-ranking officials, businessmen, and social leaders. Adding the names to her contacts from home, she was ready to make her mark on the capital.

She interviewed premier Baron Kato, who extended a rare invitation to tea at his villa with his wife and grandson; she met with the foreign minister, Viscount Uchida; and she dined on rice and raw fish at the homes of new friends. At the villa of the Viscount Takahashi, Japan's most brilliant banker, she met financial leaders and captains of industry; at the palace of Baron Iwasaki, director of the Mitsubishi Bank, she joined a reception for the secretary of the U.S. Navy; on a rainy Fourth of July, at the party hosted by the American ambassador, she chatted with Japanese officials and foreign diplomats; and she lunched at the home of a Japanese admiral and his British guest, Major Winder.

She flirted on more than one occasion with Basil Winder, who represented Vickers, a vital provider of armaments to the Japanese. So potent were her charms that he later showed her extensive amounts of secret information on his firm's dealings with the Japanese: the British planned to use Japanese middlemen in Siberia to secure trade with Soviet Russia, a worrisome prospect for the United States. She passed the intelligence to Colonel Charles Burnett, the American attaché in Tokyo, requesting that he report it to Washington without using her name.

"Major Winder has fallen head over heels in love with her," the colonel wrote in a secret memo, adding that Vickers had also offered her a position working for their Secret Service. "I advised her to take it," he said. "It would be well for us to know about such ambitious plans and that would seem the best way to find out."

Vickers and the Americans were not the only ones wanting her to share the information she reaped. The Japanese foreign office, impressed by her understanding of Russian affairs, asked her to make confidential reports on the political and economic conditions when she traveled around Siberia, and a Japanese newspaper signed a contract with her to cover a Russian–Japanese trade conference and supply other material as well.

At the admiral's luncheon table, Major Winder told jokes, imitated a monkey, and made the host laugh. But most of the time, Marguerite found the smiling faces of the Japanese men to be unreadable masks. It was not so much that they did not want to give their opinions, a Japanese friend explained; it was more that they did not know how.

"The Japanese are essentially inarticulate," the Western-educated woman observed. "They have never been able to freely express themselves to each other or to foreigners." She blamed it partly on the influence of Buddhism and partly on the clan spirit. "The Japanese are given to thinking and acting collectively," she said.

Not so for the ladies. "Feminism has never appealed to me," Marguerite said, but she was intrigued by three strong women who stood out for their individuality.

One spoke fluent English, read French and English literature, and lived in a European-style house, yet she almost never went out with her husband and chose a traditional Japanese way of life. Another, a feminist and suffragist who led the birth control movement in Japan, always dressed in Japanese clothes. The third, a well-known actress who dared to play female roles, founded a theater and school for young girls. The mélange of old and new, Oriental and Occidental, defined their lives.

The same contrast, she found, applied to Japanese foreign policy, indelibly stamped by ancient loyalty to the emperor but embossed with the goals of the modern world. Imperialistic as well as pragmatic, Japan sought territorial gains through military means and economic gains through new commercial markets. The Washington Naval Conference treaties may have dulled its military capabilities, but it seemed to be only a temporary solution for the West. A major area of contention was Sakhalin.

·   ·   ·

Before the Great War, Sakhalin Island, the strip of land above Japan and across the Amur River from Siberia, had been divided: Southern Sakhalin had been Japanese; Northern Sakhalin had been Russian. In 1918, the Allies, in need of a base to support the White Russians fighting the Red Bolsheviks, asked the Japanese to send seven thousand troops to Northern Sakhalin and Siberia. The Japanese agreed, and quickly claimed the coastline on the Siberian mainland, from Nikolaevsk down to Vladivostok, as part of Sakhalin. Within two years, they increased their troops to seventy thousand.

At the Washington Naval Conference, they consented to withdraw their forces from Siberia, but they were less than eager to leave the northern part of Sakhalin Island, insisting the Bolsheviks pay them reparations for Japanese inhabitants killed by a wild Russian commander in 1920.

Complete control of Sakhalin Island would give the Japanese a strategic position vis-à-vis Russia, and it would bring Japan a windfall of major coal and oil deposits, which, she had learned from Major Winder, they were plotting to exploit with the British. "It was a necessary stage in the trail being blazed by Japan to pave the way for her new economic imperialism," Marguerite noted. Determined to follow the trail herself, she mapped a trip to Sakhalin and beyond "to ascertain conditions on the spot."

She knew from her time in Moscow that the American government craved the same natural resources and was supporting the Sinclair Company in its negotiations with Russia for mining and drilling concessions on the same land. While the British were banking on Japanese control of the region, the United States, although refusing to recognize the Bolshevik government, was counting on Russia to gain back control of the region. Despite the conflict of interests between the United States and Japan, Marguerite convinced the Japanese to allow her to be the first foreign visitor in more than two years.

·   ·   ·

She left Tokyo in the heat of July, saying sayonara to the leafy parks filled with women and children, and goodbye to the outdoor cafés and open-air theaters. Storing most of her bags at her hotel, and accompanied by the "most delightful" Mr. Honda, a foreign office minder, she proceeded to the top of the Japanese archipelago. From there she planned to meet up with Colonel Burnett and catch a steamer boat to Alexandrovsk, the capital of Sakhalin Island, where the American attaché had scheduled meetings with Japanese officials.

On the first night of her travels, she stopped in Hakodate on the island of Hakkaido. Sleeping in her first real Japanese hotel, she lay down on a quilt spread on the floor, and with her hair wrapped in a net, she rested her head on a wooden pillow. In the morning she was brought "a decidedly unsatisfactory breakfast of bean curd soup, rice, eel omelette, pickled plums, and weak tea."

Knowing that her minder had gone off on his own, she dressed, sauntered downstairs, and told the innkeeper of her plans to explore the town and photograph the old castle. The hotel man drew back in horror: the fortress was top secret and not allowed to be seen, not even by the Japanese. What's more, he warned, photographs were not permitted: not of the fort, nor the town nor the area around it. Undaunted, she went out, camera in hand, drawing a crowd that followed in her footsteps. All went well until a policeman sidled up, seized her camera, and destroyed her film.

At her next stop, Otaru, she boarded the boat for Sakhalin. As pleased as she was to see her friend Colonel Burnett, she was not so happy to meet her bunkmates that night: thousands of roaches crawling across her body and bed. "But the food was excellent," she said, dismissing the inconvenience as she often did. The good cognac brought by the only other first-class passenger, a garrulous Japanese man, sweetened the eight-hundred-kilometer trip.

When the boat reached their destination of Alexandrovsk, a strong wind and heavy rain thrashed her as she stepped from the deck onto a tender pitching her toward the bleak harbor. Two decades earlier Anton Chekhov called the place "hell." The wretched town, rotten with smallpox and starvation, was used as a penal colony under the czar: "If I were a convict, I would try to escape from here no matter what," the visiting author wrote. Some of the current inhabitants were descended from those tens of thousands of pathetic souls imprisoned, some in leg chains, or permanently exiled to this world, at the farthest reaches of Russian soil.

Now, however, it was occupied by the Japanese, and a crisp flank of white-gloved, uniformed officers of the emperor's navy greeted the Americans on the dock. Chauffeured limousines sped them off, past the Asian neighborhood to official quarters in the Russian district. As guests of the Japanese army, they were given comfortable lodging and an unexpected teatime treat: "delicious ice cream with sponge cake, whisky and soda, and Egyptian cigarettes, as good as any to be had in New York," Marguerite said.

Fortified, they went to meet their host, General Machida, who administered the island from an old multicolored, many-domed, wooden Russian building. As Marguerite was shown later that day and the next, the polished general, who had been commander-in-chief of the Expeditionary Forces, had created a modern Japanese city out of Russian rot: new schools, hospitals, and houses, enhanced with new roads, made it habitable not just for the Japanese, and for Korean and Chinese workers imported to work there, but for the Russian inhabitants as well. Many of the latter, she learned, were comfortable under Japanese rule. One Russian peasant couple, happy to hear her speak their language, welcomed her to their home with hard-boiled eggs, bread, and tea. She asked about the Japanese: "*Neechevo*," the husband said with a shrug; Never mind, it could have been worse.

In the evening she attended a lavish banquet given by General Machida in honor of Colonel Burnett. The general had worked at the Japanese embassy in Paris, and at his elegant dinner served in Russian style, she found her place card and took her seat beside his. In front of her was the menu printed in French, and on either side of the service plate were the cutlery and crystal for an eight-course dinner with wines and champagne.

She was the only woman ever invited to dine by the Japanese general staff. Surrounded at the table by twenty officers in full dress uniforms and sculpted smiles, she said, "I had been a guest at many strange parties in many strange places but have never had a more unique experience." She had no idea what a single man was thinking as they spoke politely through their enigmatic grins. Albert Einstein, the brilliant scientist who unlocked the theory of relativity, visited Japan a few months later and was also stymied: "No one can fathom the feelings concealed behind this guarded smile," he wrote.

General Machido spent much of the dinner explaining in excellent French why the Japanese army should stay in Northern Sakhalin. As hard as he tried to persuade her that his government would leave as soon as the Russians paid reparations for the damages done two years before, she remained unconvinced.

A mad Russian ruler and his mad Russian mistress had massacred six hundred Japanese as well as thousands of Russians in Nikolaevsk, a part of Sakhalin on the Siberian mainland. But many people claimed Japanese officials were to blame for stirring up problems and then standing aside while multitudes were raped, tortured, and murdered.

Indeed, Marguerite firmly believed the demand for reparations was a pretext for the Japanese to remain in Northern Sakhalin. Its strategic location and untapped resources were unequaled. Badly in need of oil to fuel their navy and to expand their industry, the Japanese had begun drilling, knowing all along that the American company Sinclair had signed agreements with the Russians to explore the same fields. What the Japanese wanted was "annexation, by force if necessary," Marguerite said. The dragon and the bear were playing a dangerous game of real-life chess.

In his welcoming toast at the dinner, the general invited the American woman to make a full inspection of the island the next day. But when she mentioned she would like to visit the oil fields, his face froze. "Ah," he said, "it is such a pity that your steamer leaves tomorrow." And so it did.

.   .   .

She boarded the same roach-infested boat as before and headed across the river to the area of the Siberian mainland that the Japanese had claimed as part of Sakhalin. All of it had belonged to Russia until the Bolshevik Revolution, when the Allies set up their staging ground in support of the White army against the Reds and small new states began to rise and disappear like spawning salmon.

As the steamer approached the commercial hub of Nikolaevsk, she looked out from her porthole and saw sheets of burnished gold. Yellow silt from the ore ran down the hills, along the coast, and into the water, all of which the Japanese controlled.

The Japanese had promised to remove their troops, but it was easy to understand why they were reluctant to leave: fields heavily veined with gold, waters teeming with fish, forests thick with timber, woodlands covered with furred animals; the wealth of natural resources made it richer than almost any other territory in the world. This was El Dorado. It also bore the bloodstains of the massacre that had taken place.

The area, muddled with uncertainty, was now part of a Russian-designed buffer zone that lay between Russia and Japan. Called the Far Eastern Republic, it was officially recognized by the United States and its allies. For the moment, Japanese troops still ruled the mostly Russian inhabitants. Marguerite told herself she had come there to investigate and verify the Japanese pledge of withdrawal from the mainland. "But deep down in my heart," she said, "I knew that this was not the real reason I wanted to go to Siberia."

After two months living in Japan, an island of tight spaces and taut people unable to express their emotions, she missed the flood of passion and sentiment that poured from the Russian soul. She was homesick "for the sound of Russian voices, for the broad sweep of the Russian wheat fields, for the homely little villages with their wooden *izbas*, for the childlike, lovable people with whom I had lived through so much." With little success at understanding either the Japanese language or the culture, she said, "I was secretly thrilled at the idea of getting back on Russian soil."

The soil of Nikolaevsk may have been Russian, but the officers who welcomed her were Japanese. She and Colonel Burnett, the first foreigners to visit in several years, were escorted to their quarters by the emperor's troops and invited to dine that night with the commander in charge, General Saito. At her request, the general arranged for a tour of the town the next day, and she observed how the Japanese had improved the conditions, from schools to medical facilities.

Speaking Russian with local inhabitants, she heard their ambivalence about returning to Russian control: "They hated the occupation, but they were equally afraid to see the Japanese leave," she said. The massacre tainted their memories. Asked about Japanese rule, one peasant answered, "It has been bad here." But under the Russians, "it will be worse."

The residents wished for independent status and hoped the Allies would bring their dreams to fruition. Colonel Burnett's arrival made them optimistic, and when two more U.S. officials arrived from Chita a few days later, the locals' expectations rose to a fever. But Major Faymonville, a military observer, and Vice Consul Thomas had come only to collect information for the State Department about the Far Eastern Republic.

Marguerite gave them a long economic report and other material she had gathered along the way, asking once again that her name be kept off the memo. If she decided to visit Chita, they said, she was welcome to stay at their residence. Then, along with Colonel Burnett and Mr. Honda, the men all left for Japan.

She remained on her own in Nikolaevsk, writing articles on Northern Sakhalin for an English-language newspaper in Japan while awaiting the boat to take her to Khabarovsk. The city lay seven hundred miles south, halfway down the Maritime Province, the vertical strip at the eastern edge of the Siberian landmass. From Khabarovsk to Vladivostok, she planned to travel overland, an arduous journey, she had been warned, but she welcomed the experience.

Her avowed objective, she said, was to prove that the Japanese occupation, initiated by the Allies, was driving Siberia into the arms of the Soviets. In truth, she admitted that "ever since 1917 I was fed up with security, comfort and easy living." In America, "I had first enjoyed, then been stifled by material comforts. In Japan I felt cramped. Everything was in miniature: houses, gardens, countryside—even the mountains. I longed for a freer atmosphere—I craved hardships and adventure!"

.   .   .

The *Vodhinski* was an antiquated boat navigated by paddle wheel, but she considered it a comfortable old tub; although it lacked bed linens and blankets, it did provide running water and mounds of caviar for travelers. She chatted with the only other first-class passenger and befriended a few in second class, including a young Russian woman fascinated by her American styles. Tasya inspected everything in her bag, from her hairnet to her bedroom slippers, and insisted Marguerite show her how she bobbed her hair. She also recited her only English words: "Dearie, Goddam, and, kiss me quick."

Along the way, the boat stopped at small villages inhabited by the Giliaks, an indigenous tribe living in dreary wooden homes. "I shall never forget my first glimpse," Marguerite said. "It was dark and indescribably filthy." Babies swung from nets on the roof of the one-room house; one moon-faced woman cooked and rocked an infant; another lazily smoked a pipe; and a man munched on raw fish, while everyone guzzled their vodka. The whole place reeked from the odor of rotting fish, while mounds of maggots crawled through the fish waste on the floor.

On other occasions when the boat docked, she joined her fellow passengers for a stroll through the woods, and Tasya, her friend, helped her hunt for wild mushrooms. "I culled all sorts of brilliant and poisonous looking varieties," she recalled, "and ate them recklessly for supper, though not without some qualms." There was no need to worry, she added reassuringly, "there were no fatalities."

More treacherous, however, was the ticket comptroller on the boat, an amiable Russian aristocrat who sang every evening in the saloon while she accompanied him at the piano. He had attended university in Vladivostok when the Great War broke out, and first joined the Imperial Army, then moved on to the monarchists' White Army, and then signed up with the Red Army and became a Communist. At the end of the trip, when Marguerite mentioned that she had been in prison in Russia, he said casually, "I knew it all along. It is our business to know everything." She realized then that he was an agent of the Cheka.

The second day of the trip they reached a town where the Japanese troops were replaced by officials from the Far Eastern Republic. When she was asked to show her passport, one customs man noticed she was *Amerikanski*. "Do you speak German?" he asked. When she answered yes, he told her in excellent German that he had been a prisoner of war in Germany, and after the Armistice he had been sent to a hospital at a prison camp in Berlin.

Coincidentally, Marguerite had toured the same camp and visited the wounded soldiers. "I remember it perfectly," he told her. "You were the only American lady I had ever seen, and you gave us all cigarettes." The two quickly became best friends: "There was nothing he would not do for me," she said; if he could have, "he would have presented me with the Far Eastern Republic."

Her immediate destination was the halfway point of Khabarovsk, once a prosperous trading town that now showed signs it was struggling to come back. Her room at the Belvedere Hotel had a real bed with real sheets and hot water for the bath; the restaurant at the Yacht Club offered good food; the shops offered American products; and the movie theater was flourishing. But the city had been captured nine times during the war, and it was still in shocking disrepair.

During her stay, she met the Assistant Emissary of Chita, the capital of the Far Eastern Republic, whose superior was away, conferring with Japanese officials. The Emissary was trying to smooth the path for his Social Democratic Government to take charge as soon as the occupation forces withdrew. But many residents in Khabarovsk told her they saw the Far Eastern Republic as only a temporary solution: they wanted to be united with Russia, whether it be monarchist or Bolshevik. She wondered whether the attitude in Vladivostok would be the same.

.   .   .

At the station, she bought a ticket for the only train to Vladivostok and made her way across the platform through a pandemonium of humanity. Russian peasants, Japanese soldiers, university students, Chinese and Korean coolies, Cossacks, families with children, and assorted others, all hauling sacks, baskets, bundles, blankets, and food, climbed aboard the fourth-class train and plopped their belongings onto the crowded bunks.

A friendly guard led her to a special compartment for employees, and she clambered onto a berth at the top of three tiers, her suitcase, sleeping bag, typewriter, and toiletries kit close by, her feet dangling over the edge. Down below she watched passengers straggle in and out, searching hopelessly for a place to sleep.

The train started with a sputter, then lurched and crept along, until it gasped and died. Only with the help of passengers, who went outside and pushed, did the engine come alive. It bumped in fits and starts, chugging along for two days, stopping for fuel and water for the locomotive, while the travelers scrambled through the forests, picking berries and flowers under the warm Siberian sun.

"I have never seen any country as rich in wildflowers," she observed. Some species were strangers, others she recognized as old friends: shapely asters, foxgloves, lobelias, and gentians bloomed more vividly than any she had ever seen.

On occasions when the train pulled into stations, farmers offered a voluptuous array of produce. Peasants crowded around to greet the passengers, their baskets filled with fresh food for sale: melons, berries, breads, cakes, milk, honey, eggs, raw chickens, cooked chicken, and roasted pig were plentiful, tasty, and cheap.

But for stretches of time, danger lurked. On either side of the tracks, bands of Russian thieves, Manchurian robbers, and local smugglers hid and preyed on the travelers. Along the way a thief stole her typewriter, and one poor woman was robbed of six rubles of gold, her silver spoons, her best dress, and her underwear.

On the third morning out, the passengers were ordered to leave the train and climb with their bundles onto long wagonettes made of wooden planks set on four wheels. Two men at the back pushed the contraption when it climbed uphill and then jumped on board with the others when the brakeless cart went downhill. She held her breath: there was only one track, and if another wagonette sped toward them, they might crash. "There were hardships to be met, obstacles to be overcome, privations aplenty, an occasional spice of danger," she remarked.

They stopped for a night, and she stayed at a monastery run by a kindly abbot. Along with two Communist officials, a Red soldier, a Jewish scholar, two women travelers, and two other monks, who all shared a hatred for the Japanese, she ate a hearty vegetable soup, argued over socialism and Marx, and slept on a straw-covered plank bed. "I took sybaritic pleasure in my fresh straw pallet," she wrote. "Luxury is, after all, a relative thing. The only people who really enjoy the comforts of life are those who have had to do without them."

In the morning she returned to the wagonette. Once again she joggled on the wooden slats, the sun blazing above her, the bridges shaking beneath her, the mosquitoes, gnats, and other insects swarming around her face and body. As for humans, the only ones to be seen were army patrols whose uniforms changed with the territory; first came those from the Far Eastern Republic, then the Japanese Expeditionary Forces, and last, White Russian troops.

Changing to a third-class train that stopped in the Monarchist Russian zone, she was questioned for carrying an American passport that no one could read. More disturbing, she was arrested by the secret police under suspicion of being a Bolshevik agent. The charge was not absurd: her face was on the front page of the *Japan Advertiser*, the most popular foreign-language paper in the Far East; the headline read: MRS. HARRISON IS CALLED RED AGENT. Once again Stan Harding was accusing her of being a Russian spy. The article had first appeared in London, then in the United States and in Tokyo; quite possibly, the police had seen her picture.

The Japanese were surprised, and some were even shocked, the newspaper said; Marguerite had been shown exceptional hospitality during her stay, invited into the homes of the highest officials, and, as a singular privilege, allowed to take motion pictures of Premier Baron Kato and his family.

The Japanese chargé d'affaires in Washington rushed to the State Department to find out if the charges were true: "I told Mr. Saburi that the Department did not regard Mrs. Harrison as a Bolshevik spy and that there was nothing on our records against her," wrote D. C. Poole, chief of the Division of Russian Affairs. "On the other hand," he told the Japanese diplomat, she was "a very clever woman and one could not always know just what she was about." He added that he was "inclined to the belief that she was honest." But with chauvinistic disdain, he added she was "likely to be carried away by her emotions and enthusiasm."

At the same time, Colonel Heintzelman of Military Intelligence sent a secret memo to Colonel Burnett in Tokyo thanking him for the information given by Mrs. Harrison, deeming it "of great importance and highly appreciated." He repeated Major Churchill's warning, however, that "no written documents of any kind whatever should be given and confidential oral information should be carefully guarded." She has learned "so much inside information in so many countries and has had such frequent contact with many different national leaders that she might quite unconsciously make a most serious mistake."

These discussions were not known to the police who stopped her on the way to Vladivostok. Instead, she was ordered to spend the night in jail. "I have no intention of accepting your hospitality," she told the agent and demanded to see his superior. The commanding officer set her free.

The following day she boarded a "civilized train" and rode for twelve hours to Vladivostok. Originally part of China, which was only nineteen miles away, the city was claimed by Russia in 1860, and its population grew to include, among others, Russians, Uzbeks, Tatars, Scandinavians, Americans, Germans, French, Chinese, Koreans, and Japanese.

In Vladivostok, Marguerite remarked later, "Governments had a way of changing and boundaries of shifting overnight." The Japanese occupiers were still flying their flag from public buildings, but most recently, the White Russians had taken control, led by a Monarchist dictator, General Dieterichs.

She arrived at the end of August, one of the few foreigners visiting the city, and quickly arranged to interview the new Russian ruler. A former army hero under her old friend General Brusilov, the blond-haired Dieterichs had become a strange mixture of fanatic, idealist, and man of action. "He looked beyond and through you," she observed, with "a curious, fixed intensity." His motto was: "God, the Czar, and the people." Just before they met he gave a speech about his new administration: "It was about as tangible as a soap bubble!" she said.

Although the Russian city, set around a bay, had once been an international trading center and a thriving oasis of concert halls, theaters, and museums, it was now a run-down port, occupied and corrupt, with an empty treasury and a starving population. When she asked Dieterichs how he was going to handle the problems he inherited, he pierced her with his gray-blue eyes and replied, "If the people would only have faith, God would perform a miracle!" Her meeting with the mystic felt unreal.

Vladivostok's mostly male population of four hundred thousand residents had survived the difficult war years from the Russian Revolution to the Japanese occupation and many were now feasting on the moment. Bored naval officers, shady government officials, and lonely businessmen gambled their money on everything from Lotto to baccarat, dined with abandon at expensive restaurants, crowded into cafés and cabarets, and hired the whores who promenaded on once-smart Svetlanskaya Street overlooking the Bay of the Golden Horn.

At the same time, throngs of starving Russians, Estonians, Latvians, Tatars, Poles, and Finns, refugees from the wars, lined up in front of the warehouse office of the American Red Cross, eager for handouts of food. Many homeless huddled in the Railway Brigade, a length of sidelined railroad cars parked outside the city, or camped on the sidewalks, or slept on steps in front of the houses. On her way back one night from a party at a cabaret, Marguerite stumbled over a starving boy sleeping in her doorway and slipped some money into his dirty hand.

Dieterich's followers claimed the cause of the city's problems lay seven thousand miles away in Moscow, where, despite the facts, they insisted the Bolshevik government was run by Jews. Anti-Semitism ran rampant among the Monarchists. "When we come into power, we will not leave one Jew in Russia alive," a dainty woman informed her.

On Sunday, September 4, 1922, the day before Marguerite left Vladivostok, the Japanese, faced with the high cost of occupation and pressure from the United States, began to withdraw their troops. By October 25, the Far Eastern Republic was governing the city. "But behind them was the Russia bear," she said. "Three weeks later all Siberia went Red." Japanese dreams of economic expansion in the Maritime Province of Siberia were over: "Japan was checkmated at Vladivostok." Only Sakhalin remained under Japanese rule.

The tournament, however, had not ended. There were more games to be played in Manchuria and Korea and, after much hassle, with her visas and permits in hand, she set off on a steamer for Seoul. The boat sailed in the sunset out of Amur Bay and she watched "the squalor and ugliness of the town disappear, as the steep hills above the Golden Horn turned rose, then blue, then faded out of sight."

A short visit to Korea convinced her that the country had fared better during two decades under Japanese rule than it had managed for many centuries on its own. The occupiers had created a modern Japanese city, with up-to-date buildings, infrastructure, and industrialization.

In recent times, they had relaxed governmental restrictions and offered greater freedom of expression, hoping to encourage Korean friendship with Japan and discourage Korea's relationship with the Bolsheviks. Marguerite had known the head of the Korean socialist party when he lived at her guesthouse in Moscow, but Mr. Pak's dream of a Communist state in Korea was only that. As far as she could see, the Japanese had come to stay. Indeed, they did, until the end of World War II.

CHAPTER 18

A Stiff Upper Lip

Like a knight on the move, Marguerite hopped forward, backward, and sideways, chasing the players on the chess board, searching for answers. Was the whole region playing a game, and if so, who was winning? Were the Japanese and Chinese indelibly opposed to one another as well as to the Russians? Or might the two dragon countries combine against their common enemy, the bear? And where did American interests fit in? Her goal was to gauge the strength and sway of the Japanese, the Chinese, and the Russians throughout the Far East.

Her next stop was Mukden, Manchuria, the center of Japanese influence in China. The reigning Chinese warlord, once an officer in the Japanese army, had made a fierce attempt in 1921 to seize power in Peking, only to be turned back by the forces of Sun Yat-sen. In recent times the Mukden Tiger, as the warlord was known, had earned a reputation for mass executions and frequent orders to shoot the heads of his generals. A mere whisper of his name, Chang Tso-Lin, conjured images of a forbidding military man.

A few years earlier, a group of mutinous sailors were captured after attacking the government mint. One by one they were killed: "some of them shot, some of them were hung at intervals around the city wall, the rest stuffed head down into a well near the mint," she said.

Riding on streets thronged with noisy Chinese rickshaws, old Russian droshkies, and horse-drawn, covered Peking carts, Marguerite reached the Mukden headquarters of Chang Tso-Lin. With a meek smile and a moustache drooping down the sides of his bearded chin, the dictator hardly looked like the fierce Manchu she imagined. Nor did he give the appearance of a man with one wife, five concubines, and fourteen children.

Welcoming her to his French-style château, his back slightly bent, his body small and seemingly frail, he wore a black satin coat with long black sleeves and bore a black skull cap on his head. In a gesture of friendship, he offered her his usual gift for a journalist: a big black cigar. She was the first female ever to interview him.

She turned down the cigar but quickly informed him she was on her way to Changchun, three hundred kilometers to the northeast, where she had a Japanese newspaper assignment to cover the upcoming Russo-Japanese trade talks. When she mentioned that she knew Adolph Yoffe, the leader of the Russian delegation, the Chinese kingpin implored her to speak to him.

With help from his English-speaking adviser Mr. Wong, a graduate of Columbia University, Chang Tso-Lin made clear that in the event of a trade agreement between Japan and the Far Eastern Republic, all imports and exports would have to travel between China and Japan and would be transported part of the way on the Chinese Eastern Railway. The railroad ran across Chinese turf, and the warlord wanted Yoffe to know that this swath of Chinese territory belonged to him.

China was not unified, he explained carefully, nor did he think it should be. While his rival Sun Yat-Sen held the power in Peking and to the south, he himself controlled Manchuria, the land of the former Manchu dynasty, made up of the three provinces northeast of the Great Wall. "The strong man of China," as he was known, wanted to make certain that his adversary, Sun Yat-Sen, laid no claim to management or earnings from the railway.

Tell Mr. Yoffe, he said, toying with his long silver pipe, that if the head of the Russian negotiating team "thought that Peking was entitled to dispose of the question of the Chinese Eastern Railway, he was very much mistaken." The territory was his. Marguerite, an intermediary in the game, promised to deliver his message and return to Mukden with her report.

. . .

In Changchun, a Chinese town which she found "inconceivably ugly, inconceivably dirty," she spent time with the correspondents from the Associated Press and the English-language *Japan Advertiser.* Together with them, she attended press briefings, ate tasteless meals, and played poker in the cheerless lounge of their gloomy hotel.

A highlight of her stay was a dinner given by Mr. Yoffe, the new Russian ambassador to China, for all the journalists. To the dismay of the Japanese, who knew that Marguerite was accused of being a Soviet spy, she was seated to the left of the host. The two renewed their acquaintance, discussing politics, about which he was resolute, and the Russian theater, which he loved.

She had known him from her days in Moscow at the Horitonevsky guesthouse, where he often made visits to his ex-wife and daughter. Marguerite had also seen him frequently at the Savoy Hotel where he had led the Soviet delegation in peace talks with the Latvians. The Soviet government considered him one of its most gifted diplomats, and he arrived in Changchun with a delegation of one hundred political and military experts and spies.

Short and stocky, with thinning dark hair and a pointed beard like his mentor Trotsky, Yoffe peered through his wire-rimmed glasses and assured her he knew of her efforts on behalf of the Soviet government. He acknowledged that she consistently spoke in favor of U.S.–Soviet trade relations and urged American recognition of Soviet Russia. She brightened when he described how, with Lenin's blessing, the country was prospering, attitudes in Moscow were changing, and the government had become more lenient. White Russian officers were receiving permission to enter the country and, most likely, he said, she would be allowed in also.

Before heading back to Mukden, she made a detour north to the Chinese city of Harbin, the headquarters in China of the Chinese Eastern Railway and, she noted, "the center of Russian intrigue in the Far East." Russian workers had arrived two decades earlier to build the railway line, and up until the Great War and the Bolshevik Revolution, when the Japanese stepped in and took over the commerce, the city had been the heart of Russian influence in Manchuria. Now seething with intrigues and schemes, a snarl of Bolshevik, White Russian, Jewish, Japanese, Chinese, American, and other foreign spies snooped on one another, spreading rumors and competing for everything from furs to weapons to the railway.

On her return to Mukden, she assured Chang Tso-Lin that she had delivered his message to Mr. Yoffe and apprised the warlord of the results of the conference. The outcome had been disappointing: the Russians refused to negotiate until the Japanese announced a date for their withdrawal from Sakhalin, and the Japanese refused to set a date until the Russians paid reparations for the massacre at Nikolaevsk.

There were sights to see in Mukden, from the bustling shops tucked inside alleyways of the walled inner city to the ancient Manchu palace within the outer walls, and from the cages balanced at the ends of poles on cricket sellers' shoulders to the Japanese coal mines where Chinese workers were digging out black chunks from bottomless pits. In addition, a charming Chinese official smoothed her visit and showered her with attention.

On her last night in the city, the delightful official bade her a fond farewell. The next day, however, when she boarded the train to Peking, it took her aback to see him ensconced in her compartment. He, too, was on his way to Peking, he announced.

They chatted and lunched, and after dinner together it was clear he intended to stay, not just for a while, but all through the night. Mulling over her dilemma, she worked out a solution and left her seat in search of an Englishman who had been speaking Chinese in the dining car. She soon found the fellow in the corridor, emerging from the lavatory in a pair of gorgeous purple pajamas.

Explaining her situation, she asked him to tell the guard to come to her carriage and express his horror at seeing such a distinguished man having to share his space with another passenger. She gave the Englishman two Mexican dollars, the accepted trading currency used in China, to give to the guard with instructions to offer to move the high official and his baggage to a private compartment. The ploy worked. The Chinese dignitary could not refuse the proposal from the guard, and Marguerite could bolt her door, safely alone for the rest of the night.

. . .

Peking swooped her up in a swirl of parties, dinners, and teas. Her hotel, the Wagon-Lits in the Legation Quarter, served as the center of social life for foreign envoys, and she slipped into place with the silken ease of a diplomat. Her charming conversation combined with her intellectual bent made her a good partner and guest. Gliding from English to French to German and Russian, she could engage acquaintances with chilling tales of Russian prison or little-known tidbits about well-known prime ministers.

Flooded with invitations from foreign emissaries, businessmen, and others posted to Peking, she bobbed her hair, rouged her cheeks and lips, put on her best silk frock, and set off to cheer at the polo matches, play out her bids at the bridge table, dine with officials, foxtrot to jazz bands, picnic by moonlight at the Jade Pavilion, and stay the night at country houses or Chinese temples.

Enchanted as she was by the romantic evenings and inner-city excursions, she soon found the social routine repetitious and dull; every event brought together the same people in the same places eating the same foods, playing the same games, discussing the same topics, and sharing the same gossip. As Somerset Maugham, who had been in Peking two years before, observed about the legation crowd: "They were bored to death with one another."

More vexing for Marguerite, she had come to the Far East not to party with outsiders but to penetrate the minds of the insiders. During her monthlong stay, she met the travel writer Harry Franck and the paleontologist Roy Chapman Andrews. The future head of the American Museum of Natural History and the Explorers' Club, Andrews was based in China and had worked as a spy for MID during the World War. He had just motored from Urga, the capital of Mongolia, through the Gobi Desert to Peking, and had faced mass graves crammed with bodies half eaten by hungry wolves; sheltered against ferocious sandstorms; gazed at glorious rainbows; and unearthed the skull of the largest mammal ever to stalk the earth. His exploits were like magnets drawing her to Mongolia and beyond.

Along with meeting the two daring Americans, Marguerite encountered the impressive foreign minister Wellington Koo and his rich wife, a "fascinating creature" who slinked in a silver sheath and smiled with enameled red lips. In addition, she interviewed the Chinese premier, the president, and many officials who served up superficial talk like a handful of peanuts when she hungered for a sirloin steak.

She wanted to pierce the mysteries of the ancient Chinese culture, which had reached its apex long before Western civilization began. In 1500 BC, scraps of Chinese silk were found in tombs in Afghanistan; in 1000 BC, mummies wrapped in Chinese silk were discovered in Egyptian tombs; and in AD 1200, Chinese paper arrived in Europe, but the Chinese had invented paper more than a thousand years before, and by AD 600 the Chinese had so much paper they were using it to cleanse the bottom reaches of their torsos. In AD 800, Chinese emperors garbed in brocaded silk gave orders printed on paper scrolls to shoot their enemies with gunpowder.

The complexities of China eluded her. It had taken her two years to get a real insight into conditions in Russia, and, she acknowledged, China was far more complicated. Making matters worse, she was unable to speak the language. "It was impossible to get even a rudimentary idea of the intricacies of Chinese politics," she said.

Harry Franck quoted an old China hand: "You can easily tell how long a man has been in China by how much he doesn't know about it. If he knows almost everything, he has just recently arrived; if he admits that he really knows nothing whatever . . . he has been out here a very long time."

Although she stayed for only a month, Marguerite sensed an Asian renaissance. "I felt there were great things stirring in China, but," she admitted, "I could only guess at it all." China was the great unknown in the Far East game. It might be, she opined, that Sun Yat-Sen and Chang Tso-Lin would combine to form the basis of a new federal republic; or there might be a rapprochement with Japan; or a Communist state might emerge.

Indeed, the creation of the modern Chinese Communist Party had taken place the summer before and included the young Mao Zedong, who would later go on to rule the People's Republic of China for nearly three decades. "In the East," she said, unaware of the future leader's reign, "Communism existed long before the dawn of West-

ern history and people have been thinking collectively for centuries."
With so many possible political mixtures, "it is difficult to predict
which combination on the Chinese chessboard will eventually win."

. . .

The bags she had left in Tokyo were lost en route to Peking, and
she was obliged to stay longer in the Chinese capital than she wished,
but by early October 1922 she was on her way north. Her initial idea
had been to cross the Pacific and return home from Vancouver, but
she was too intrigued by Mr. Yoffe's assurances of a Bolshevik welcome, and too tempted by the invitation to stay with the American
officials, Major Faymonville and Mr. Thomas, in Chita.

She canceled her plans to travel by ship, and in Peking she received
a visa to return to the Far Eastern Republic; there she expected to
obtain permission to venture into Russia. She had written to her
stepfather-in-law, Dr. Ames, that she hoped to get permission to pass
through Russian territory on her way to Constantinople.

She had been told that under Lenin the Communist government
was making great strides. Capitalism and free-market enterprise had
been reintroduced, and she hoped to capture a firsthand look and
bring her lectures on Russia up to date. Her plan was to trek across
the great Gobi Desert to Outer Mongolia, make her way to the Siberian border, and continue onward to Moscow. Told by friends it was
safest to take the traditional route of the Trans-Siberian Railway from
China to Chita, she scoffed. It may have been "a foolhardy and sense-
less undertaking from many points of view," she admitted, but hers
was "a much more romantic and adventurous route."

The sun sparkled, and the air snapped with a chill as she set off
northward to the Chinese town of Kalgan, the first big stop on her next
adventure. From there, at the outer ramparts of the Great Wall, she
would make her departure for Inner Mongolia, still a part of China.
She had not received permission to enter Outer Mongolia, which, with
help from Russia, had only recently broken away and declared itself
the independent nation of Mongolia; its relations with the Chinese had
ended, but she counted on her American passport to get her through.

She knew she was taking a risk, yet, she confessed, "the lure of Mongolia was irresistible, and I yielded."

The American consul in dusty Kalgan advised her to avoid the regularly scheduled cars to Urga, the longtime capital of Outer Mongolia, soon to be renamed Ulaanbaatar; the Chinese men drove recklessly over the perilous roads, their vehicles crammed with passengers. Instead, he suggested she travel with an English fur trader who had his own car and chauffeur. Mr. Smith was leaving in a few days for Urga. Come to dinner, the consul said, and you will meet him.

It was not easy for her to persuade the Englishman to take her along. His last female passenger had suffered hysterics on the hazardous roads, and he wanted no part of such an experience again. But Marguerite assured him that she had calmly survived far worse. He would be leaving in a few days, he allowed; he sent a message to meet him at nine a.m. on the appointed day at his office outside the city gates.

She stuffed her sheepskin sleeping bag with her fur coat and felt boots; filled her duffel with underwear and silk stockings, warm clothes, a fancy dress, a camera, a Sterno stove, and a collapsible rubber tub; loaded her toiletries kit with cosmetics, a first-aid kit, and emergency medicines, closed her new typewriter in its hard-shelled case, slung her bags into one rickshaw, and climbed into another.

For half an hour she bumped along in a mess of traffic amidst a cacophony of blue-clad Chinese coolies driving bullock carts, deafening shouts of men pulling rickshaws, herds of bleating goats and baaing sheep streaming to market, and long caravans of noisy camels carrying brick tea to Urga or leather hides to Peking.

At last, just beyond the city gates she saw Mr. Smith, his Russian driver, and his brand-new open Dodge, piled so high with bags and boxes that she had to crawl through a narrow space to reach the back seat of the car. She settled in, wrapping herself with furs against the wintry chill. A Swedish missionary, also going to Urga, did the same.

The driver maneuvered the car past the throngs of beasts and men, and it wound its way through a narrow valley and upward, clinging to the edge of steep, curving mountain roads made of rock and gravel and climbing through a long mountain pass. It took four bullocks to pull the car up more cliffs until, three thousand feet high, they reached the summit. Wherever she looked, she saw the empty steppes of Inner Mongolia. By nightfall, they stopped at the house of a Swedish missionary, where they slept. Rising early, they set off once again, and by noon they had left Inner Mongolia and entered the arid wilderness of the Gobi Desert.

She had pictured the desert as a sprawl of shifting sands, but the Gobi, the largest desert in Asia, proved far more beautiful than anything she had envisioned: purple shadows hung over crimson and gold hills, grasses shimmered like fine silk carpets, stepped ledges wavered in colors of granite or red clay and led to surfaces coated in pebbles sparkling in a rainbow of colors. Each time the driver stopped the car she got out and picked up handfuls of the tiny stones, slipping them through her fingers into her pockets, like birthday jewels as she turned forty-four. "I can recommend nothing more thrilling than a motor trip across the Gobi Desert," she wrote.

No sounds broke the hush of desert silence, save for the occasional bullock cartwheels that creaked and the camel bells that tinkled as long caravans driven by Mongol men went by. Dressed in bold red or yellow silk robes and black saucer hats crowned with yellow cones, the men circled the auto. They stared inquisitively at the car, as incongruous as a camel in Manhattan. "*Sein beno,*" they said to the passengers. Walk in peace.

After two more days the car reached the frontier. Despite some earlier worries, she showed her passport, paid one Mexican dollar, and slipped effortlessly across the border, setting her foot in Mongolia, the land once ruled by Genghis Khan. The fifteenth-century empire, the largest that ever existed, had stretched north to the Arctic, south to the Levant, west to Poland, and east to India. Now, freed from China, it was an independent republic led by the ill and elderly Living Buddha, the third most important figure in the Tibetan Buddhist world. But the real administrators were a group of educated men who supported the Bolsheviks and hoped for a Soviet Republic.

As they neared the capital, Urga, the Gobi sands drifted behind them. Riding through rolling hills with high sweet grass, Mongolian men and women traders passed them by, their faces like golden moons, their bodies wrapped in brilliant silk robes lined with fur, their legs covered in embroidered leather boots, the women's jet-black hair wound like the horns of mountain sheep and held by jeweled silver clips. They paid no attention to the filth that covered their clothes and hair.

Bare, windy, dust-covered Urga swarmed with traders from far and wide: Mongol princes on horseback, wearing peacock-feathered hats and fur-trimmed silk robes held in place by belts holding carved silver knives; Russians in thick fur coats; and Chinese shopkeepers in padded blue denim all buzzed about the open market, a frenzy of narrow alleys filled with stalls brimming with piles of goods.

Marguerite wandered around the shops with Mr. Manning, an American who had bought a gold mine near Urga before the Revolution and was trying to retrieve his rights from the Bolsheviks. On their long walks she joined the shoppers bargaining for magnificent brocades, boots, embroidered robes, aigrettes, American cigarettes, packs of chewing gum, beads of glass, lapis lazuli, malachite, and much more.

A few minutes away at the base of a mountain stood Lama City where a sixty-foot gilded bronze statue of the Buddha protected the Living Buddha and the twenty thousand lama priests who resided there. The Sacred City of the Living Buddha contained a cluster of gold-roofed temples and colorful monasteries surrounded by a string of felt-covered yurts where Mongol prostitutes, their tight-skinned golden faces sometimes flaming with red, filled the needs of the celibate men.

Like all the inhabitants, the women obeyed the Mongolian motto "Water washes away happiness." From the time they were born until the time they died, they never bathed or used soap, and rarely let water touch their faces. They replaced their inner garments only once a year but almost never changed their outer clothes, which were covered with dirt and insects. Yet, thanks to the hot sun and the dry air, Marguerite said generously, "they were not particularly odiferous." The paleontologist Roy Chapman Andrews disagreed: "One Mongol in a closed room is equivalent to one skunk in the same space," he wrote.

The city's smells were worsened by the piles of waste and offal that made up the unpaved roads of Urga. Crowds of faithful followers kneeled in the litter whenever the Living Buddha came down from the mountain and drove by in his Dodge. Alongside his car rode his horsemen, all dressed in red satin robes and sable-edged caps adorned with peacock feathers. But like everyone else, their robes bore the stains of food and the soil of bodily functions. The city had no toilets, and people crouched in the streets or in front of their doors to relieve themselves.

Nor did Urga have proper burial sites. Instead, the bodies of the dead were carted away and dropped outside the town, where their evil spirits were left to be eaten by packs of savage mongrel dogs. After ten days in Urga, with little amusement but shopping and playing poker, Marguerite was ready to move on.

Mr. Lubarsky, head of the vast Soviet consulate, told her she would have an answer to her visa request for Russia when she arrived in Chita, the Far Eastern capital. She hired a *yamshik*, a driver, who promised a comfortable ride and swift horses for the thousand-*verst* trip. Instead, he brought an old troika, three horses abreast—one that was twenty years old, one that was an unbroken colt, and one that was lame in two legs. The Russian carriage had no springs, and its four wheels sat on two poles, a bouncy ride at best. "It looked like a relic of the days of Catherine the Great," she said.

She climbed aboard and unrolled her sleeping bag across a sack of straw in the back. The temperature was close to zero, but enveloped in her fur-lined coat, fur hat, and her high felt boots, and jammed between one sack filled with tea and sugar, a leg of lamb, and a large loaf of black bread for the passengers, and several sacks of oats for the horses, she dismissed the wintry cold with a shrug. "The air was deliriously dry, the sunshine dazzling and the spell of the open road was on me," she said. With a farewell wave from friends and the jingle of bells, the carriage set off at a brisk pace.

November had arrived, and she knew she could never make it back to New York in time for her scheduled lectures, but she did not care. "*Sudba!*" It was fate, she exclaimed. She had become like a Russian, resigned to the inevitable.

Over the course of two weeks, they crept along a mountain range covered in piles of snow, rode through a blinding blizzard in a driving wind, and walked cautiously across a frozen river. At one point she had to wait for a week until a river froze, or she might have fallen through the ice and drowned. Setting off again, she saw little of human life, but she feared the strange wolves with "pinpoint flames of phosphorescent green eyes," that passed her by.

They stopped for food and drink at filthy post stations, and at one the heat was suffocating and the air held the stench of several Mongol customers. At night she slept in *izbas*, one-room log cabins, sometimes lying on the floor with animals, other times stretched out on wooden planks side by side with strangers so close she could hardly move.

In one old village she had a room of her own. "I was able to take off my clothing and bathe in my collapsible rubber tub," she recalled. They reached Miamachen, the last Chinese stop, and a few *versts* farther down, a Russian soldier asked where she was from and waved her on; she had entered the Far Eastern Republic without so much as a glance at her papers.

In the town of Troitsk-Kosavsk they took on a Russian passenger, Yevseev, a young Cossack courier who carried the diplomatic mail to Chita and made good company along the way. Even more comforting, he carried a rifle and a revolver that came in handy when they spotted a band of highway robbers hiding in the bushes. "Take the reins," he told her, and climbing up nervously to the high seat, she felt like a target in the driver's box. Yevseev and the driver stood in the back and cocked their weapons at the cowardly bandits, who saw the guns and ran away.

Exhilarated by the open air and the dry cold, exhausted by the ride, she slept well at night, not even bothered by the fleas and lice crawling beside her. She stayed in *izbas* owned by Old Believers, a Russian Orthodox sect. Exiled to Siberia in the eighteenth century, they still clung to their refusal to accept early church reforms.

On the road she lived on tea, rye bread, and frozen meat dumplings she heated in boiling water. With that, and a well-stocked supply of chocolate and cigarettes, she found the journey through Siberia "a rare and delightful experience," she said. "To tell the truth, I was enjoying myself immensely. I did not mind the cold or the discomforts, I was not homesick, lonely or afraid. This vagabond life had a curious fascination for me. I did not want to go home!"

Seeing the rooftops of the nearby town of Verkhne-Udinsk, where she would say goodbye to the troika and board the train for Chita, she heaved a sigh of regret. "I thought my adventures were over. In reality, they were just beginning."

.   .   .

The first hint of trouble came with the bang of a door in her face. The Communists had seized control of Verkhne-Udinsk, and a woman whose home had been recommended refused to take her in for the night. Strangers were eyed with deep suspicion. She finally found a Jewish woman who agreed to rent her a room, but minutes later a member of the Political Police arrived and demanded that all residents of the house appear at the Revolutionary Tribunal in the morning. Feeling certain she would be arrested as a spy, Marguerite left the house with Yevseev as fast as she could.

They had nowhere to go and two days to wait until the train to Chita arrived, but the Cossack came up with an idea: he knew a house run by a Chinese man who rented rooms to ladies of the night. Glad to have a warm room, she took it, and ignoring the women in their dirty peignoirs and the sounds of merriment filling the hall, she locked the door and drifted off to sleep.

The following night while having dinner in her room with Yevseev, she heard a knock on the door. A sly-looking man announced himself as a local reporter, asked too many questions, and left, leaving behind a strong whiff of suspicion. Her companion went out and soon came back reporting that the visitor was an agent of the Communist police. They paid their bill in a rush and left for the train station, where she spent the freezing night trying to sleep on a waiting-room bench. Early in the morning they boarded the train for the twenty-four-hour trip to Chita.

She had no idea if the Communists had thrown their reins as far as the capital, but along the way, when the train pulled into a station, she bought a newspaper and learned that the day before, on November 14, 1922, the Far Eastern Republic had turned Soviet. She, who had been barred from Russia, was now a trespasser on Russian territory. She sent a telegram to her American hosts asking that they meet her at the train station in Chita. If there was any problem, at least she would be assured of their protection.

Mr. Faymonville greeted her warmly on the snowy platform and drove her to the apartment, where she and Yevseev enjoyed breakfast. Weary from the stress, she spent the remainder of the day resting, but after dusk, with the plumbing out of order, she ventured outdoors to the public baths. She had nothing to worry about, Thomas and Faymonville assured her: The new Soviet government would take no heed of her entry and most likely would issue her a visa. If not, the two men planned to leave in a few days for Peking, and she could travel with them back to Harbin in Manchuria.

The head of the Far Eastern forces invited the Americans to dine at his house the following evening, and she enjoyed a reunion with Mr. Yanson, the former foreign minister of the Far Eastern Republic and now a Soviet commissar of foreign trade, whom she had met in Changchun. When she paid a visit to his office the next morning, he promised to inquire about her visa to Russia. Later that day Yevseev, who was returning home, asked her to go with him to a photographer to develop pictures she had taken on their trip.

Cloaked in her beaver-collared coat, black hat, black stockings, and black shoes, her face covered with a thick black veil, she walked down Irkutsk Street with Yevseev, talking and laughing about their adventures. Suddenly, a Red soldier stepped in their path. "Hands up!" he ordered, pointing a cocked gun at their heads. "Hand over your revolver," he commanded Yevseev. When he turned to Marguerite, who expected the would-be robber to take her purse, she heard him ask instead, "Are you Citizeness Harrison?" "Yes," she replied. "*Vui arrestovanna*," he announced. "You are arrested."

With that he pushed them both into a carriage parked at the curb and ordered they be driven to the local prison of the Cheka, now renamed the Governmental Political Department, or GPU. There, the commandant informed her he had orders from Moscow to arrest her for espionage for the United States government. But why? she asked. "You are going to Moscow by the next train. You will know all the details when you get there," he snapped.

She was allowed to see Faymonville and Thomas, who protested her arrest and brought her belongings but offered her little comfort. "You will have to go through with it, Mrs. Harrison," Thomas said. "But keep a stiff upper lip."

She said goodbye, claiming to be baffled that she had been arrested for reasons she did not comprehend. It hardly seemed warranted, and the tension brought her "nearer to breakdown than I had ever been in all my life. The iron self-control to which I had schooled myself almost gave way," she said. "I could not understand why the old charges had been revived against me." Later she would learn more.

After three nights in the local Cheka jail, she boarded the Trans-Siberian Express, not as the privileged passenger she dreamed of being as a girl, but as a political prisoner bound once more for the dreaded Lubyanka.

CHAPTER 19

Return

Marguerite left Chita assured by her American hosts that they would report her arrest to Washington. But shortly after the train pulled out of the station, she was stunned to learn that the plans for her trip had been deliberately changed: she would not be taken directly to Moscow; instead, she would be diverted to Novo-Nikolaevsk, the largest city in Siberia. She realized that no one would know where she was, and that if she were smuggled into Moscow, Soviet officials could claim they had no idea of her whereabouts. They could put her on trial in secret. Without means to contact anyone, she was a mouse in the paw of the Communist cat.

Despite her fears, she managed to have some amusement along the way. Installed with two guards in a first-class compartment reminiscent of czarist days, she found it well heated, fitted with carpets and tasseled velvet curtains, and lighted with electric brass lamps gleaming in wood-framed mirrors. Not permitted to leave the carriage alone, she negotiated with her guards to walk unescorted to the bathroom or sit silently in the carpeted corridor. Most of the time, settled in a plush chair in her compartment, she played cards with her wardens and ordered meals from the restaurant.

She savored the dinners of consommé or thick vegetable soup, beefsteak or mutton, rice or potatoes, green vegetables, and blancmange or American canned fruits, and coffee. For supper she chose from cold meats, fried calves' brains, or an omelette, along with stewed fruit, white rolls and butter, and tea. Paid for with her own money, the meals, including breakfast, cost 26 million rubles a day, the equivalent of two dollars, slightly more than a steak at Delmonico's.

As the train skimmed around the southern end of Lake Baikal, she looked out the window of a train on the world's longest railway and cast her eyes on the world's largest lake. The sight of the white mountains, sharp black cliffs, and sapphire water brought a drop of tranquility to the fateful ride. The words of "Holy Baikal," the song of Siberian prison escapees, came to her mind:

"I've been wearing heavy chains for a while . . . I'm not afraid anymore."

The train stopped at Irkutsk, the westernmost point to which the Japanese had sent their troops, and she saw burned freight cars and ruined train depots left from the Russian civil war. It was here that General Kolchak, leader of the White Army, was executed by the Bolsheviks in 1920. At Krasnoyarsk, where the bleak forest overshadowed the city, more traces of fighting between Whites and Reds still sullied the woods and snow. On the fourth night, the train chugged into Novo-Nikolaevsk.

In the cold and dark Marguerite was bundled into a sleigh and taken to the office of the Cheka commandant, where she spent the rest of the night sitting on her bags on the floor. At sunrise, a guard led her to a frigid, putrid-smelling log cabin and locked her in a prison cell with four other women. The windows were boarded up, and she could hardly make out the others; it took a while before she saw they were lying on bare wooden plank beds in the dark, dank, filthy place, the cell and their clothes crawling with vermin. "In all my experiences I had never seen anything so horrible," she recalled.

The women had been there as long as three months and were not permitted fresh air, or light, or books, or exercise or activities of any kind. A once-pretty Jewish woman asked if she had a mirror. When Marguerite drew out a pocket glass, the inmate took it to the window and burst into tears.

Late that afternoon she was ordered to leave, and two new, gruffer guards, pressing a gun at her back, led her onto the train for five more days of travel. When one of the men awoke the next morning with a high fever and a swollen face, she treated him with aspirin and boric acid, but to no avail. His condition worsened, and at one stop they learned he had a highly infectious disease and needed to be hospitalized. But there was no hospital, no doctor, and no separate compartment available for him. Instead, the threesome worriedly journeyed together on through a landscape of endless snow and leafless trees. "It was a ghastly experience," she said.

On a Sterno burner she had brought with her she made coffee, and from her bag she pulled out American magazines and Sunday newspapers given to her by Mr. Thomas. The train rolled on, first to Omsk, where Dostoevsky spent five miserable years buried alive in exile, and then to the ancient city of Ekaterinburg, where the guard pointed out the house of Czar Nicholas II.

Only four years earlier the monarch and his family were murdered by the Bolsheviks; the gunshots of the firing squad still echoed through the bare birch woods. They stopped at Perm, where the famine she had once described in her reports had decimated the population; and at Novgorod, where she had traveled with the British labor delegation under orders to spy on them for the Cheka.

On December 3 they reached Yaroslavl station in Moscow, where the sick man was taken off while she and the second guard awaited an official car. She was surprised to find the waiting room warm and clean, and the newsstand filled with an array of the latest newspapers and magazines for sale.

At the restaurant where she had a cup of tea, well-dressed people sat at white-clothed tables, and waiters wearing white aprons with black jackets, a white napkin spread across the sleeve, took their orders. The buffet offered a variety of sandwiches, cold meats, cakes, bread, and fruit, and a separate case presented cigarettes and chocolates. The startling difference from the empty waiting rooms two years before, when travelers were scarce and food and newspapers nonexistent was proof that Lenin's New Economic Policy had brought an encouraging change to the economy.

Riding in the automobile, she saw the transformation outdoors; where Stygian darkness and dirty snow once covered the roads and sidewalks, there were now bright, clean streets; electric lights were burning, electric trams were running, and official vehicles as well as private cars with liveried chauffeurs drove past. Restaurants and tea shops were open, stores were selling bread, cakes, and foodstuffs, others were offering books, boots, millinery, furs, and jewels. The ride was over too soon; she longed to see more of the city, but a crooked finger beckoned her to Lubyanka.

After four days in the prison, she heard the familiar call, "Pack your clothes," and, with trespassing the only apparent reason to keep her, she felt sure she was going to be released. Instead, she was ordered to climb into the big black van to Butyrka, where she had once delivered weekly packages to British and American prisoners; stunned, she told herself it was better than Lubyanka.

Locked in a room with eleven other women, mostly political prisoners, she spent morning after morning playing cards, sewing, and gossiping, and afternoon after afternoon walking in circles in the courtyard. For amusement she read people's palms, and when the brutish matron put out her hand, she told her she saw a second husband and lots of money in her future; the Bolshevik woman softened her ways.

Several days later, she was told once again, "Pack your clothes," and this time her experienced cellmates offered their congratulations. "*Na voluy*." You are going to be released, they shouted, giving her hugs and kisses while she threw her clothes in her bag and dared not think. "I was not as optimistic as my roommates," she said.

Again, she was taken to Lubyanka and ordered to wait for hours in the administration office. Then, although the strain of waiting and imprisonment had made her ill and weak, she was forced to climb four flights of stone steps to the commandant's office. Rather than being released, she was questioned and searched. At the end she was ordered up more steps to an attic room close to the one where she had stayed in 1921.

The horrid surroundings were familiar: the cell crammed with inmates, the plank beds, and the stinking *parashka,* the metal can for urination; the locked doors and dim light; the banning of books, paper, and pencils; the rules for silence and the threat of solitary confinement. Overall, the food had improved, even though she still faced the revolting herring soup, but the vermin had disappeared, and she was even able to take a bath every two weeks. Christmas came and went once again without her son, but with the addition of a new judicial system that gave her a regular cross-examiner. The man informed her that she was being indicted on three counts.

Knowing that in Russia the accused is considered guilty unless proven innocent, she realized she did not have much of a chance. In fact, she began to believe there was no exit: she would be there until she died. She heard nothing further until a few days after New Year's, 1923, when she was summoned to the office of the presidium. She saw a familiar face.

With a bow, her old foe Mogilevsky showed her a seat and uttered a casual "Good morning."

"Will you kindly tell me why I am here?" she replied. Protesting her arrest as irregular, she repeated the counts of indictment: the old charge of espionage to which she had already pleaded guilty; and two new charges: one for espionage, which she refused to accept, and another for entering Soviet territory after she had been expelled. They were "preposterous," she declared.

"I admit all that," Mogilevsky said with a sly smile. "But when you know why I committed this trifling irregularity I think you will agree with me that it is a great compliment to your ability."

"What do you mean?"

"Just this. When you agreed to work for us two years ago you double-crossed us. But during our conversation I became aware of the fact that you could be exceedingly useful if you could be made to work seriously. When you put yourself within our reach once more the opportunity was too tempting."

"Then it was you who ordered my arrest?"

"Certainly." He had been following her since October, when she was in Peking and applied for a visa to the Far Eastern Republic. He did not tell her that agents in Harbin and Peking sent urgent messages to Mr. Lubarsky, the consul in Urga: "One of these days the famous American Mrs. Harrison will come to Urga." When she did, "Install surveillance. Suggest she is a spy."

On November 11, instructions sent to the courier Yevseev in Troitsk-Kosavsk ordered him to accompany her to Chita "to ascertain the identity and purpose of her visit to Soviet Russia." Along the way, the courier reported, "I found out she is the daughter of a famous capitalist." Furthermore, he wrote, "She was sent to Soviet Russia to inform America of the political and economic life of Russia." He learned that she had statistics on fishing in Nikolaevsk, information on gold mines, and details on cattle breeding in Mongolia.

On November 19, Yevseev arrived with her in Chita and turned the case over to the GPU agent, who shadowed her movements. Two days later, she was arrested for being a spy. There was little she could say except "What are you going to do with me?"

"That depends on you," Mogilevsky replied. He was head of the GPU in the Caucasus and had traveled some two thousand kilometers from Tblisi to make her an offer. If she accepted, he claimed, she would be set free.

"What is the offer?"

"You will remain in Russia," he said. She would work as an informant spying on Russians. "You speak the language almost perfectly. They will trust you as a foreigner and give you information which they would not give to any Russian." In return, he promised, "You will have a comfortable apartment, all your living expenses and a salary paid in gold equivalent to two hundred and fifty dollars a month in American money."

Appalled, she stared at him in horror. She may have been weak, but her rage gave her the strength to respond: "So that is it! You want me to give up all hope of ever returning to the United States. What about my son? Am I never to see him again?"

"Why, certainly you shall see him," Mogilevsky answered in a heartening tone. "He will be brought from America at our expense, and he can finish his education at the University of Moscow. This is the country for youth. He will have limitless opportunities."

"Thank you," she answered. "I prefer to remain in prison." She would never spy again, she declared, not for America, not for Russia "I would rather die in prison. And as for my son, I want him to grow up where he is free to form his own political opinions."

Mogilevsky shrugged. If she refused his offer, he countered, he would not help her. He reminded her that she still carried the old charges of espionage and treason. "You will still be brought to trial. You will probably be sentenced to death." At the best, he said, she could expect ten years' imprisonment in Siberia. "You don't want to change your mind?"

"No."

"Then it is useless to prolong our interview. Au revoir, madame."

A few weeks later she was called to the GPU office of foreign espionage. Hour after hour, day after day, she was grilled, her inquisitors demanding she admit to spying for the American military. Plied with cups of tea and puffing on endless cigarettes, again and again she described her trip to the Far East, until finally they announced that the date for her trial had been set. If she were found guilty, she would receive the death sentence. At the very least, she would be sent to Siberia.

She knew she would receive no help from a court-appointed lawyer, nor from the Russian foreign office. True, the Soviet laws had been modified, but, she said, "the Russians were still obsessed with the traditions of the old regime. Just as they had lived in fear of the Okhrana under the czar, they still lived in fear of the GPU. The old man of the Lubyanka was their old man of the sea."

. . .

Back in her cell, she lay in a stupor on her plank bed, thinking endlessly about Mogilevsky, admitting that "in a curious fashion" her old enemy had always attracted her. She sensed he had been attracted to her as well and questioned the reason he had brought her back. "I wondered as I lay staring into the darkness what were the motives that had impelled him to follow my movements . . . and to scheme and plot to get me back again to Moscow."

She had two weeks before her trial would begin. But Washington still refused to recognize the Soviet government, which meant that on the slight chance the State Department knew where she was, they still had almost no influence in gaining her release. Her best possibility for freedom was with the American Relief Administration, but even they might not know she was there.

She was ill with pulmonary tuberculosis and a collapsed lung, kidney disease, and gynecological problems when she was summoned once again to an interrogation. In her feverish state, she was taken aback by what she heard: "Citizeness Garrison, I know that you will be glad to hear that I have an order for your release."

"What?" she asked, not sure if she was hallucinating.

"You are free," the man repeated. "Here is your discharge."

She had fought hard never to show her captors any signs of emotion, but this time, "it was only by superhuman effort of the will that I refrained from bursting into tears." Her fingers trembling, her knees quaking, she took the document and shook hands with the man. "I will probably be back again," she said. He smiled.

She had five days to procure her papers and put them in order. She spent hours trudging through the snow, going from office to office, filling out forms for her passport and visa and trying unsuccessfully to retrieve her camera. The rest of the time she saw old friends and observed the scene around her.

It was mid-February 1923. The Union of Soviet Socialist Republics had been formed with Russia, Ukraine, Byelorussia, Georgia, Armenia, and Azerbaijan; and Lenin's New Economic Policy was flourishing. Commercial banks were open; restaurants were thriving; well-dressed people were dining on imported foods and champagne; theaters and cabarets were sold out; gambling halls were full; beauty parlors were busy; luxury shops were selling splendid furs and brilliant jewels; customers were cramming the aisles of bookstores, buying books in Russian and other languages, foreign news magazines, and even the French edition of *Vogue*.

And yet, despite the economic success and the improvement in the standard of living, the spirit of the people was gone. The GPU, successor to the Cheka, kept watch on everyone; freedom was kept tightly in check, and the oligarchy was in control. "People had resigned themselves to the new despotism," she noted.

Thousands of students attended schools, but they were all stamped out from the same mold. Journalists, playwrights, and novelists were all forced to write with a Marxist pen. Artists painted with a propaganda brush. "The Dictatorship of the Proletariat had turned into a bureaucratic autocracy," Marguerite noted sadly. "Individualism and independent thinking were ruthlessly suppressed."

Nevertheless, she lingered in the city, hating to leave. With her time running out, and only minutes to spare, she reached the train station, papers and passport in hand, bound for Riga on the Diplomatic Express. She was free. But she would never see Moscow or Mogilevsky again.

Part Four

CHAPTER 20

Somewhere, Anywhere

On the sun-splashed morning of October 2, 1923, outside the sprawling Dolmabahce Palace in Constantinople, Allied troops, one hundred
each from Britain, France, and Italy, stood at attention, while behind
them Allied warships sat in the Bosphorus awaiting sail. Masses of
Turks packed the surroundings, eager to bid them farewell.

A bugle blasted, drums boomed, and trumpets blared as the *mehter
Takumi*, the Turkish military band, marched in the square. Standing
on the palace grounds with a coterie of guests of the American high
commissioner, Marguerite Harrison watched the celebration marking
the end of four years of Allied occupation and the beginning of a new
Turkish era.

Crowds gathered on the grass while some, eager for a better view,
clung to the limbs of the leafy plane trees, hung on to lampposts and
telegraph poles, or peered from the rooftops of nearby buildings. All
kept their voices hushed as the rugged Turkish troops saluted the
flags of the withdrawing Allies. Then waving their fezes they cheered
loudly as the band played the Turkish anthem and British, French, and
Italian generals saluted the white crescent and star on the red Turkish
flag. "It was a day never to be forgotten!" Marguerite said.

A momentous period had come to a close for the Turks. Like a
fallen majesty, the large and powerful Ottoman Empire that began
in fourteenth-century Anatolia and at its height spread across Asia,
Europe, and Africa was gone. Imperial Turkey, whose capital, Constantinople, straddled the shores of Europe and Asia—and whose ter-

ritories once included Greece, the Balkans, and Hungary westward to the gates of Vienna in Europe; Egypt, Palestine, Syria, and Mesopotamia in the Middle East; Mecca and Medina in the Persian Gulf; and Libya and Tunisia in North Africa—was now a diminished state. After six centuries of rule by sultans and viziers, ornamented with harems and overseen by eunuchs, the last sultan, Mehmed VI, had abdicated, and the monarchy had tumbled down.

The Ottomans had cast their fate with the wrong side in the World War. Even before the conflagration, large chunks of the empire had melted away like ice floes. The bloody battles with the Allies caused even more damage: the League of Nations imposed a British mandate on Palestine and on Mesopotamia, renamed Iraq, and forced a French mandate on Syria.

But the Turkish picture improved when the rebel fighter Mustafa Kemal declared "Turkey for the Turks!" and defeated an invasion of Greeks. The Treaty of Lausanne, a peace pact with the Allies and Greeks signed in 1923, confirmed the rise of a newly independent Turkish state, and the new parliament elected Kemal to show the way. The emerging nation would become a modern, secular republic, and Kemal, adopting the name of Ataturk, "the Turk," would become the most admired leader in the Muslim world.

.   .   .

Marguerite had arrived in Constantinople on the Orient Express from Paris; she came seeking permission to travel to Anatolia, the Asian region of Turkey, where she hoped to make a film with Merian Cooper. She had helped the American when he was in prison in Russia, and in the late spring of 1923, after a phone call to reconnect, the two lunched together in New York. He told her he had recently returned from a trip to Asia and Africa, and he talked about his travels sailing from Singapore to Arabia.

The place that intrigued him most was Abyssinia, an empire dating back to King Solomon's days. In Addis Ababa, its capital, he met Prince Ras Tafari, the small, slight, French-speaking regent who would become the emperor Haile Selassie; Cooper reported to the State Department about the larger-than-life leader and his independent country, and along with a cameraman he made a film about the exotic nation, a feudal state in the modern world.

"Having seen a bunch of travelogues," he said, in a southern accent tinged with northern prep school and tough West Point, "I thought this was a great opportunity to make a feature picture. I had a tremendous advantage—I had probably seen fewer pictures than just about any man alive and was therefore unspoilt by what I considered the phony stuff of Hollywood." But when a fire broke out on their ship, the footage they shot disappeared.

Now back in New York, Merian, like Marguerite, was restless and craved adventure. "He felt as I did," she recalled. "He had just come back but he was dying to get away again." He wanted to make another movie, and he would go anywhere, do anything that was distant, difficult, and dangerous.

Marguerite had returned from her second Russian venture in March 1923, receiving far less fanfare than she did the first time. Friends, family, and the press welcomed her with a hint of suspicion, curious to know more details. Why had she gone to Russia again? Why had she taken such risks? Why was she arrested? Was she still a spy?

It was only the reason for her arrest, she said, that made the story dramatic. But, she added, "that I kept to myself." She wrote about her experiences with a fluid pen, but she often left blank spaces on the page. Like others in the murky world of espionage, she would take her secrets to the grave.

"I do not know whether I shall ever unravel all the mysteries connected with her," wrote Dr. Ames, her father-in-law, to the head of the Department of Commerce. It was Dr. Ames who had first introduced her to MID.

.   .   .

Upon her release in February from Lubyanka prison, Marguerite had gone directly to Riga and Berlin, where she was confronted by the press. It appeared that she continued to be the target of Stan Harding's rage. The British woman was still on the attack, rallying journalists and members of Parliament, demanding compensation from Marguerite for being imprisoned in Moscow. If Marguerite was nervous and ill before she arrived in Riga, the harassment made her even more so.

Back in the United States she went at once to Washington to report on her Far East trip and to attend government training sessions; now that the Russians had broken her codes, she would need a new set of instructions. But her primary goal was to discuss the problem that shadowed her: Marguerite wanted the United States to protect her from Mrs. Harding's charges.

The State Department must persuade the British foreign office to put an end to the matter, she told William Hurley, the official in charge of counterintelligence; otherwise, she herself would be forced to reveal her own connections to MID. It was because there were leaks inside MID that the Russians had learned Marguerite was a spy. And it was because the Russians had arrested Marguerite and put her in prison that, under threat of being shot, she denounced Mrs. Harding. Marguerite wanted her own name cleared by the State Department. But American officials refused to do so.

She was a living example of Somerset Maugham's *Ashenden:* "There's just one thing I think you ought to know before you take on this job," she was told by British intelligence. "If you do well you'll get no thanks and if you get into trouble you'll get no help."

In desperation, Marguerite revealed to the press that as a journalist in Germany she had collected information and sent it to MID. She also described her friendship with Stan Harding in Berlin, acknowledged that the Englishwoman had introduced her to socialist groups, and noted Mrs. Harding's close relationship with British army officers. The woman, Marguerite declared, was a British agent and may have been sent to spy on her in Germany.

Tainted by Stan Harding, and by Russia's knowledge of her work, Marguerite claimed she could no longer serve the U.S. government. But what would she do now? At forty-four she was still attractive and smart, flirtatious in drawing rooms, unflappable in deserts, a stimulating speaker with a theatrical flair, and a successful author. She enjoyed writing and lecturing and still drew large audiences to her talks, but this time when she spoke, the reaction was different. Americans were less sympathetic to her message.

. . .

On her way back from Russia she had stopped in Berlin. Staying at the luxurious Fürstenhof Hotel on Leipziger Platz, she heard "lurid tales of French oppression and persecution" swirling around the city. "Every German citizen was up in arms about the highhanded attitude of the French," she said. As she had predicted, the Germans had failed to make the payments on their heavy reparations, and in response the French government had sent in troops, taking over the mines and factories in the Ruhr valley. "I felt an uncontrollable desire to investigate conditions in the Ruhr for myself," she recalled.

In Essen and Düsseldorf, the heart of Germany's coal and steel production, she found that the French were treating the German workers with contempt, shutting down the Krupps factories or running them "at the point of the bayonet," and in some cases even shooting employees. German workers had gone on strike, and the French had arrested many strike leaders and local officials.

With most of the people hungry and unemployed, the government was forced to pay their salaries, but production of its most essential industries had slowed, and the German treasury was compelled to print more money to pay them. The cost of bread rose faster than the loaves in the oven. Hyperinflation was nightmarish: a loaf of bread that cost 163 marks in December 1922 jumped to 250 marks in January 1923 and would skyrocket to two billion marks by November 1923. People's bank accounts were collapsing, and the middle class was becoming poor. In return, German militancy was on the rise: secret societies were forming and extremists were gaining an upper hand. Talk of revolt was in the air. In November the Nazi party would attempt a putsch. Marguerite considered the French behavior "appalling," and wove her observations into the lectures she would deliver when she went back to America.

Her audiences, however, did not want to be told why they should feel sorry for their former enemies, the Germans who were responsible for the war. Nor did they want to know why the attitude of their allies, the French, was wrong. If France treated Germany with contempt, Americans believed it was well deserved. If the French demanded reparations the Germans could not afford, so be it. Americans saw those claims as vindication for German aggression, not as provocation for another war. Marguerite was taken aback when she was hissed by her audience. Later she would write about the conduct of the French: "No better way could have been found to stimulate the movement which eventually led to Hitlerism."

It was not long before she felt her lectures were less an assessment of world affairs and more an occasion to attack her. And then there were her repeated statements about the Russians: America must recognize the Soviet government, she insisted; commercially and politically, recognition would benefit the United States and bring about a shift in the Russian system.

"I firmly believe," she wrote, "the re-opening of trade relations will strengthen the peasants and the intellectuals and give them the ability to bring about radical political changes." If other nations gave them a chance, she said, the Russian people would create "a form of government which will retain the good and eliminate the evil brought about by the Revolution." Her opinions put her further out of favor with the public.

She gave many of her talks in New York, where she was sharing an apartment again with her son. Despite her absence in his life over the past few years, she contended they had always been the closest of companions. "He had always understood with a wisdom far beyond his years the impulse that was forever driving me to wander over the face of the earth," she said. In fact, Tommy wrote to a family friend who had helped with Marguerite's release: "Inasmuch as my mother has apparently an incurable desire to get into jail, I hope that she will select an American one the next time."

But her desire for distant travel prevailed. "I should have been content to live with my boy in New York where I had made hosts of friends, but I could not settle down," she noted. Disheartened by American attitudes, bored by the routine of daily life, she reacted as she had in the past: she sought escape. She was impatient to go "somewhere—anywhere." She lay in bed at the Hotel Schuyler and heard the horns of the ocean liners leaving the piers for foreign ports, an echo of the trains calling out to her when she gazed out the window of her mother's bedroom. "They were truly sirens to me, urging, enticing, irresistible."

She could write articles for magazines, but the prospect seemed dull. She met with Merian Cooper at lunches and dinners, and they discussed ideas for a travel movie, not just a glance at unfamiliar places, but a silent motion picture with a story line. He had heard about a colorful tribe of Kurds in Turkey, he said, and thought they would make an interesting subject. He was inspired by *Nanook of the North*, the acclaimed new film depicting man's struggle with nature.

As a wartime censor for the state of Maryland, Marguerite had viewed hundreds of films and seen the allure of actresses like Lillian Gish, Mary Pickford, and Theda Bara. She was intrigued with the concept of making a movie and enticed by the idea of acting on-screen.

As they talked, she and Cooper developed his vision of a nomadic tribe in migration. This would be a true tale imbued with its own drama: the essential battle of mortal man against the eternal force of mother nature. They would make an epic documentary that would show the tribe's fundamental struggle for existence. It was a grand and romantic idea, and she saw herself playing a central role. The key questions were where to go and whom to film.

On a trip to Washington, she consulted the State Department expert Harry Dwight, a diplomat born in Constantinople and familiar with the Near East. Like Europe and Asia, the region was undergoing transformation. In the aftermath of the World War and the dismantling of the Ottoman Empire, the area from Turkey to the Persian Gulf was roiling with uprisings for self-determination and demands for the creation of new states. Moreover, it was awash in conflicting claims on its increasingly valuable oil deposits.

From the moment in World War I when First Lord of the Admiralty Winston Churchill switched the fuel for British warships from coal to oil, petroleum became significant. When airplanes, automobiles, and armored vehicles, all fueled by oil, were added to the weapons of warfare, oil went from significant to indispensable. Officials in Washington watched the situation in Iraq, where the British had quickly established control, and in neighboring Persia, where a battle was taking place in the north.

Foreign companies were bidding against each other for enormously valuable oil concessions that were held by the British and coveted by the Russians and the United States. Harry Dwight suggested that Marguerite and Cooper film the Bakhtiari, a fierce, independent tribe that lived in Khuzestan, a mountainous part of southwest Persia. Not incidentally, and of considerable interest to the American government, the Bakhtiari controlled major amounts of land containing vast reserves of oil.

But, Harry Dwight acknowledged, the trip to the remote region of Persia would be arduous and long; as an alternative he suggested Anatolia, where, to the fury of the Turkish government, the Kurds were eager to form an independent state of Kurdistan with their Kurdish cousins in Syria and oil-rich Iraq.

When Marguerite met with Merian Cooper again in New York, the two agreed that as enticing as the trip to Persia might be, the journey would be expensive and, as Merian had explained, he had no means to fund the endeavor. What's more, he had little experience aside from the small film he had made in Abyssinia with the cinematographer Ernest Schoedsack. Marguerite offered to raise ten thousand dollars, half as a loan, half in outright payment, just enough to cover their expenses, But she had two stipulations: she wanted to be a partner and she wanted to be on the screen. Cooper accepted her proposal.

. . .

As noted in the *New York Times*, on August 4, 1923, Marguerite Harrison and Merian Cooper embarked for France on the SS *Lafayette*. At thirty years old, he was small and muscular, sandy-haired with deep blue eyes, equipped with a bare minimum of work clothes plus a dinner jacket and a pair of patent leather dancing shoes; she, at forty-four, was tall and shapely, with a new permanent wave and a stylish wardrobe including a wool coat, fur-trimmed coats, fur hats, velour hats, pith helmet, pongee britches and riding jackets, corduroy suits, daytime and evening dresses, corsets, nightgowns, scarves, boots, shoes, theatrical makeup, toiletries, medicines, books, and a collapsible rubber bath.

In Paris, they met up with Ernest Schoedsack, the Hollywood cameraman whom Cooper had invited to join their team. Cooper, however, had neglected to tell his friend that their third partner was a woman, nor was it clear how much she had provided for the venture: instead, he said that she had given half the money and that his own family had furnished the rest. When the tall, breezy midwesterner saw the chic New Yorker, he was dismayed: "a lady journalist" would only get in the way.

Despite Schoedsack's protests, Cooper insisted on her presence: not only was she financing the film, he felt indebted to her for saving his life. Indeed, she would turn out to be an asset: her linguistic talents and medical skills would help attract friends along the way.

Schoedsack teased the loyal Cooper, accusing the former airman of being in love with the much older Marguerite. She, however, had a far different view of her relationship with Cooper. "He never thought of me as a woman at all," she said. "That was why we were able to get on together." She continued: "We had furious arguments about women, but they were never personal."

For Schoedsack and Cooper, the teasing served as a male bond. Though physically opposite and temperamentally at odds, they were a complementary team. The five-foot-eight-inch Cooper, with his muscular frame and pugnacious jaw, had disdain for the soft life and preferred to be seen as aggressive. At six foot five and known to his friends as "Shorty," Schoedsack, with his dark, curly hair, was more like an overgrown boy with a cheerful air and a penchant for jokes. Compatible working partners, the two men spent ten days in Paris buying film and camera equipment, while Marguerite went off to Constantinople to arrange for travel permits. Along the way she completed *Red Bear, Yellow Dragon,* a book she was writing on the Far East.

.   .   .

Constantinople, the queen of two continents, offered a Turkish delight of Byzantine and Ottoman arts and architecture. Few visitors could resist its mosques and palaces, its golden domes and slender minarets, its gardens, waterways, and ornamented wooden boats. But most interesting for Marguerite was her front-row view of the political changes taking place. In Warsaw, she recalled, she had seen a resurrection of the Polish nation; now she found the rebirth of the

Turkish nation to be even more romantic. She would write about it in magazines and books, but whether or not she was reporting back to Washington she did not reveal.

Her education about Turkey had taken place more than two decades before when, as a debutante, she was courted by the charming Reshid Sadi Bey. The Turkish diplomat had played a part in the early movement to reform the monarchy. A member of the Young Turks and a friend of their leaders Enver, Djemal, and Talaat Pasha, he had fought for the constitution that was established in 1908.

Although he was no longer at the forefront of events, his fervor had left its mark on Marguerite. She was intrigued by the social changes and pleased, she said, "to see the new Turkey in the making." Mustafa Kemal's moves toward Western modernization were affecting everything from the elimination of the fez and the removal of the veil to the equality of females, the use of the Latin alphabet, and the secularization of the law.

While she waited in the Ottoman capital for Merian and Schoedsack to join her, she tried to attain their travel permits to Anatolia. But her frequent trips to the Turkish foreign office led nowhere. The new government had its offices in Angora, later called Ankara, an arid town on a mountain plain almost three hundred miles away. Best known for the long hair of its cats and the soft fleece of its goats, it was stymied by poor communications made worse by the strained relations between the new regime and the old. Permission to leave Constantinople was not forthcoming.

In the interim, Marguerite dined with foreign envoys and partied on the American high commissioner's yacht, meandered through the bazaars, met leaders of the Turkish women's movement, and spent time with teachers and students at the American-run Robert College, where she quickly learned to converse in the Turkish language.

When Merian and Shorty arrived, eager to begin their exploits, they were sorely disappointed; approval to travel still had not been sent. "Time was money with a vengeance," Marguerite noted. Their limited funds left them with little time to waste. After a frustrating week of waiting and watching while their liras diminished, the threesome held "a council of war" and resolved to begin their work.

Sketching out a rough scenario, they planned to film Marguerite as an up-to-date but disenchanted Western woman on a search for the forgotten people of her ancestral past.

As Shorty filmed the opening scene, Marguerite, looking glamorous and starry-eyed, fluttered her eyelashes, puckered her cupid lips, and disembarked from a modern steamer at the busy port of Pera. She was on the European side of the Bosphorus, where, behind the camera, cosmopolitan life flourished.

The Pera Palace Hotel welcomed foreign travelers from the Orient Express, while the embassies of France, Italy, Britain, and the United States reigned over residents' social life. Locals rode the tram to Taksim Square to bargain with Armenian merchants selling finely woven rugs, or buy wine in the shops of Greek merchants, or scour the shelves of Jewish book dealers, searching for new volumes and rare editions. Diplomats and politicians, intellectuals and artists, lawyers and merchants sat at smart cafés and lingered over chocolate-smothered profiteroles, or gossiped between sips of sweet tea or argued while they gulped down thick Turkish coffee.

At the Pera port, swarms of porters hovered as Marguerite stepped onto an old caïque steered by six swarthy oarsmen who sailed the gondola to the Golden Horn. There, at the inlet of the Bosphorus, she alighted at Old Stamboul on the European shore. "We made some lovely pictures of the Golden Horn with its tangle of masts and its picturesque craft, against a background of domes and minarets," she said. Behind her were the exquisite church of Hagia Sophia, the Blue Mosque, and the Palace of Topkapi.

But on the other side of the Bosphorus a different life existed. The next scene showed Marguerite standing on a balcony, looking out across the narrow waterway to the sparsely settled rolling hills of the Asian shore. Gazing intently toward the rugged East, she longs to begin her pursuit of the forgotten people. The scene served as an introduction for the movie, but it was hardly the exciting adventure the filmmakers craved.

After weeks of work their travel permits arrived, and with papers in hand the Americans piled onto the train for Ankara, bringing along hand-cranked cameras, heavy wooden tripods, extensive film equipment, bedrolls, duffel bags filled with gifts including watches, knives, beads, and scarves for the tribes, necessities for themselves, a few clothes for the men, and Marguerite's elaborate range of attire.

They reached Ankara in mid-October 1923, just as it was officially anointed the capital; "the greatest day in its history," Marguerite called it. But the town's population had doubled in one year, and the streets were overflowing with thousands of Turks who had come to fight the old government and support the new. Far removed from the modern world of Constantinople, Ankara had no electric lights, no running water, no sewage system, no taxis or trams, no shops or coffeehouses, and no modern hotels. The mood in the drab, muddy town was hardly celebratory.

Nevertheless, with help from the local office of the Associated Press, the threesome found space at the Turkish Club, a journalists' nest of tiny rooms, and soon received an invitation to meet the foreign minister. They were expecting to hear good news from Ismet Pasha, the brilliant diplomat responsible for the Lausanne Treaty that ended Turkish hostilities with the Allies and Greeks, but he gave them instead a blunt reply: "We cannot allow you to film a movie in Kurdistan," he said flatly. English-speaking people, they learned, were suspected of stirring insurgencies among the Kurds, and rumors were flying that another uprising was imminent.

They heard, however, that other groups of nomads lived on the far side of the Taurus Mountains in the southeastern corner near Adana. Once again the men were eager to be off, but to Merian's irritation, Marguerite insisted they wait: she wanted to interview the new president, Mustafa Kemal. The men chafed at the delay. A woman did not belong on the trip, Shorty said again, and Merian was adamant that Marguerite's fascination with politics had to be put aside. They were here to make a movie, he argued. Everything else must be ignored.

But she persisted. Propelled by her interest in world affairs and determined to interview the leaders wherever she went, she arranged a meeting with Kemal. Their encounter took place at an exhibition of Turkish art, where she expected to see a dark, swarthy Turk, but the man who appeared was blond-haired with intense blue eyes. Direct and dynamic, with the determined look of a German officer. He described his plans for the new capital and for the up-to-date farms he wanted to create for the people. But he refused to talk politics, and the meeting provided little information.

It was mid-November, and now all three were ready to leave, but once again the trip was delayed: Merian was ill and required an operation. The miserable hospital conditions in Ankara, along with a lack of medicines and morphine, left him weak and in pain after the surgery, but after a few days he refused to stay in the town. At risk to his life, he insisted they set off.

. . .

The first step in their plan was to cross the barren Salt Desert, a dry sea of salt and shale, and make their way south through ancient Konia to the western part of central Turkey, where they would begin their search for the nomadic tribes. They hired a brightly painted araba that had neither springs nor passenger seats; instead, sitting on a hard bench in the covered wagon, they bounced through the desert, filming scenes along a caravan trail that had been used since the biblical times of Nebuchadnezzar. Their driver, Saladin, named for the Muslim ruler who defeated the Christian Crusaders, was given a role as Marguerite's guide in the movie.

Most nights Marguerite slept in the araba while the men lay on their bedrolls under the wagon. They spent one night at a sprawling stone caravansary, an old travelers' inn, where they joined a group of weather-beaten Turkish camel drivers for dinner. Marguerite squatted on the ground, a fashion plate in her corduroy safari jacket and long skirt and wearing a pith helmet draped in a long scarf. In front of her the men prepared food on a campfire made from chunks of camel dung, and she ate as everyone did, using only her right hand, chewing the thin, flat bread baked on an iron sheet over the fire.

As the blaze flickered in the dark, the only things visible to her were the strange shadows made by the flames on the faces of the men, and the only sounds she heard were the snuffles of the camels and the tinkle of their bells. In that stillness and quiet, she said, "I felt transported to another age and another world."

In the morning they rode again in the araba, jolting and lurching, stopping along the way to eat rice or mutton or balls of dried camels' milk. They were on the route to Konia, where they hoped to receive permission to continue their trip. After five nights, they arrived in the early Seljuk capital only to find the *vali*, the local governor, was friendly but too fearful to sign any papers. They would have to wait three more weeks for permission. In the meantime, they finished filming their desert scenes, planning to end the sequence with a dramatic, blinding sandstorm. But it was December, and the rainy season had come; the soil was damp and hard, and not a speck of sand blew in the wind.

Using a Hollywood technique to simulate storms, they hired a group of *halal*, local porters, and after waiting for a day when the wind blew strong, the men brought dozens of large sacks of bran into the desert. When a gale erupted, Saladin drove Marguerite into the center of the squall. The porters opened the sacks and shoveled out the grain, sending millions of tiny bits swirling in the windstorm. Marguerite was enveloped in bran: it drenched her clothes, stuck in her hair, and filled her nose and her mouth. The sandstorm looked realistic on film, she said, but "I almost choked to death." It took days to get rid of it all.

That night she settled into her sleeping bag on the floor of a small inn. From the barn stalls on the other side of a partition, she heard the snorts and snuffles of the horses and smelled the warm milk and fresh straw. It was Christmas Eve, and looking up at the sky through a hole in the roof, she felt certain she saw the twinkling star of Bethlehem.

There were no lights, no decorations, no sweet carols for Christian believers in Konia. Nonetheless the Americans' spirits were high. Marguerite found a lemon tree and strung it with blue beads while Merian and Shorty wrapped some gifts they plucked from their bags, put on their crumpled dinner jackets, pulled out a phonograph and some records, and wielding a long cigarette holder as a baton, marched into a warm room for dinner. To their surprise they found Señora Marguerite dressed in a décolleté evening frock with her hair piled high and held in place with an elaborate Spanish comb. With jazz music for dancing and local foods to savor, the threesome celebrated Christmas.

On a Friday they joined throngs of locals on their way to prayers. This was the place where Rumi had lived, entranced by the whirling dervishes and writing the poems that brought him world renown. Here old men dressed in long cotton gowns and turbans, young men wearing baggy trousers and broadcloth boleros, and women in dark cloaks and thick veils still streamed to the mosque to watch the dervishes.

Shoeless and sitting cross-legged on a platform for guests, Marguerite listened to the orchestra and watched the dancers perform the ritual for Sufi believers: dressed in flared skirts and short jackets, the men gathered in a circle, stretched out their arms, and spun like tops, whirling around the floor.

The dervishes may have been an early sect, but the French-speaking *Chelebi*, their religious leader, had a modern outlook and a belief that there was truth to be found in all religions. A man of the world, he discussed the Great War and its aftermath and invited Marguerite's opinion: "When will the world become civilized?" he asked.

"Only when we have progressed far enough in the way of international understanding and cooperation to make future wars impossible," she answered.

"That will not be," he said, "till sun and moon stand still in the heavens."

.   .   .

The Americans planned to venture through the Taurus Mountains and go east from there to Adana, close to the border with Syria, hoping to find an interesting group of nomads to film along the way. But after their three-week wait and their waning patience, their plans were stymied: the permission they received stated they were to travel directly to Adana.

With foreigners still under suspicion, the government refused to allow them to make any stops on the railway and ordered them, instead, to stay on the train until they reached the Syrian border. Defiantly, the two "jailbirds," as Marguerite described herself and Merian, agreed to the orders but plotted to sneak off the train when it stopped at some small village station.

On a bitter-cold morning thick with January snow, the trio and their interpreter, Fettah, boarded the train for Adana. That night, when the train stopped for fuel and water, they gathered their belongings and snuck off, only to discover that the station was locked and there were no hints of houses, no signs for inns. They were stranded in an empty village with nowhere to go.

Happily, they spied a tiny shack on the side of the road selling odds and ends to passing caravans. The owner peered at them with his one good eye and, after some bargaining, agreed to let them sleep on the floor. In the morning, he brought them tea, and when they asked to find some horses and drivers, he offered to help, but the horses were decrepit and the drivers looked dangerous. And then, Marguerite grumbled, he charged them an exorbitant amount of money for his efforts.

As they sat at a table inside his shack, a bearded hunter walked in. With a rifle on his shoulder, he bowed: "*Salaam Aleikum*" ("Peace be with you"), he said. "*Aleikum Salaam*," they replied. After a chat with Fettah, their interpreter, he introduced himself as Halil and offered to guide them to his village. It was thirty miles away through mountains covered in deep snow, but the people there, he assured them, would be welcoming. When the Americans asked how much they would have to pay, he took offense. "My services are not for sale," he said. "The *effendi*," he called them respectfully, "will honor my village by accepting its hospitality."

"It was snowing! Lord, how it was snowing!" Merian recalled, the heavy snow preventing them from leaving the village for three weeks. But the villagers were hospitable, and not only did they give the foreigners a guesthouse to stay in, they agreed to take part in the movie. Dressed in baggy trousers and coarse white linen coats that served as camouflage in the snow, the men invited the visitors to go with them and join the hunt for goats. "It was hard work!" Marguerite said. "I wallowed in snow drifts," sometimes riding her horse, other times walking a mountain pony, searching for goats that weighed as much as 150 pounds.

Afterward the five men invited the trio to join them for a meal around a fire. While one of the tribesmen played a version of the banjo and Merian and Shorty filmed the scene, Marguerite sat cross-legged on the ground, wearing her fur-trimmed coat and large fur hat, high boots, and britches, watching the hunters skin the goat and cook it. Then she daintily ate the meat with her fingers, chatting with her hosts as though she were at an embassy dinner.

The hunting sequence went well, but the long stay had raised the risk the trio would be discovered by government agents. At last the weather turned warm, and with the snow melting, they prepared to move on. But the day they were leaving, a posse of armed police appeared on horseback. They had been searching for the foreigners, their leader announced: they had orders to arrest the Americans if they had broken the rules and were found in the mountains.

"Quite right, my man," Fettah responded. "But we have left. We are on our way to Adana. You arrived too late." Those words and a handful of Turkish *lira* brought a grin to the face of the leader. "I understand *effendi*. You left yesterday," he declared. With that, he took the money, ordered his men to turn their horses around, and galloped away. The Americans quickly left too, accompanied by the hunter Halil, who escorted them through the snow-covered mountains all the way to the border town of Adana. There they thanked him with a big new silver watch.

They had hoped to locate a colorful tribe near the town, but the best they could find was a collection of bedraggled men, "a squalid, moth-eaten lot," said Marguerite. The group's annual migration consisted of a short route across an easy mountain path, scarcely the bold exploits the filmmakers sought. With their Turkish efforts now thwarted, the Americans elected to journey the twelve hundred kilometers through Syria and Iraq to Persia. They simply had to find the Bakhtiari or another noteworthy tribe. If they were unsuccessful, they did not have enough money to return to Turkey to continue their search.

They took the Berlin to Baghdad railway from Adana and rode across the Syrian border southeast to Aleppo. From there, they received permission from the government of the French Mandate to ride through the desert to the border of British-mandated Iraq, where they planned to hire a car and drive to Baghdad. From Baghdad they would make their way to Persia.

Most travelers took the safe and busy route, driving from Aleppo to Beirut and Damascus and on to Baghdad, but these were no ordinary voyagers. Instead, they left Aleppo in a war-beaten Ford and rode alongside the Euphrates River, passing through poverty-ridden villages and driving for miles through land uninhabited save for hidden bandits and hijackers. The car was so decrepit it was held together with ropes, and the route so dangerous it was patrolled by a camel corps of desert police who declared it unlawful to travel after four p.m.

Five days later they reached the Syrian border and crossed into Iraq. At a British fort nearby, they filmed Marguerite in full makeup, dressed in a safari hat, patch-pocketed jacket, pants, and boots, riding a camel that she called a "Bedouin airplane." Later, Shorty commented on one of her outfits. Those "damn white britches," he complained. "They always made the picture unbelievable."

CHAPTER 21

Friendship

Baghdad! The very name conjured romantic visions of Scheherazade and the palace of the caliph Haroun al Rashid, of beautiful women and powerful men, of a past dating back more than five thousand years; and a well-earned respect for its invention of writing and creation of books, its early methods of banking and mathematics, its advances in medicine, and its expressions of art. But all of that was gone. In its place, Marguerite found a drab city in decay, a disappointing array of ugly houses and unpaved streets, people in turmoil over their sovereignty, and tribes seething with conflict between the Shiite and Sunni sects.

If Baghdad had lost its captivating air, the British in charge had not lost theirs. The Americans carried a letter of introduction to Sir Percy Cox, a tall, dignified man who had distinguished himself in the British Indian Army, overseen British oil interests in Persia, and held the position of British High Commissioner in Iraq. Among his hobbies were a pet bear and collecting birds, including an eagle that he fed with live bats, which, to the horror of his wife, were kept in their kitchen refrigerator.

In the meeting with Marguerite and Merian, Sir Percy suggested they speak to Sir Arnold Wilson, who worked with the Anglo-Persian Oil Company in Tehran and was knowledgeable about the Bakhtiari tribe. Their territory contained "the greatest oil field in the world," Wilson wrote.

Most important, Sir Percy said, they must meet Miss Gertrude

Bell. She had not only served as chief intelligence agent in Baghdad during the Great War; she was the greatest tribal expert in the region.

Indeed, she was so forceful that after she spoke to the huge Anazeh tribe, loyal allies of the Turks, their powerful and chauvinistic sheikh told his men that they must switch their allegiance to the Turks' enemy, the British. "You have heard this woman," he said. "If all the Englishwomen are like her, their men must be like lions. We had better make peace with them."

Marguerite was curious to meet the legendary Miss Bell. She imagined her to be tough and masculine, but the woman who greeted her was as feminine and fashionable as one could imagine.

"A daintily manicured hand was stretched out to meet mine," Marguerite wrote. "I looked into a pair of keen gray-blue eyes set in an oval face with regular features crowned by a mass of softly waved, perfectly dressed hair. This redoubtable lady who had made such an impression on the Arab chief was as feminine a person as I had ever met in my life."

Gertrude Bell invited her to dine that night at her home, a meandering Arab villa set in a verdant garden behind a stone wall on a narrow street. The guests included Kinahan Cornwallis, the British ambassador during the war and now adviser to the king; Captain Iltyd Clayton, significant shaper of Arab policy for the British; Lionel Smith, adviser to the ministry of education. Mrs. Harrison was a triumph, holding the men in thrall with tales of her adventures in Turkey and beyond. "It was a rather remarkable evening," Miss Bell wrote home.

The next day Marguerite spent time at her office, hoping to learn as much as possible about events in Iraq. But as eager as she was to ask questions, Miss Bell quickly took control. A border dispute with the Turks was troubling her, but even more concerning was the secular Kemalists' abolishment of the caliphate. Who would take on the role of caliph, the spiritual leader of the Muslims, she worried. The hard-line Wahabis of Arabia were likely to seize control and strengthen the pan-Arabists, causing serious problems for the British. She pummeled her guest with questions, and Marguerite provided her with keen observations about the new government in Ankara. At the end of their two-hour conversation, she asked the American to dine once again at her home.

That evening, Marguerite kept the guests so engrossed with her stories that they leaned across the dinner table and rocked with laughter. "I have never had such an uproarious dinner. She was extraordinarily amusing," Miss Bell said, "but the tales she told us would make the hoariest official blush."

Afterward they went off to a ball at the British Residency, where King Faisal was in attendance. Faisal, who had unified the Arabs and led them in their revolt against the Turks, had never set foot inside Iraq until Miss Bell helped the British arrange a referendum in 1921 that made him king. Now, knowing he was curious about the American woman, she led Marguerite to his side and then took her around the room and introduced her to all the guests. "She had a great success," wrote Gertrude Bell.

When Marguerite asked about the Bakhtiari, Miss Bell assured her they were an interesting group and confirmed that their migration over the mountains was a drama well worth filming. In a meeting with Sir Arnold Wilson, Merian Cooper received a similar nod of approval for the tribe, along with a letter of introduction to the sheikh of Mohammerah. The potentate's emirate served as the port for the British oil company as well as the entryway to the Bakhtiari terrain.

But they had better hurry, Miss Bell advised; it was the end of March, the sun was heating up, and the grass was beginning to burn. Without grass the animals would die, and without the animals that supplied their food, the people would die as well. The migration would start in early April.

The Americans packed up quickly and set off for Persia, the two men taking the scheduled weekly steamer sailing five hundred kilometers south from Baghdad to Basra. Marguerite chose a riskier course, motoring with Mr. Fuller, an American diplomat, through desert and ditches, taking in historic sites along the way. They stopped at Ctesiphon, capital of the ancient Medean and Persian empires, and ate lunch at the palace arch amidst the imposing ruins. The massive brick arch and yellow brick vault were reminders of the legions of Muslim soldiers who, fifteen hundred years earlier, had marched from Mecca to Iraq. Then, for Marguerite and Mr. Fuller, it was on to Babylon and the Hanging Gardens, and to Kish, the earliest Sumerian city that had been discovered.

Leaving Kish they drove for two days on a road pitted with muddy ditches, slogging through some by foot. At others, deep and as wide as twenty feet, the driver stopped the car, opened the door, reached to the running board, and took down two piles of planking and wire ropes. He rolled them out on either side of the ditch and banged them into the ground with wooden pins. Slowly and carefully, the passengers rode over the newly created suspension bridge.

Afterward, they reached Kut, where during the Great War, the British, under siege from the Turks, suffered their worst defeat: twenty-three thousand soldiers were killed by Ottoman troops. Kut was one hundred miles from Amara, close to marshlands that were impossible to drive through. But a steamer came the next morning and they managed to put the car on the riverboat. "This was by no means a simple matter," Marguerite said. "There was no wharf at Kut." From there they sailed to Basra, the main Iraqi city on the Persian Gulf, where Marguerite took a launch to Mohammerah and met up with the men.

CHAPTER 22

Wild Men

The nineteenth-century archaeologist Henry Layard had spent months with the Bakhtiari and spoke of their savage countenances and swift sword blows, noting that the Persians called them "a race of robbers, treacherous, cruel and bloodthirsty." The British oil company representatives at Mohammerah knew little about them but warned that the tribesmen were known to be "a wild, unruly lot."

The only way to travel safely through their region, the British advised, was with permission from their rulers, the khans. Suave, polished Persian princes, they resided in Tehran in sumptuous villas filled with French paintings and ormolued furnishings and entertained their friends with good food and games of poker. But at least once a year they left their wives behind and made a visit to their tribes to collect their taxes and hear their petitions.

The khans were now on the annual trip around their territories. Captain Peel, a British political officer who knew the Bakhtiari rulers, agreed to contact them and ask for their consent. Without such approval, he warned, the foreigners would be robbed and likely murdered. With that, he sent the Americans to see the governor general in the dusty town of Shushtar, near the khans' encampment.

. . .

"Good afternoon," said a dark-eyed, handsome stranger. Marguerite put down her cup of tea. Smooth-shaven and self-assured, dressed in European riding clothes and carrying a riding crop, he appeared in the garden of the house where they were staying. He was responding to the request from Captain Peel, he explained: "I am Rahim Khan, and my uncle is the Il-Khani, the chief of the Bakhtiari. He has sent me to ask if you will do him the honor of visiting him at his camp."

Too stunned to reply, the Americans stared in disbelief. The man not only looked like the hero of an operetta, he spoke excellent English with an American accent. He had been educated at the American College in Beirut, he told them, and wanted nothing more than to see the pretty girls in New York and hear the jazz music on Broadway. Nonetheless, he was living with his fellow princes in the province of Khuzestan in the mountains of Persia, on an annual trip from Tehran overseeing the rich and extensive family realm.

Early the next morning they rode with him toward his uncle's camp, listening to the lively prince describe the wealth of the Bakhtiari ruler, Il-Khani. Pointing his riding whip at the villages, he declared they paid $40,000 a year in rents; directing attention to the fields, he announced that the rulers received a third of the income from the crops; and as for the oil wells, they provided $65,000 a year for Il-Khani and $25,000 a year for each of the dozen princes.

"What about government taxes?" the Americans asked. "Do you pay them?"

The independent Bakhtiari princes refused to pay any duties, Rahim replied. But there was a problem, he acknowledged: the reformist Reza Shah, appointed minister of war, wanted to centralize the Persian government and nationalize the army; worse, he was threatening to attack the tribe for its feudal system. The khans were inclined to submit rather than lose their territory. But the government wanted to take away the tribesmen's weapons, and the peasants refused to surrender.

A few days later the Americans heard a Bakhtiari declare: "Every man of us will die before we will give up our guns." Arms were their most valued possessions; indeed, the size of the tribes was counted not in men but in rifles.

The peasants may have defied the shah's wishes, Rahim said, but they paid total obeisance to their Bakhtiari rulers. Along the way to Il-Khani's camp, he showed the Americans a display of the people's fealty. Stopping at a village guesthouse, they were welcomed into a room covered in rugs and comfortable cushions, where they were each offered a seat.

Barefoot tribesmen entered with platters of food on their heads and placed the obligatory gifts on a cloth on the floor. Laid out before the guests was a feast of roast chicken, mutton, basmati rice pilaf with raisins and spices, curds, sour milk, lime drinks, date juice, nuts, raisins, sweet cakes, and bonbons stuffed with nuts. "We ate ravenously," Marguerite said. Tradition called for the guests to be served first; after them, the local men ate their meal, and after that it was the dogs' turn. Whatever was left was given to the women.

In the morning they rode with Rahim toward the Zagros Mountains and arrived at the sprawling camp of Il-Khani. Five princes and their cooks, barbers, bodyguards, and other servants, along with three hundred swarthy, black-robed men, lazed in front of their fires or rode their horses across miles of open land.

White, brown, or yellow goatskin tents dotted the scene, and in one far section Rahim showed them their quarters: one tent decorated with rugs and cushions and draped with heavy white cloth served as a sitting area; another, for Cooper and Shorty, offered rugs on the floor for their bedrolls; and the third tent was for Marguerite, the only woman in the camp, who was given a sleeping cot. Servants brought them each a silver pitcher and basin, and Marguerite quickly washed her hands and face, changed from her dust-covered riding clothes to a smart day dress, and joined the men to meet the ruler, Il-Khani.

Bodyguards bearing silver-topped staffs marched in advance, and the old chief of the Bakhtiari appeared. A powerful-looking Persian with a commanding air, a sunbeaten face, and a sweeping white moustache, he was dressed in the Bakhtiari costume: short black toque, black coat wrapped with a white sash, billowing pants, and white canvas shoes. With him was his cousin, Amir Jang, the second most powerful ruler of the tribe. Known as Il Begi, he had a shrewd and citified air. Stout and middle-aged, with a short black moustache and keen black eyes peering from gold-rimmed glasses, he wore a black frock coat, gold wristwatch, and big diamond ring.

"*Salaam aleikum,*" both men said. Peace be with you. "*Aleikum salaam,*" the trio replied, and after the requisite flatteries, with Rahim

serving as translator, they told the rulers why they were there. They
had come to join the tribesmen to film the migration over the mountains. But, they explained, they did not wish only to observe the tribe,
they wanted to live with the group: eat the same food; sleep in the
same tents; and travel with them on their most difficult route, the one
where no European had ever journeyed.

Amir Jang burst out laughing. "You brave people," he said and
laughed even harder. He and his family would never take such a dangerous path, he avowed: "very, very bad road. Big mountains, big
wood, big river, then big, big mountains with plenty snow." No foreigners had ever been there, he assured them, and only some of his
tribesmen chose that route. "Wild men, very," he said. "We call them
'Bears.'"

The discussion continued; the rulers explained that five clans
belonged to their tribe, but only one clan, the Baba Ahmedi, took that
perilous path. The Americans could go with them if they wished.

Yes, they wished, they said, and offered profuse thanks.

Two days later, much relieved and eager to start their work, they
said farewell to Il-Khani. With an invitation to travel with Amir Jang,
they set off on their return to Shushtar, close to the Baba Ahmedi
camp. Tribesmen led them to the shallow edge of the Karun River, the
largest river in Persia, where a big raft sat in the icy water. No ordinary flatboat, it looked more like Cleopatra's barge: made from one
hundred inflated goatskins and attached to the underside of a woven
wood frame, it was crowned with a canopy made of tasseled red satin
and clad with a floor of thick rugs and cushions.

Marguerite was the first of the group to board: climbing onto the
shoulders of a tribesman, she wrapped her legs around him and rode
piggyback through the frigid river, sliding off as he stepped onto the
barge. The others followed until there were twenty people seated like
royal guests, all plumped on stacks of silken pillows; up front the
attendants joined the four oarsmen paddling the raft, floating down
the swirling river on the swollen goatskins.

Servants brought them small glasses of tea and a tray from which
Amir Jang offered a special treat. "You join me?" he asked. Marguerite and the men nodded yes and watched him open a small silk bag of

opium; with a set of tongs, he retrieved a pellet, placed it carefully in the small bowl of a pipe, and heated it over a charcoal brazier.

They were each given their own pipe. Reclining on the cushions, they sat back and drew in the pungent smoke. With the sun baking, a breeze blowing, and the strong current pulling them through a narrow, rock-lined passage, Marguerite felt a wave of calm set in. "The opium had soothed my nerves and relaxed my muscles," she said. "I felt a delightful sense of peace and contentment."

It wasn't just the opium: she felt at ease just as she had in Russia and Turkey. "I experienced the same sensation of complete and absolute familiarity with my surroundings. When I arrived in Moscow, I knew that I had seen it before." It was the same in her travels through Turkey: "I could sit cross-legged or on my heels for hours at a stretch without feeling fatigued."

She imagined her forebears fighting with Darius and Xerxes, ancient Persian rulers, or sweeping across Asia with Genghis Khan and the Golden Horde. "I suddenly felt very old and very young— old because of all I remembered, young because of all I had forgotten!" Now she accustomed herself to Persia. She learned the language quickly, understood the thinking and customs, and ate the food readily, as though these were her roots and she was at home.

.   .   .

They reached Shushtar and stayed at the comfortable home of a merchant, lazing through Ramadan, the time of year that Muslims spend in daylight spells of introspection and fasting, and nighttime streams of celebration and feasting. After several days they received word that the chief of the Baba Ahmedi clan was waiting for them.

Led by their head driver, Hadji, and their interpreter, Mohammed, a new and necessary member of their group, they left and spent the night in a small village, sleeping in a filthy one-room mud hut. Within moments of their arrival, the mayor paid a visit and begged for their help: his people were suffering from malaria, dysentery, and eye diseases and were desperate for medicines, he said.

Marguerite was prepared; she had been advised to pack quinine pills, boric acid, and cathartic tablets to give to the tribesmen and she offered the mayor a large supply. Only later, when she was besieged by a mob of women and children, did she learn that the village official kept it all for himself.

The following day, the Americans came upon the familiar sight of the tents of Il-Khani; the leader and his men were moving from clan to clan to collect their money, hold audiences, receive petitions, and settle complaints. They had chosen this new location to be near the Baba Ahmedi.

Welcomed by their friend Rahim Khan, the Americans were introduced to a fierce-looking man called Haidar Khan, chief of the wild Baba Ahmedi clan. "He will be at your disposal," Rahim said. "You have only to tell him what you want done. He has orders to conform to your wishes in every particular." Clearly unhappy with playing host to the *ferengi,* the weather-beaten chief, ruler of five hundred rifles, glared silently with his hard black eyes, thrust his forceful jaw at the foreigners, and bowed.

Amir Jang had given the visitors two white tents for the trip, and as Marguerite readied herself for bed that night, with mosquito netting safely around her, she heard a man's plaintive cries, followed by Rahim's harsh replies. When the man's pleas turned into screams, she stepped outside her tent and, dismayed, saw an older man laying prostrate on the ground. Rahim was standing nearby with arms folded, supervising as his servants beat the helpless tribesman with a club. Afterward, Rahim turned to Cooper, who was also watching. "I hope the singing over at my tent did not disturb you," he said with a smile. The gracious cosmopolite had turned into the brutal tribal chief.

Later they learned that the older man, chief of his village, had been ordered to provide food for the animals. He protested strongly, insisting his people had barely enough grain to feed their own herds. But after the lashing, he assured his ruler the food would be delivered the next day.

In the morning, Marguerite awoke to find that the camp had broken and hers was the only tent still standing. An hour later she, Merian, and Shorty said goodbye to Rahim as he rode off and they prepared themselves to go with Haidar. They carried two wooden hand-cranked movie cameras and one still camera, two extremely heavy wooden tripods, four large boxes of film, three open-topped development tanks, and their personal necessities: a minimal amount of underwear and clothes, including one linen suit for Shorty and one pair of dancing shoes for Merian; a light quilt to sleep on and a single blanket for each man; and Marguerite's wardrobe, toiletries, cosmetics, and rubber bath. All of it was carried by the mules.

Mounting their animals, the threesome followed as an angry Haidar led them through a narrow mountain pass. On one side of the trail, Marguerite looked down on a deep valley, where the grass was turning brown; on the other side she looked up at a steep mountain range with snow-covered peaks looming above.

They soon reached their destination, a small camp composed of only four black goat-hair tents. Similar camps of the Baba Ahmedi were scattered for miles around, assuring the three hundred families that there would be enough grazing grass for the goats, sheep, and cows that provided them with sustenance. As Vita Sackville-West wrote from Persia two years later, they were far away in distance and far back in time. The main impression was isolation.

As darkness fell, the Americans joined Haidar and several tribesmen, squatting outdoors for a feast prepared in their honor. Seated on rugs on the ground with Merian and Shorty, Marguerite was given a place of honor next to the chief and his men. A servant carried a silver ewer and poured water on their hands; other servants carried bowls piled high with fresh food and set them down. This was the sort of romantic life with a tribe that Marguerite had envisioned: living in the present yet dwelling with an ancient people and their customs from the ancient past. But there was nothing romantic about the meal.

Flies swarmed all around them as they each used one hand to dig into communal dishes, tearing off chunks of sheep and rolling balls out of rice and ghee. Instead of a sweet jug of wine, they drank sour milk from a shared bowl; and instead of a loaf of bread, they chewed on unleavened bread so hard that Marguerite broke a tooth. From then on, at every meal Shorty used the butt of a rifle to crush the round of flat bread that Cooper called "cast iron pancakes."

Talk was minimal until dinner was over and the conversation turned to concerns about Reza Khan. The Persian war minister wanted to modernize his country and make it a republic. What was a republic? the men wanted to know. Were there any kings left in Europe? they asked. When Marguerite told them that one country had a woman ruler, Haidar ridiculed the notion. "It was evident he had his own ideas about the place of women," she remarked. Nonetheless, he was more than pleased when she presented him with a gift of ladies' gold-tipped cigarettes.

In the morning Marguerite met Haidar's wives. Like all the women in the camp they were tall and strapping, barefoot and unveiled. They wore their hair in two long braids tied under the chin and dressed in full ankle-length, dark-blue or black cotton skirts, floral jackets, and brightly colored head scarves.

Wife Number One, a handsome woman with intense black eyes and thick black brows, seemed to be well regarded by her husband. She had borne four children, including her husband's favorite, Lufta, a nine-year-old boy who idolized his father. But Haidar's younger Wife Number Two had not produced any offspring, and for this she was poorly treated by her husband. Like all the second wives, she was ordered about as a slave by Wife Number One.

Women carried out most of the work at the camp. They spun the wool, wove the yarn, drew water, washed the clothes, milked the sheep and goats, made the sour milk that was a staple of their diet, prepared the food, and looked after their babies. Marguerite was also put to work after Wife Number Two came to her tent with a plea on the second day at camp. "Four years I have been married and I have no child. Will the *Khanum*, the Lady, give me medicine that I may have one?" she begged. Marguerite could only shake her head. "God alone can do that," she replied.

Other women soon followed: some prevailed upon her to cure malaria, which was common among the tribespeople; others to heal the sores of another frequent ailment, venereal disease; some asked her to treat snake bites or dress wounds, or even act as a surgeon for a necessary amputation. When a mother brought her dying son who had shrunk to almost a skeleton, Marguerite found out the boy had swallowed a leech. Not knowing what else to do, she gave him warm salt water to drink, hoping he would vomit up the parasite. "Then a miracle happened," she said. "Up came the leech, quite dead. After that the boy improved rapidly and soon recovered completely."

Men, too, joined the daily cluster of patients who came asking for her help. She dispensed quinine pills to the feverish and took them herself as a preventive, bathed sores, and cleansed sufferers' eyes with boric acid. When long lines of men showed up complaining of liver disease, she gave out silver coated pills but soon learned they were stashing away the tablets to use as silver currency for sugar and tobacco.

She had played a medical role in earlier years as well, nursing those in need: she tended a British journalist who took sick in Russia, winning the praise of Bertrand Russell; healed the wounds of Russian peasants in the Far East; and looked after the gravely ill sentinel who guarded her when she was a Soviet prisoner on the Trans-Siberian Express to Moscow.

The Bakhtiari soon gave her the name *Hakim Khanum*, Lady Doctor, but she shook off the title, claiming she knew nothing about medicine. "Luckily none of my patients died," she said. The work gave her a closer look at the people, and the picture she saw was not one she liked. "They were not a lovable or an interesting people. They were hard, treacherous, thieves, and robbers," she said, brutes who treated their women like cattle.

As for the men in the camp, consisting of four of Haidar's married brothers and their helpers, they lolled about, smoked their *kalyan* (water pipes), drank strong tea with chunks of sugar, cheated at cards, and sometimes rode off to neighboring camps to visit six more brothers and their families; the siblings, including sisters, totaled twenty-two, all produced by one haggard mother.

At the end of a week, with the early April sun already baking the fields and the grass turning from green to brown, the brothers gathered at Haidar's camp. They smoked the *kalyan* and made their plans: in the morning they would break camp and begin the migration. That night male musicians played the flute and the drums, women danced and sang in a circle, and the men acted out a duel. Only a few hours later, before sunrise, the tribesmen pulled the pegs from the ground, and the goatskin tents collapsed into crumpled squares.

CHAPTER 23

Where the Soul Flows

A group of 150 men, women, and children gathered at the onset and grew within days to five hundred people. Leaving behind their folded tents, they made their way on the trail, each family bringing with them only their saddlebags filled with rugs, rice, and grain, pots and pans, and water pipes.

Barefoot humans and thousands of bogged-down animals carrying babies and baggage formed a long line that wound for miles around the curves of mountain passes. Men led the way, marching across the rocks, clearing a path, or beating the animals to keep them in tow. Women walked, some pregnant, others, having recently borne their infants, carried wooden cradles strapped to their backs; toddlers sat tied on the backs of cows or donkeys; older children tramped, some guiding the goats and sheep.

Haidar, his son Lufta, the other khans, and their trusted men rode tall on their Arabian horses, rifles slung across their shoulders; a rare wife rode astride. Marguerite, Merian, and Shorty rode with their interpreter, Mohammed, their muleteer, Hadji, and Marguerite's servant, Niaz Ali, each on a surefooted mule. All around them were swarms of flies and thick dust that blasted their faces. Handkerchiefs covered their mouths.

At night they all lay on the hard ground, except for Haidar and Marguerite, who slept in tents, her cot well wrapped in mosquito net. She used the space under her bed as safekeeping for the many bags of silver coins needed to pay the tribesmen for labor and food, for which the *ferengi* were excessively charged, and as a hiding place for the cans of film, developed or new, that were precious and irreplaceable. They could never reshoot the scenes, nor could they purchase fresh film anywhere nearer than Paris or Rome, five thousand miles away.

They weren't the only ones who valued the cans of film; rumors spread that the cases contained gold and jewels. At any moment some tribesman was likely to try and steal them. The interpreter Mohammed told the Americans, "They'll steal anything. A boy can't sit with his elders, he isn't a man, until he has stolen a horse." Thievery was a point of pride. Decades earlier, the explorer/statesman Lord Curzon wrote that the name "Bakhtiari" was synonymous with "robber." Robbery was a game; winners were looked upon with admiration.

The procession grew as more Bakhtiari clans joined the Baba Ahmedi, reaching a total of five thousand humans and fifty thousand animals—goats, sheep, donkeys, and cows, along with chickens and dogs—all trudging in a long line, zigzagging their way by day through eight to ten miles of rough mountain paths and sleeping at night on the hard ground of grassy valleys.

The same scene was repeated along a stretch of a thousand miles from the Black Sea in the north to the Persian Gulf in the south. A million Bakhtiari, Kurds, Lurs, and other ancient tribes trekked across the mountains going from west to east in the spring and back across the mountains in autumn, always seeking grass, always struggling against the forces of nature. But no tribe's path was as treacherous as that of the Baba Ahmedi.

. . .

In mid-April, two weeks after they set out, the route of the Baba Ahmedi stopped. The mountain trail came to an end, and in its place they faced a seething section of the icy Karun River. There on the riverbank sat a rough version of Il-Khani's regal barge. Days earlier, the men had blown up big goatskins, tied them together, plugged the punctures, and attached the inflated skins beneath large sections of wooden dowels.

Now the crude rafts were ready to ferry the Baba Ahmedi through freezing whirlpools of racing current that heaved the flatboats off the side of the bank, careened them spinning half a mile down the S-shaped river, and tossed them onto the opposite side. And while the people and the goats, the only animals unable to swim, were pitched out on the rafts with a shout of "Yo, Ali!," the sheep, donkeys, horses, and cows were pushed into the churning waters by men paddling furiously on inflated goatskins, driving and beating the animals to swim to the opposite shore.

Women shrieked, children screamed, animals bayed and moaned as they shook from side to side on the spinning rafts or swam in the ferocious river. But they had no choice. This was a matter of life and death: to survive they needed grass, and where they were, the grass was dying. The only way to reach the grass growing on the other side was to cross the Karun.

Hours flew by like minutes as Marguerite watched the scene, mesmerized by the same routine that took place every year, twice a year, and had been repeated for centuries. Nervous and doubtful, she waited to be called. "When I saw the first rafts set out, it did not seem to me that they could ever reach the opposite bank," she said. "Finally, it was my turn. I piled into a raft with half a dozen saddlebags, my own belongings, three women and five goats. It shot out into the current, whirled round and round dizzily until I had to shut my eyes to keep from falling off into the water, and at last it reached the opposite bank."

In charge of it all was Haidar, transformed from an indolent bystander to an assertive commander. Rushing into the frigid water, he ordered his men about, overseeing their actions as each man blew up a pair of goatskins and tied the ends together, then flung them into the river and climbed on top, putting his knees on the float and his feet in the flow, his legs and arms free to swim and to push the petrified animals into the surging stream.

Haidar took complete control, leaping into action, swimming nearly naked through the harrowing current, then carrying his raft half a mile back up the riverbank, making eight trips a day, assuring the survival of the Baba Ahmedi.

The maneuvers continued for almost a week until the entire clan and their animals had crossed the river and landed on the jagged shore. Merian and Shorty filmed it all. It was "the greatest piece of continuous action I have ever seen," Merian recalled. Later, film critics concurred.

From there the tribesmen faced a perpendicular mount. Climbing upward, they struggled for several miles on steep, rocky trails. At last, they reached a broad stretch of flat fields where they set up camp. Worn out from the events, Marguerite went to bed that night and quickly fell asleep, only to be awakened by a loud commotion. Was it tribesmen stealing the film cans? Were the men looting the money bags?

The whole tent was collapsing around her. But the noise was not coming from a fumbling burglar. It was one of Hadji's mules that had broken away, raced around the camp, landed at Marguerite's quarters, and caught his foot in the rope between the flap and the ground. In the confusion, he had brought down her tent. It took some time for Cooper and Shorty, along with the muleteer, to free her from the morass.

Most nights at the camp, the Americans gathered in Marguerite's small white tent and ate a supper of sour milk, rice, and flat bread served by Niaz Ali. Once in a while they feasted on a chicken or berries, given as a thank-you to Marguerite from someone she had attended. After the meal, they were joined by Haidar and his brothers, who sat for hours, the clansmen puffing on their hookahs and all of them sipping strong, sugary tea.

As always, Marguerite was the only woman, except for one special female who came to visit from another camp. "She was a hideous old crone, bent and wrinkled. Her hair was dyed bright red and her lips were drawn tight over her toothless gums, but she was a real person," Marguerite said. This was Haidar's mother. "She took part in the councils and her advice was always heeded."

The rest of the women, however, were regarded scornfully by the Bakhtiari. Although no man would ever approach another man's wife, they treated their own women like chattel. When Wife Number One lost a donkey that roamed from the camp, Marguerite watched, horrified, as Haidar beat her without mercy. No pleas from the *Hakim Khanum*, the Lady Doctor, could stop him. Later when the woman came to her for help, Marguerite found two broken ribs, which she wrapped with adhesive tape. But when she suggested to Haidar that his wife be allowed to ride on a horse over the rough trails, he refused: the anguished woman was forced to walk.

Haidar was not the only one whose attitude was offensive. Marguerite called Merian's opinions of women a combination of "southern chivalry and Oriental contempt." He believed that "nice women" were made to be worshipped on pedestals, but he considered them "brainless creatures fit only to mind home and bear children. We had furious arguments about women," she said, but because he did not see her as a female, the arguments were never personal. "To him I was simply a boon companion, a business associate, and the person to whom he claimed he owed an eternal debt of gratitude."

Marguerite saw herself in a different light: smart, capable, nurturing, and empathetic, she also had a penchant for fashion and a strong desire to look attractive. "I had never lost my feminine fondness for clothes, and even when I was in prison I clung to my pocket mirror and my last grains of face powder, and I waved my hair on bits of rags or papers. These things had always helped me to keep up my morale."

Her arguments with Merian Cooper went beyond the treatment of women: they quarreled over their approach to making movies. As a reporter, she said, she sought the truth; as a filmmaker, he sought a story. But if she felt disgust when he shrugged off veracity, she did respect his talent for drama. Indeed, a few years later, with his vivid imagination, he created the movie *King Kong*.

·   ·   ·

The tribesmen spent several days in the camp sorting out their animals and their belongings, gathering strength to start the next phase of their journey. The Americans were sitting with Haidar one night when a stranger came to the tent asking for Marguerite's help. His son was ill with an infected wound and needed medicine. Marguerite gave him the treatment, but she warned that the medication was only to be used on his skin and not to be swallowed. It was poisonous if taken internally. The man thanked her and spoke for a while with Haidar, who offered him tea and a smoke with his *kalyan*.

When the stranger left, Haidar turned to Marguerite: "I am sorry you told that man that the medicine you gave him was poison."

The words took her aback. "Why?" she asked.

"Because he is our enemy. He belongs to a hostile tribe that steals our cattle and has slain many of our best rifles."

If his tribe killed your men, then why did you not arrest him? she wanted to know.

"Because he managed to slip past our outposts," Haidar replied. "I could not harm him while he was in our tents." The tribal laws required hospitality, he explained. But, he added, "if I meet him on the trail tomorrow, I will shoot him dead."

. . .

With the days growing hotter, it became too difficult to march the animals under the blistering sun. Instead, they broke camp earlier and set off at midnight. Awakened in the pitch dark, Marguerite joined the march through a mile-long narrow gorge where people and animals squeezed one by one through the slim pass, emerging into a narrow valley. But at the end of the valley, they faced the first of three sky-high mountain ranges spread across 150 miles. These unmapped giants were the great challenge that would lead to the treasured green fields.

In early May, they were ready to attack the first of the mountains. Marguerite dressed carefully and applied her makeup for the morning film shoot. She had clothes for every type of weather: light-colored pongee riding suits for the hot sun; wool coats and furs for the cold and the snow. But she had only one type of mascara and greasepaint for her face.

When the temperature hovered around a hundred degrees, her makeup began to melt. Intent on pleasing the camera, she carried the box of cosmetics in her saddle crupper and, stopping along the way, she balanced the tin on her donkey's neck and repaired her face. And then in the evening, with help from servants who brought in a pitcher of water heated over a fire of dried dung, she bathed and washed her clothes, ready for the next day. Later, some critics snarled that she looked too clean.

. . .

They were trekking in the blackness of night, climbing from the bottom of the mountain straight up a sheer cliff when one of the animals lost its footing. Down the side the donkey fell, another nearly falling too, the women shrieking and sliding, unable to stop its death. The march continued up the rock face, and all along the way, tribesmen beat their animals and sang out, "Yo Ali, Ali," until Shorty taught them a different tune: "Yes, we have no bananas," he sang, and the women repeated his words with a Bakhtiari accent. Marguerite could hear the popular song, as ludicrous as a sailboat floating across the cliff: "Yes, we have no bananas. We have no bananas today."

At the end of the first week of May they were in the Shimbar Valley, where the sweet spring in the Zagros mountains served as a meeting place for all the tribesmen. "Where the water of life flows, no illness remains," wrote Rumi. But fighting among the Bakhtiari was inevitable, and the gathering itself was almost a guarantee of stealing and warring. As a British officer had written years before: "They may be considered the most wild and barbarous of all the inhabitants of Persia. They pursue their blood feuds with an exterminating spirit."

Little had changed since then. A night of duel fighting over a horse led to the stabbing of one tribesman. The man was bleeding to death when Marguerite was called to his camp for help. With her surgical skills and a pair of sewing scissors, she held his dangling fingers, severed one of them with the scissors, sewed up the wounds, and tended to deep gashes in his back and neck. The man thanked her with a promise to send her a sheep.

. . .

Often, Merian and Shorty went ahead of the camp and spent days setting up their shoot and filming, while Marguerite stayed behind. Haidar, always impatient to lead the tribe, had vowed to Il-Khani that he would look after her, and unhappy though he was, stayed back as well. Days after the tribe broke camp in the Shimbar Valley, the two rode together and soon faced a rocky cliff that continued upward for fifteen hundred feet. As they reached the summit, Marguerite looked out and saw the fearsome Zardeh Kuh. Only after they conquered that mighty snow-covered Yellow Mountain would the tribe be near their precious goal. But their march toward grass was halted when Marguerite took sick.

She had been careful to take quinine tablets every day and sleep under the mosquito netting every night, but the dampness and the endless heat had won out and brought her down with malaria. For three days she burned with fever that reached 106 degrees, all the while shivering with cold or dripping with perspiration. They had been ready to break camp, but she was too weak even to lift a finger. And she had given away so much quinine that now, when she needed it badly, she had none left for herself.

She knew that Haidar was eager to continue the migration and that Merian and Shorty wanted to film every step of the way, and she worried when Haidar came to her tent. She expected a fit of temper, but instead he stopped the march. Telling his men to turn in all their quinine pills, he announced they would stay in camp until she felt better. What's more, he checked on her every day as did his brothers, who offered anything they had to make her better. "Haidar Khan was almost human," she said. "It was the only time I ever saw him display any decent feeling." Perhaps it was the gold-tipped cigarettes that stoked his heart.

Desperate to lower her fever, she asked Niaz Ali to bring her a pitcher of cold water and poured it over herself. "I nearly fainted from it," she said, but the method worked. Her vision was blurred from all the quinine, but by the fourth day she had just enough strength to crawl out of her tent and onto her mule.

They were back on the trail, in one of the hottest regions on earth, surrounded by snow-covered peaks. And then for three days the skies opened, the rain poured down, and the ground was drenched. The trek came to a halt. She stayed in her tent while Haidar and his men set out up the rocky mountain. Barefoot, with ice picks, poles, and shovels they cleared a path through the thick blankets of snow.

· · ·

As soon as the rains stopped, the tribe set off on the new trail. A cold wind blew as the shoeless and coatless people, wearing only their cotton clothes, trekked thousands of feet above a precipice across snow-covered cliffs. Their bare feet bled and their lips were blue and blistered, but they kept on going because there was nothing else they could do. Shorty wore boots with his only outfit, the Palm Beach linen suit, Merian wore warm clothes with his only shoes, his patent leather dancing pumps, and Marguerite looked smart in riding boots and britches, her fur-trimmed coat, and brimmed hat. They all hiked for four days, and, at one point where the snows rushed down the side of the mountain and formed a river, the barefoot tribe, along with the trio, sloshed with their herds through the glacial water.

They made camp, then soon set off again, thousands of people marching single file on a narrow trail that stretched for miles below, a skinny black snake crawling slowly up the side of the white mountain. And then they were climbing on a coat of snow as hard and smooth as glass, making their way to twelve thousand feet above sea level. All the while, the Bakhtiari voices rang out, "Yes, we have no bananas."

On the last day of May, they climbed to the summit of Zardeh Kuh. With the wind bellowing and the snow melting in the sun, they began the descent downward. They slipped and walked across rugged stretches, sometimes treading over ground covered with thousands of purple wildflowers. After six weeks, they had reached the land of plenty. They would make their camps, the men would relax, the women would do their work, and they would remain until the grass began to wither and the other side of the mountains beckoned them to return.

"Here it's spring, my friends," wrote Rumi. "Let's make our home in the cypress grove and wake our sleepy destiny till it surges skywards like these trees. Just like them, we are bound to the ground heading to groundless ground, where the soul flows."

CHAPTER 24

Disillusion

With no regrets and a sigh of relief, Marguerite turned her back on the Zardeh Kuh and left the Bakhtiari behind. The Americans had accomplished a major feat and made a film that would be unique. "We had crossed a country which had never been crossed by Europeans and we had been able to record a phase in the evolution of civilization," Marguerite said. They had come to a place "where civilization had stood still for two thousand years."

Nonetheless, she had found the tribe offensive in almost every way, from the contempt they held for women to their callous disregard for each other. They were amoral, arrogant, and aloof, "hard, treacherous thieves, crassly material," interested only in stealing goods and animals, ready to use their knives and guns on anyone, and trusting of no one. They had developed no higher culture: no written language, no art, no music, no poetry, no verbal lore. Like all humans, their basic intent was to survive, but they were "devoid of sentiment or spirituality," she said, lacking any of the elements that enrich civilized experience.

Pleased to be on her way, she traveled with Cooper and Schoedsack, first by mule for three days and then by taxi to the ancient city of Isfahan, where they stayed in the princely palaces of Rahim's family. In a luxurious guest room fifty feet long where gorgeous rugs hung on the walls and hand-blocked-printed curtains covered the windows, she bathed in a tub filled with hot water and attar of roses and slept on silk sheets and a satin pad. At another castle they stayed in even more sumptuous quarters, but it was time to move on. For two days they rode by car, through the holy city of Qum, where she sensed the hostile attitude toward infidels, to the capital, Tehran. The city was an oasis of modernity that offered electricity, trams, and even movies.

While Marguerite was the guest of an American serving as a finance adviser to the Persian government, Cooper and Schoedsack stayed with the America diplomat Robert Imbrie. At the trio's request, Imbrie certified a letter from Amir Jang, the powerful commander of the Bakhtiari tribe, and Haidar Khan, the ruler of the Baba Ahmedi clan, stating that the three Americans were the first foreigners ever to have made the forty-six-day migration with the Baba Ahmedi across the Zardeh Kuh mountains.

For Marguerite, the highlight of her stay in Tehran was a meeting with Reza Khan. Eager to learn his intentions and perspective on the world, she interviewed the military man who would soon depose the Shah. At his summer villa in the mountains, under a striped marquee tent in the garden, she observed the future ruler who would take the name Shah Reza Pahlavi and wrote about him for the *New York Times:*

> His face was heavy, almost sullen—hard boiled is the American word that best describes it. His skin was tanned as if from exposure to sun and wind in innumerable campaigns; his mouth was set in rigid lines under his close-cropped mustache, but his eyes were his most remarkable feature. They looked straight at you and through you from under thick, level brows, unwavering, appraising, inscrutable. Nothing could escape eyes like those.

Next to him stood his young son, Mohammad Reza, dressed exactly like his father, who would follow him onto the peacock throne. Mohammad Reza's future wife, Queen Soraya, and his prime minister, Shaptur Bahktiar, were both from the Bakhtiari tribe. In 1979, the Shah would be deposed. Reza Khan took a seat and gestured for his guest to do the same. Tea was ordered, but there was an awkward silence until Marguerite spoke a few words in Persian to the child, bringing a hint of admiration from the leader. "You are the first *ferengi* lady I ever met who could speak our tongue," he said.

Although he did not know English, Reza Khan spoke fluent Russian learned during his early work as a soldier guarding the Russian embassy. Making their way in Persian and Russian, the host and guest conversed, somewhat stiffly, about family, and about her travels with the Bakhtiari. After tea, they walked around the garden, and as he talked about the flowers, she noticed he was more at ease. "The constraint had entirely disappeared. He was altogether human and altogether delightful," she said.

But aside from a few comments about the Bakhtiari, who, he insisted, whether by free will or by force must pay their taxes and join the modern system of government, the political discussion she tried to encourage was not forthcoming. Indeed, she sensed that, like the other men she had encountered on her trip, he was dismissive of women. A few minutes later, when a male guest appeared, he moved away to speak with the man.

Still, Persia intrigued her, and she left the country reluctantly, spending her last night asleep on the roof of a caravansery looking out over mountains that stretched to Iraq. She felt pulled in opposite directions, eager to be on her way to Baghdad and her "workaday world," and longing as well to go back to the east, to the land of Marco Polo, "a world of dim ancestral memories."

In Baghdad, she hoped to visit again with Gertrude Bell, but the British lady was on holiday in England. With the daily temperature hovering at 110 degrees, Marguerite left the city with Cooper and Schoedsack, and the threesome motored through the sweltering Syrian Desert to Beirut. Faced with the real possibility of their precious film melting in the heat, the men caught the next boat out for France, where they planned to edit the movie, while Marguerite, insatiably curious about the people and the politics, moved on to Syria.

Motoring to Aleppo and Damascus, she met the French governor, General Weygand, who gave her a cursory view of the political situation. But on her own she witnessed the disastrous state of life under the French Mandate, where incessant fighting over religious and nationalist beliefs kept Arabs, Druze, Christians, and Alaouites at each other's throats. The tensions were even greater in Palestine.

There in the holy land, the Arabs and Jews living under the British Mandate battled over disagreements embedded in the ancient soil.

She felt sympathetic to the Jews from Eastern Europe whose suffering she had witnessed in Poland and Lithuania, and she understood that "a reconstituted Zion" was their "only hope and solace." She also admired the Jewish intellectuals who came from America and Western Europe to establish a "cultural center." But she was certain that the small group of political Zionists who aimed to create a political state would cause many problems in the future. With the Arabs in the majority of the population, and the land as holy to them as to the Jews, she predicted that Palestine "would never cease to be a battleground of faiths and races."

By the end of her trip, she felt disillusioned. The guns of the Great War had been dismantled and the ink had dried on the peace treaties signed at Versailles and Lausanne, but Woodrow Wilson's idealism had been destroyed, replaced by political intrigues and corrupt ideology. Whether in the Near East, the Far East, or Europe, the American dream to advance democracy and encourage self-determination had turned into a nightmare in which the oppressed became the oppressors. "Kings had been overthrown, but dictators had taken their places," she wrote.

Turkey, Persia, Russia, and Italy were all under the thumb of authoritarian rule, and Germany was following suit. "Moral chaos and political chaos seemed to have engulfed the world." Democracy was failing; fascism and Bolshevism were on the rise. "We were destined to live out our lives in a period of transition," she noted. "Our era had ended. The new era had not yet begun." Uncertainty muddled the air.

She returned to New York with Cooper and Schoedsack in September 1924, knowing only that she would not stay long. "I had become a confirmed wanderer," she said. She would let fate determine what came next; for the immediate term, she had much to savor. She would complete the film with her two partners; she would write and lecture; she would spend time with friends, and she would be with her boy, twenty-two-year-old Tommy, the person she considered "closer to me than anyone else in the world."

Part Five

CHAPTER 25

Transformation

In the past Marguerite pushed aside thoughts of her son and chose the pull of adventure until, returning home each time, she berated herself for being a bad mother. Now she took an apartment with Tommy and his friend, but the arrangements were short-lived. If she had thoughts of making amends and focusing time and attention on her son, it was too late: he was engaged to be married.

Only a month after his mother's return, Thomas Bullitt Harrison married Marjorie Devereux Andrews, a young socialite whom Marguerite "loved and admired." The wedding, held at St. Thomas's Church with a reception at the exclusive Colony Club, was followed by a honeymoon in Europe. The couple came back to a home on Long Island and a life of their own.

As always, Marguerite had plenty to keep her busy. For a year she had been engaged in the making of *Grass*. Her partners had finished editing the footage of the silent film, and the time had come to write the titles for the screen. As a journalist, she knew exactly what to do: "We had made an authentic record of a stupendous, natural drama," she said. "I felt it should be treated in an absolutely natural manner." She planned to write dialogue that used the actual words of the nomads. But she was overruled.

Cooper and Schoedsack insisted on subtitles that were "melodramatic and artificial," she complained. "They put impossible speeches into the mouths of the Bakhtiari tribesmen, whose language was as primitive as their lives." The men were "quite right from the point of view of the theater," she acknowledged, but "I simply could not collaborate with them."

Marguerite attended the premiere of *Grass* at the Plaza Hotel in New York in February 1925. From there the epic documentary opened at the Criterion Theatre to wide acclaim and a four-month run. *Life* magazine called it "a genuinely great picture"; the explorer William Beebe pronounced it "one of the greatest pictures ever produced"; and the film critic for the *New York Herald Tribune* deemed it "the most important achievement of the motion picture camera." Marguerite watched the movie once but could not bear to see it again.

.   .   .

She was busy the winter of 1925 writing magazine articles, and represented by the prestigious Pond Lecture Agency, whose clients included Mark Twain and Winston Churchill, she toured the country as a speaker on the lucrative lecture circuit. In her privileged childhood she had been introduced to a world far beyond the boundaries of America, and now as an adult she felt compelled to bring that world of international affairs back home. But she shared her observations on this period in history with a public that had little understanding of events far from its shores.

Her remarks were shrugged off by audiences with preconceived notions of faraway countries and foreign people. Worse, as had happened before, her insights were ignored by reporters with more prurient interests in her affairs. The newsmen covering her talks or interviewing her for feature stories wanted to know about the indignities she suffered from prison guards, love intrigues they imagined with Soviet commissars, and the steamy passions of Persian sheikhs. While she was discussing the weakening of democracy, they asked if she wore lipstick in the desert.

The demeaning attitude of the men on her trip had made her seethe, and her fury only increased at home: The salacious questions thrown at her would never have been flung at men. What's more, Merian Cooper was welcomed to join scientific groups and geographic organizations, particularly the prestigious Explorers Club, whose president, Roy Chapman Andrews, Marguerite had met in the

Far East. But while Cooper was invited to become a member of the club, she was barred. She had survived tuberculosis and a collapsed lung, isolation, solitary confinement, hunger, cold, heat, wet, and weeks of wandering through unmapped lands. But Andrews had a different view. "Women are not adapted to exploration," he told the female students at Barnard College.

Marguerite had outwitted lotharios in Europe and Asia, outfoxed male guards at remote frontiers, outmaneuvered male thieves on crowded railroads and deserted highways, outshone male colleagues in foreign languages, outpaced male riders on horseback, and outdistanced male travelers through treacherous lands. But the crusty men who belonged to the Explorers Club could not conceive of a female doing such things. It simply was not possible for a woman to equal— and certainly never possible for a woman to outdo—a man!

In her travels she had met female activists in Russia, Japan, and Turkey who worked staunchly for women's rights, yet it was true, she admitted in her writing, that she had never been an active supporter of feminist ideas. More intent on asserting her individual rights, she admired women who stood on their own, like Gertrude Bell. There were others too, like some of the friends she had in New York.

At tea with chums on a wintry day, she expressed her anger at men's attitudes toward her achievements. Her accomplished colleagues responded in kind: they had been similarly ignored. "It was difficult for any woman to get the proper sort of recognition for her work," Marguerite said.

Speaking with Blair Niles, a travel writer who made expeditions to Ecuador and Haiti; Gertrude Emerson, an Asia expert and editor of *Asia Magazine;* and Gertrude Shelby, a geographer in the American Southwest, all of whose groundbreaking work had been diminished or dismissed, the group agreed to start an organization for "women who had done unusual things, and blazed new trails in geography, ethnology, natural history and kindred sciences." Their purpose was to raise the level of recognition for their work and establish the place of women in the scientific world.

They would provide an opportunity for women to support each other: to share ideas, compare experiences, contribute financing, and collaborate on future projects. With the addition of Har-

riet Chalmers Adams, who explored vast areas of South America
and served as its first president, the Society of Women Geographers
(SWG) became an international body with over five hundred mem-
bers including Amelia Earhart, Margaret Mead, Jane Goodall, Mary
Douglas Leakey, Eleanor Roosevelt, Mary Ritter Beard, and Margaret
Bourke-White.

The women who founded the Society of Women Geographers
were part of a larger circle of colleagues, male and female, authors,
journalists, and adventurers, whose conversations she found stimulating and whose company she enjoyed in the months after her
return. One of those men was the struggling novelist, James Cain, an
acquaintance from their reporting days in Baltimore who went on to
write prize-winning books and movies such as *Double Indemnity* and
Mildred Pierce. Among the others she socialized with at posh Society dinners or at inexpensive restaurants, some were poor, some were
brilliant, and many of them were as restless as she was.

Some of the relationships with men were platonic; others slid
toward the sexual. She always had a flurry of men who held her close
on the dance floor, and undoubtedly there were a few whose limbs
entwined with hers in the night: but she never allowed the liaisons to
go beyond the transitory. "Men had always played a large part in my
life," she said. "My friendships with them had been merely interludes,
some of them very charming, but a thing apart." The loss of her husband had left her unable to set her emotions free. A serious attachment
was out of the question. There had not been another man to whom she
had yielded her love.

She sought the companionship of friends from earlier days in
New York and Baltimore, but their lives had taken far different turns,
and she soon realized they had little in common. "My friends had
died, married, divorced, remarried, lived through domestic idylls or
domestic tragedies, and had accumulated a wealth of memories and
experiences in which I had no share." They spoke of events she had
not heard about, books she had not read, plays she had not seen. They
dropped from her life like rose petals falling to the ground.

She felt like an outsider, and once again her thoughts turned to
distant places. Yet her fascination with world affairs had waned, and

the allure of wandering alone around the world had lost its appeal. "I was puzzled, even a little frightened by my state of mind. All at once, my life that was so full, had become quite empty." She hungered for something to fill her life, but she had no idea what that might be. "I still shrank from the mere thought of love. It had once made me suffer too much, and I vowed that I would never let it touch me again." Besides, she valued her independence over mutual reliance. The idea of another marriage never occurred to her.

. . .

Arthur Blake was six feet tall and broad shouldered, with a thick head of iron-gray hair and a small, groomed moustache to match. British by birth, fluent in French, German, Spanish, and Italian, he had crewed for his Oxford team, fought for the United States in the Spanish-American War, and acted on the New York stage. They met soon after she returned to New York and found they had much in common. "He, too, had lost many of his illusions and he too was unconsciously seeking something that would give a new meaning and purpose to life."

He swept her off her feet. She was terrified. She had never considered giving up her personal freedom or her "hard won happiness" for any man after the death of her husband. But she was lonely, lonelier than she had ever been in Russia or in Asia. The better she knew Arthur Blake, the stronger her sense that she would someday marry him. But she trembled at the prospect.

Despite the life she had made as an independent woman, cavalier about her relationships with men, she had an old-fashioned attitude toward marriage. "I believed that people who marry voluntarily assume certain mutual obligations that cannot be shirked or ignored." She wanted no part of those obligations; she had paid too high a price with the illness and loss of Tom.

Instinctively, she wanted to run away. Reminiscent of her debutante days when her mother hurried her off to Europe to rid her of any youthful passions, she seized upon an offer to write about the work of the Near East Relief Society and rushed to go abroad.

. . .

The collapse of the Ottoman Empire and the subsequent signing of the Lausanne Treaty between Turkey and Greece in 1923 resulted in new borders being drawn and masses of people resettled. More than one million Orthodox Greeks who had lived for generations in Turkish areas suddenly lost their homes. Hundreds of thousands of families in Constantinople and hundreds of thousands of farmers in Anatolia were uprooted to Macedonia, Thessaloniki, Athens, and elsewhere inside the new Greek lines. At the same time, four hundred thousand Muslim Turks who had lived in Europe were expelled to Anatolia in Asia Minor.

Many on both sides did not speak the new language or have the capability to earn a living or educate their children in their new homelands. Some of the Greek refugees were helped by the American government and the League of Nations. But little was provided for the Turks and Armenians until the Near East Relief Society created camps and schools and orphanages for the displaced. The agency's money came from private sources, and it needed publicity to help raise sufficient funds.

Traveling in Turkey from Broussa to Smyrna, Marguerite was saddened to see the helplessness of Turks who had farmed their old land but did not have enough money to buy seeds or livestock or equipment for their new soil. In Saloniki she was distressed by the sight of poor Greeks who had been shipped from Anatolia and cast off into run-down barracks in the run-down town. At the same time, she was amazed at the ingenuity of others, such as the thousands of Armenians who, unloaded into concentration camps in Aleppo, managed to earn a living as traders.

On one subject her feelings remained constant: every day she thought of Arthur Blake, and every day, as promised, she wrote him a letter. It was as though she had brought him along on her travels. By the time she boarded the ship to come home she knew that they would marry. She would be transformed, "like a moth breaking out of a cocoon," she said. "Marguerite Blake would not bear the faintest resemblance to Marguerite Harrison." She recalled the words of

Richard Wagner inscribed on the wall of his villa in Beyreuth: "Here where my restless soul has found peace."

Mr. and Mrs. Arthur Blake were married in February 1926, but their souls were still restless. Shortly after their small wedding, they set off on a six-month honeymoon to Morocco. The trip was extended, and Marguerite published her most scholarly book, *Asia Reborn,* with a dateline of August 1, 1927, Rabat, Morocco.

"The history of Asia," she wrote presciently, "has been largely determined by two factors which we do not always take into account: climate and geography." And she noted two other factors had also taken their places on the global scene: science and economics. Modern science, she said, was "breaking down all barriers of distance and inaccessibility." Additionally, people around the world were becoming economically interdependent. If those ties were broken, the cataclysmic results would affect all humanity. The critically well-received volume served as a textbook at Harvard.

For several years after the publication of the book, Marguerite and Arthur Blake spent time in Europe, working on a series of travel films for Fox Studios. In 1930 they bought a château nears Tours in France, but a few years later, with their finances weak and war on the way, they left for America. Marguerite returned to speaking on the lecture circuit, but Arthur's attempts to establish himself as a movie actor in California were unsuccessful.

Like many spies, Marguerite retired to a quiet life. After her husband died in 1947, she went back to Baltimore, where her son, divorced and remarried, had moved with his new wife and their young daughter. Tommy, kind and gentle by day, drank too much every night and argued bitterly with his wife. Although his friends knew he was angry and felt abandoned by Marguerite, he never bickered with his mother. But the only photograph he kept on view was of his grandmother.

Even into her eighties, Marguerite continued to travel the world on her own. Although some of her forays with Arthur Blake may have been for the government, her greatest escapades remained mostly in her memories and took shape as objects around her house: woven textiles on the walls, rugs on the floor, silver bowls and samovars on shelves; pieces bought in the open stalls of Russia and the flea markets of Asia.

Those were her glory days, packed with a lifetime of adventure, yet they had spanned less than a decade. It was in 1918 that Marguerite Harrison slid her typewriter into its case, slipped her code book inside her bag, and stepped aboard the magic carpet that lifted her out of Baltimore society and onto the world stage. In her time she had played many parts: a journalist, an author, an explorer, a filmmaker, a public speaker, and a spy.

Before women had the right to vote, and long before married women in the United States could open their own bank account, she determined her own course and boldly pursued her own goals. A woman of contrasts, she was raised amidst plush surroundings with patrician parents and countless servants to care for her, yet she chose to live in rough environs and spare quarters. Accustomed since childhood to transatlantic voyages on her father's fleet of ships, she trudged as an adult across vertiginous mountains in far-off lands. Tutored to be a charming ornament in sugar-coated settings, she used a steely intellect to slice through enameled facades. Prepared for a life of leisure, she toiled tirelessly at her work. Accustomed to great wealth, she chose arduous pursuits instead of money. "I craved hardships and adventure," she said. She longed for the "blurry beyond."

.   .   .

Her whole life was blurry: the mother who rarely saw her child; the lover who would not let herself be intimate; the patriot suspected of being a double agent; the spy who omitted more than she told. In her autobiography, written in 1935, she drew parts of her life in sharp black and white, but key elements were left in a murky gray. She skirted around her relationship with her sister, skipped over the unhappiness of her son, never fully revealed her work as a spy. Her father-in-law, the scientist Joseph Ames, had unraveled the complexities of aerodynamics, yet though he was her close confidant, he could not fathom her actions.

Described as "the essence of femininity," she crashed through sexist barricades and stamped her footprints on unmapped paths. She was a white-gloved socialite who saw herself as a socialist tinged with pink, an individualist who stood up for feminists, a traditionalist who created an unconventional life. "Long before cigarettes or alcohol touched a lady's lips," said the *Baltimore News American*, "she chain smoked and drank alcohol and left a trail of broken hearts."

With a sympathetic ear and a skillful way with words, in English, French, German, Italian, Russian, Turkish, Persian, and a smattering of Japanese, she wrote about, spoke about, and spied upon a world in turmoil. The first woman sent overseas as an intelligence officer to spy for America, the first American woman to enter Germany immediately after World War I, and one of the few females in the small group of American correspondents in Europe during the crucial years from 1919 to 1922, she was an early witness to the bitter resentments, deprivations, and despair that followed in the wake of the First World War and the Russian Revolution.

Those conflicts shattered empires and splintered nations: monarchies ceased to exist; states were overturned; national identities were put in question; ideologies were upended. Resentment was rampant, and the winners were piling on the building blocks for disaster: Germany demoralized by the Great War; Russia ensnared in upheaval and internal strife after the Bolshevik Revolution; Turkey in shards after the collapse of the Ottoman Empire. In addition, Persia was consolidating its feudal society into a centralized, oil-rich state; Japan was pumping its postwar muscles well beyond its narrow borders; and China was at war with itself.

At a time when women of her class did not work, she built an astonishing career. As an espionage agent she conveyed vital information about foreign countries: she uncovered secret data on the composition of their populations; the capabilities of their militaries; and the personalities of their leaders, along with their methods and their results. She won the praise of American intelligence officials at the highest levels.

An independent thinker with strong convictions, she chose action over celebrity. As a patriot, she risked her life to serve her country. Aware that her government might not come to her rescue, she endured two separate sentences in Lubyanka, one of the world's most harrowing prisons, and refused to surrender to the demands of the enemy.

As a journalist with an internationalist point of view, she was always ready to travel and introduced her readers to little-known regions and powerful rulers around the world. In numerous articles for the *Baltimore Sun*, the *New York Times*, *Cosmopolitan*, *Asia*, and other magazines, she told of the dangerous rise of nationalism and the equally dangerous fear of socialism, the importance of economic security for every country, and "how the rise and fall of civilizations dovetailed into one another." She explained complicated issues in accessible language, tried to show the humanity of the enemy, and kept a keen eye on friends.

As an author she published five well-received books concerned with world affairs; two volumes on Russia, two on Asia, including *Red Bear or Yellow Dragon*, a significant source of information on Japan, and her autobiography, *There's Always Tomorrow*.

As a lecturer, she sounded warning bells. She told how harsh punishment of Germany after World War I turned its people against the world; how extreme sanctions against the Russians tightened the Soviet grip on power; how economic needs in Asia encouraged expansion. She warned of the dangers of populism and the risks of only looking inward. She cautioned against the rise of fascism and fought Soviet attempts to infiltrate American thinking.

As a filmmaker and one of the first female film producers, she made a landmark contribution to the fields of ethnography and documentary movies. *Grass*, the film she funded and appeared in, is now in the archives of the Museum of Modern Art.

Her work with three other women in founding the Society of Women Geographers helped highlight the pioneering efforts of female explorers, writers, and scientists and countered the effects of similar clubs available exclusively to men. Her work with children too ill to attend school gave the youngsters the opportunity to exercise their brains as they strengthened their bodies.

Both the Society of Women Geographers and the Children's Hospital School in Baltimore, which Marguerite helped establish as a young society wife in 1905, provided opportunities and encouragement for people whose abilities were derided and voices were suppressed. Through these organizations women received the recognition they deserved for their outstanding work and children received the education they needed to develop their potential skills.

Marguerite considered these institutes to be two of her most important accomplishments. Later she wrote: "I always think of them as two distinct clear patterns in a life that is a medley of confused particolored designs like a carpet that has been worked on by many hands!"

But she set the course of her life by her own hand. She wrote and spoke for what she believed in and tried to bring the world closer to home. She lived each day to the fullest, and when she died in 1967, she asked that her ashes be spread across the sea.

Acknowledgments

Marguerite Harrison first came to my attention when I was writing a biography of Gertrude Bell. Poring through Miss Bell's letters at the University of Newcastle, I was struck by her description of an American woman who visited Baghdad in 1924. Who was this woman, and what was she doing there? Certain that these escapades were more than an ordinary adventure, I became convinced that the exceptional lady was a secret agent. But an early search led me nowhere.

Frustrated in attempts to uncover her, I wrote several other books, yet she still lingered in my mind. At last, I discovered the evidence at the National Archives, where papers stamped "Classified," "Secret," or "Negative Intelligence" produced the proof: the socialite was a spy.

With encouragement from the indomitable Lynn Nesbit and an enthusiastic response from Nan Talese, I began an exciting adventure of investigation and exploration. The coronavirus pandemic stifled my travel, but I trekked and steamered around the world, led by the first woman sent overseas to spy for American Military Intelligence.

Early on, Kris Puopolo came aboard as editor and took on this project with passion and gusto. Her excitement bounded through her emails and along the airwaves from the remote reaches of upstate New York to my desk in New York City. I am grateful to her and all the Doubleday team: Ana Espinoza helped me through my technological limitations; Nora Reichard and the production group, along with Tricia Cave and Lindsay Mandel, showed great enthusiasm in bringing this book to life. My thanks also to Mina Hamedi at Janklow & Nesbit.

I was fortunate to have generous help from new friends and old and am indebted to them for their wise advice and gentle critiques. Susan Richards offered insights and recollections of her great-grandmother Marguerite and her grandfather Tommy. Nancy Harrison was kind enough to share photographs and memories of her grandmother and her father.

Elihu Rose kindly read drafts and provided his expertise on military history in Europe and the Far East. Simon Serfaty offered keen suggestions and tutored me on the Bolshevik Revolution, European relations, and the world in upheaval after the Great War. Judith Kalb saved me from placing St. Petersburg streets and buildings in the center of Moscow and from twisting the spellings of Russian names.

At MoMA Ann Temkin and Starr Figura shed light on Käthe Kollwitz and the Bauhaus. Rajendra Roy and his team graciously made available the original footage of *Grass*. Glenn Lowry, knowledgeable about the great and small, amazed me with his familiarity with the Bakhtiari.

My gratitude to Kai Byrd, who gave me moral support along with help finding research assistants. Gahl Burt connected me with colleagues in Berlin. Mark Stout provided information on Military Intelligence; Suhu Haniolglu furnished obscure facts on Turkey; Dennis Doros, Bahman Maghoudlou, and Patrick Montgomery all offered valuable observations on the making of *Grass*. Carolyn Waters welcomed my inquiries at the New York Society Library.

Sara Lukinson joined me for bottomless cups of tea and endless discussions on music, literature, poetry, and the pleasures and pains of writing. Susan Flamm, Elaine Abelson, Dini von Mueffling, and Ted Sann kept my spirits buoyed.

As always, my sons, David Allyn and Michael Wallach, listened patiently to my plaints. My granddaughter Jordan Allyn taught me to see every day as an adventure. Their love fortified me whenever I felt stymied by the mysterious Mrs. Harrison.

Notes

CHAPTER I: *WILLKOMMEN*

8   peace and order: Harrison, *There's Always Tomorrow* (hereafter cited as *TAT*), 109.

8   Workmen's and Soldiers' Council: Harrison, *TAT*, 109. Based on the Russian Soviet, it was the only body in the city with any authority.

9   first American woman: *Baltimore Sun*, August 31, 1919.

9   droshky: A four-wheeled open carriage with a long bench for seats.

9   *"Gnadige"*: Harrison, *TAT*, 112.

9   "We have won our position": von der Goltz, *Nation in Arms*.

10 Spartacists': Members of the Spartacus League, the German Marxists' organization.

11 "Long live the German Republic!": Schönpflug, *World on Edge*.

11 "wax mightier in our hearts": von der Goltz, *Nation in Arms*.

12 "Long live free Germany!": "Berlin, 1918–1919: Käthe Kollwitz, Witness to History," *New York Review of Books*, October 18, 2015.

12 "We see light": Kollwitz, *Diary and Letters*, 90.

14 "Engine trouble": Harrison, *Baltimore Sun*, May 18, 1918.

14 at a shipbuilding plant: Harrison, "The Story of a Woman Who Worked in a Shipyard," *Baltimore Sun*, May 18, 1918.

15 "my whole life": Harrison, *Baltimore Sun*, May 18, 1918.

15 *Pirates of Penzance:* Harrison, *TAT*, 32–33.

15 Winston Churchill: FBI report, August 12, 1941, FBI file 100 HQ 40298, National Archives and Records Administration (hereafter cited as NARA).

16 "greatest men in the world today": FBI report, August 12, 1941.

16 "idea of Queen Empress": Harrison, *TAT*, 38.

17 she applied to the navy: Up until this time military intelligence was conducted by the navy.

17 "lose my life": Harrison, *TAT*, 90.

17 "take you much farther": Harrison, 20.

17   "as Swiss German": Harrison, Naval Intelligence application, September 15, 1918, RG 165, File PF 39205, Military Intelligence Division files (hereafter cited as MID files), NARA.

18   something for her country: Harrison, Naval Intelligence application.

19   "bagged for sheer sport": Harrison, *TAT*, 46.

19   "I have ever known": Harrison, 48.

20   "safe for democracy": Harrison, 95.

21   "at an end": President Woodrow Wilson, speech to Congress, January 8, 1918.

CHAPTER 2: UNDERCOVER

22   "at their peril": Woodrow Wilson, amplification of the Fourteen Points speech to Congress, February 11, 1918.

24   Charlottenburg: Neighborhood in the western section of Berlin.

25   which name to choose: Harrison, *TAT*, 136.

27   "ally of her husband in the field": de Beaufort, *Behind the German Veil*.

28   behind the new government: Harrison, *TAT*, 115.

28   "the Jewish race": Harrison, 34.

29   in chocolate sauce: Harrison, 119.

29   Red Terror: Russian period of assassinations, mass shootings, and arrests.

29   Deutsche Bund: Harrison, *TAT*, 115.

30   "sometimes witty": Harrison, 129.

31   escaping Allied lips: Harrison, 130.

32   "obtaining credit": Harrison, 142.

33   "not nearly so well off": Harrison, 123.

34   paper shoes: Harrison, 126–27.

34   "going to bed hungry": Harrison, 119.

CHAPTER 3: THE BIRTH OF WEIMAR

36   only female foreign correspondent: Harrison, *TAT*, 158.

37   "obvious sincerity": Harrison, 159.

37   photograph outdoors: *Baltimore Sun*, August 31, 1919.

38   "fine, sane people": Hecht, *Child of the Century*, 282.

40   blown to bits: Harrison, 147–48.

40   "stone a cherry": *Baltimore Sun*, September 17, 1919.

40   give a damn: Schönpflug, *World on Fire*, 155.

41   "His face was a study!": Harrison, *TAT*, 135.

41   "peanut gallery": *Baltimore Sun*, September 14, 1919.

41   continued onstage: *Baltimore Sun*, September 14, 1919.

42   added to the mix: Hecht, *Child of the Century*.

42   "rattling machine guns": Kessler, *Berlin in Lights*.

43   "dam will be broken": Harrison, *TAT*, 167.

43   "treatment by the Allies": *Baltimore Sun*, September 14, 1919.

44   "settled by Americans alone": Henry Cabot Lodge, *Senate and the League*, 227–61.

44   "of the German government": MID files, NARA.

CHAPTER 4: ENTANGLEMENTS

46   "released from a cage": King, *Lady Is a Spy*, 37.

47   "chosen my victim": Harrison, *TAT*, 45.

47   "by my indifference": Harrison, 45

47   "had hysterics": Harrison, 45.

47   his "Mardie" Harrison, 55.

48   ever held in the city: *Baltimore Sun*, June 6, 1901.

49   collapsed in her bed: Harrison, *TAT*, 49. Elizabeth Baker suffered from a chronic thyroid condition.

50   "mournful name": Harrison, *TAT*, 161.

50   proudest achievements: Harrison, 62.

50   "Johns Hopkins": Harrison, 121.

51   "raw materials": Harrison, 66.

52   "Peace of Europe": *Baltimore Evening Sun*, June 29, 1914.

52   "Heir to Austrian Throne": *Washington Post*, June 29, 1914.

52   "with passionate interest": Harrison, *TAT*, 65.

52   "gentle, kind Germans": Harrison, 66.

53   temper tantrums: Harrison, 67.

53   "both of us" Harrison, 11.

53   blind and paralyzed: Harrison, 69.

53   "words he spoke": Harrison, 69.

53   "like that again": Harrison, 70.

55   all raised eyebrows: King, *Lady Is a Spy*, 42–47.

55   "courageous Englishwoman": Kollwitz, *Diary and Letters*, 6.

55   "adroit little snake": King, *Lady Is a Spy*, 39.

55   "kinds of strikes": Harrison, *TAT*, 166.

55   others from the Entente: The Entente was composed of Britain, France, Italy, Russia, Japan, and the United States. It was formed to oppose Germany, Austria-Hungary, Bulgaria, and the Ottoman Empire.

CHAPTER 5: OMINOUS HINTS

58   "German-Polish question": Harrison, *TAT*, 168.

58   down to Silesia: Harrison, 169.

59   "the old imperialism": Harrison, 178.

59   "rising tide": Harrison, 178.

59   "an official report": Harrison, 172.

60   "speak to Colonel Bouvier": Harrison, 173.

60   "with money furnished me": Harrison, 173.

60   "plenty of bedfellows": Harrison, 174.

62   "forerunners of the Brown Shirts": Harrison, 168.

63   "ugly frame of mind": Harrison, 175.

63   its overthrow: Harrison, 184.

64   "in your memories": Schönpflug, *World on Edge*, 161.

64   "the Jewish problem": Harrison, *TAT*, 177.

64   "overlordship of the Jews": Harrison, 181.

65   "brown shirt meetings": Harrison, 186.

65   two hundred million rubles: *Baltimore Sun*, March 12, 1919.

CHAPTER 6: SPIDER'S WEB

67   high on the list: Van Deman, *Final Memoranda*, 84–85.

67   combat the Bolsheviks: Talbert, *Negative Intelligence*, 155.

67   *Why American Soldiers:* Talbert, 154.

68   "could not be missed": Harrison to Churchill, October 10, 1919, MID files, NARA.

69   weakness of their army: Harrison, *TAT*, 194.

69   "and no jubilation": Harrison, 195.

70   "led him to believe": Harrison, 197.

70   incriminating evidence: Harrison, 197.

71   "under her petticoat": Harrison, 198.

71   "stand in politics": Harrison, 197.

72   "Women of Germany": Harrison, 192.

72   "sap has dried up in me": *Berlin in Lights: The Diaries of Count Harry Kessler*, June 22, 1919.

72   "prefer my bacon": Harrison, *TAT*, 192.

74   "passionate devotion": Harrison, 9.

74   "dared not think": Harrison, 104.

74   details on his shirt cuff: "Catonsville" Wise, *Catonsville*.

75      $150,000: *Baltimore Sun*, August 23, 1919.

75   "intolerance": Harrison, *TAT*, 209.

76   "I had experienced": Harrison, 210.

76   "exceptionally good service": William Hurley, secret memo to Ambassador Winslow in London, April 17, 1920, stating, "She is long known to M.I. having rendered exceptionally good services with A.E.F. and is known to be highly reputable and exceedingly efficient."

76   "equipped for it": Colonel David to Director for MI, July 30, 1919, MID files, NARA.

76   "flux and change": Harrison, *TAT*, 210.

76   "breathless interest": Harrison, 210.

CHAPTER 7: AGENT B

79   "champion of Causes": Harrison, *TAT*, 299.

81   Why did men fear it?: Harrison, 211.

81   cypher tables: Memo on ciphers, October 22, 1919, MID files, NARA.

82   around her corseted waist: Harrison, *TAT*, 284.

83   headed for slaughter: Harrison, 15.

83   across the deck: Harrison, 15.

83   "keen sportsman": Harrison, 55.

83   "Mardie": Harrison, 52.

84   "playmates and comrades": Harrison, 52.

84   revolution in America: Harrison, report to MI marked "Negative," SS *Adriatic*, October 28, 1918, MID files, NARA.

85   "in the dark": Harrison, report to MI marked "Negative."

85   Associated Press: Harrison, *TAT*, 213.

86   four empires: Germany, Austria-Hungary, Ottoman, Russia.

86   "back by Easter": Harrison, *TAT*, 220.

CHAPTER 8: INTO THE UNKNOWN

88   "ideals and ambitions": Harrison, *TAT*, 223.

88   "in abundance": Harrison, 223.

89   Poland was *Popsuta:* Harrison, 225.

89   "until further notice": War Department Telegram, Coxe to Miles November 26, 1919 MID files, NARA.

89   information to the Poles: Harrison, *TAT*, 229.

90   life in Poland: Letter to Frank Burke, Bureau of Investigation, Department of Justice, January 27, 1920, MID files, NARA.

90   "friction was inevitable": Harrison, *TAT*, 236.

90   "pogroms in Poland": Van Deman, *Final Memoranda*, 94.

90   "something of my boy": Harrison to Dear Friend, December 1919, MID files, NARA.

91   grant her permission: Harrison, *TAT*, 250.

92   "stone floor": Harrison, 252.

93   "the Soviet government": Harrison, *Marooned in Moscow* (hereafter cited as *MIM*), 35.

CHAPTER 9: A CLEVER WOMAN

94   the foreign office: Harrison, *MIM*, 58.

95   "all your papers": Harrison, 58.

96   "complete social upheaval": Harrison, *TAT*, 278.

96   she was safe: Harrison, 279.

97   "political meetings": Harrison, 282.

98   found "appalling": Harrison, 289.

98   "our dolly": Harrison, 289.

99   "chic and charming": Harrison, 296.

99   "law of eugenics": Harrison, 296.

100   "very clever": Berkman, *Bolshevik Myth*.

100   "sweet-tempered person": Harrison, *MIM*, 149.

101   "anyone else with bombs": Harrison, 149.

101   "day of my life": Berkman, *Bolshevik Myth.*

102   "middle-class businessman": Harrison, *TAT,* 294.

102   "sure of himself": Harrison, 294.

103   "bobbing up and down": Harrison, *MIM,* 81.

103   "sleep in their shawls": Harrison, 91.

104   "anything she pleases": Harrison, 92.

104   "plucky": McCullagh, *Prisoner of the Reds.*

105   "That's Trotsky": Harrison, *TAT,* 304.

106   kissed it: Harrison, 306.

106   was worth it: Harrison, 306.

CHAPTER 10: SAFE DREAMS

107   "of the drama": Harrison, "The Bolos and the Arts," *The Bookman: Review
        of Books and Life,* December 1923.

107   "amusing companion": Harrison, *TAT,* 300.

108   "our Soviet epoch": Chantal Sundaram, *Manufacturing Culture.*

108   "than the ensemble": Harrison, *Bookman,* December 1923.

108   professional pianist: Author interview with Nancy Harrison, Marguerite's
        granddaughter, December 2018.

109   "dream of my life": Harrison, *Bookman,* December 1923.

109   "news in the Truth": Harrison, *TAT,* 314.

110   three thousand rubles: Harrison, *MIM,* 158.

110   "bizarre and somewhat bewildering": Harrison, *Bookman,* December 1923.

111   "bizarre effects": Harrison, *Bookman,* December 1923.

111   "monstrously decadent": Harrison, *Bookman,* December 1923.

111   "under the sun": Harrison, *TAT,* 299.

112   "through that country": A. B. Coxe to William Hurley, memorandum,
        April 26, 1920, MID files, NARA.

112   "You are arrested": Harrison, *TAT,* 308.

112   "insure your lfe": Harrison, 309.

113   "point of view": Harrison, 309.

113   "suspense was trying": Harrison, 310.

113   "American Secret Service": Harrison, 310.

114   "What is your proof": Harrison, 311.

114   "your own attitude": Harrison, 311.

114   "Certainly not": Harrison, 312.

115   "useful you are to us": Harrison, 312.

115   "your proposition": Harrison, 313.

CHAPTER 11: NIGHTMARE

116   *koshmar:* Same as French *cauchemar.*

116   discovered at the Kremlin: Memo, April 14, 1920, from Berlin to Washing-
        ton, MID files, NARA.

116   foreign bank notes: Confidential memo to London, November 26, 1920, MID files, NARA.

117   "will not last long": Hurley to Coxe, memo, April 27, 1920, MID files, NARA.

117   "known of her": Joseph Ames to General Churchill, April 13, 1920, MID files, NARA.

118   "upon her for guidance": Coxe to Ames, April 16, 1920, MID files, NARA.

118   "at four o'clock": Harrison, *TAT*, 315.

118   "Any news": Harrison, 315.

118   "You be first wife": Harrison, *MIM*, 196.

119   Austrian officer: Cheka files, Central Archive of the Federal Security Bureau, Moscow.

119   "quite limp": Harrison, *TAT*, 316.

119   "not cruel or bloodthirsty": Harrison, 316.

119   "sort of camaraderie": Harrison, 316.

120   "back to Lubyanka": Harrison, 320.

120   "yielded to despair": Harrison, 320.

121   "Revolutionary light": Emma Goldman to Maxim Gorky, Goldman, *Living My Life*, chapter 52.

121   "sympathetic soul": Harrison, *TAT*, 325.

122   human dignity: Harrison, 324.

122   "much better American": Harrison, *MIM*, 150.

122   "impartial listener": Harrison, 147.

123   protection money: Harrison, 160.

123   sweet Russian pastries: Harrison, 163.

124   toothpaste and soap: Harrison, *TAT*, 338.

124   high-level positions: Harrison, 323.

124   "free citizen": Harrison, 323.

124   her own trial: Harrison, *MIM*, 114.

125   Bolshevik life: Harrison, 109.

125   brilliant leadership: Harrison, 109.

125   to every Russian: Harrison, 109.

126   life in America: Harrison, 112.

126   "I am a soldier": Cockfield, *Russia's Iron General*, 329.

126   "get ourselves out": Harrison, *MIM*, 111.

126   Marguerite was interrogated: Cheka files.

127   political situation: Harrison, *MIM*, 215.

127   material for Washington: Memo from military attaché in London to director of MID, June 21, 1920, MID files, NARA.

CHAPTER 12: SHOCK

128   Vladimir Lenin: Harrison, *TAT*, 329.

130   handed to Marguerite: Harrison, 329.

130   reason for her visit: Harrison, 330.

131   "a good chance": Harrison, 330.

131   "double-cross the Cheka": Harrison, 329.

131   "their opinions": Harrison, 330.

132   her British counterparts: Harrison, 331.

132   "air we breathed": Russell, *Autobiography*.

133   "political views": Harrison, *TAT*, 331.

133   the riverboat: Harrison, 335.

133   "to escape from Russia": Russell, *Autobiography*.

133   slap in the face: Harrison, *TAT*, 332.

134   "Mrs. Stan Harding": Harrison, 337.

134   the right effect: Harrison, 337.

CHAPTER 13: A BRAVE FRONT

135   "out of this mess": Harrison, *TAT*, 341.

135   "beyond words": Harrison, 341.

135   "you are arrested": Harding, *Underworld of State*, 64–65.

136   "without speaking to her": Harrison, *TAT*, 343.

137   "cake of soap": Harrison, *MIM*, 217.

137   Red Cross ball: Harrison, *TAT*, 349.

138   "pipe and tobacco": Harrison, 348.

138   back in prison: Harrison, 351.

139   "Eugene Debs": H. M. Brailsford to Joseph Ames, October 25, 1920, MID files, NARA.

139   "very intelligent": Harrison, Cheka files.

140   again and again: Cheka files.

140   "look bad for 'B' ": MID files, NARA.

141   "kept in prison": Harrison, *MIM*, 114.

142   "fair-minded person": Harrison, 223.

142   "dazzled by her": Harrison, *MIM*, 223.

142   thirty-three years old: Louise Bryant, "The Last Days with John Reed," *Liberator*, February 1921.

143   "on American soil": Harrison, *MIM*, 224.

CHAPTER 14: ORDERS

144   tall Cheka caps: Harrison, *TAT*, 352.

145   dreaded Lubyanka: Harrison, *MIM*, 229.

145   they scoffed: Harrison, 229.

145   to be asleep: Harrison, 230.

145   Prisoner 2961: Harrison, *TAT*, 359.

146   Rabelais and Voltaire: Harrison, 366.

146   "deserves a trial": Harrison, 361.

146   "won't need that": Harrison, 361.

147   solitary confinement: Harrison, 234.

147   waiting for the end: Harrison, 363.

147   "fortune of war": Harrison, *MIM*, 235.
148   "spiritually limitless": Harrison, *TAT*, 363.
148   "have to tell me?" Harrison, *MIM*, 239.
149   grilled her for hours: Harrison, *TAT*, 366.
149   "counterrevolutionary activities": Cheka files. Central Archives of the Federal Security Bureau, Moscow. Moscow.
150   tapered coffin: Harrison, *TAT*, 367.
150   "in Russia": Harrison, 368.
151   way to pray: Harrison, 371.
151   "scissors could be put": Harrison, 373.
152   "some hairpins": Cheka files.
152   secret message: Harrison, *TAT*, 420.
153   laughing and left: Harrison, 377.
153   cell next door: Harrison, 376.
153   "I won't go": Harrison, 378.
154   "came crowding back": Harrison, 384.
154   Virgin Mary: Harrison, 386.
155   each of their pillows: Harrison, 388.
156   The letter was signed: Chicherin to Ames, April 26, 1921, MID files, NARA.
157   "pluck and morale": Riga to Washington, memo, April 29, 1921.
157   ask his superiors: Harrison, *TAT*, 405.
157   comprised the Novinksy: Harrison, 406.

CHAPTER 15: *DO SVIDANYA*

158   tea and a bed: Harrison, *TAT*, 408.
158   she could hope for: Harrison, *MIM*, 277.
159   "being fond of her": Harrison, *TAT*, 413.
159   "in penal institutions": Harrison, 415.
159   try to see her: Harrison, *MIM*, 292.
160   secure her freedom: Harrison, 292.
160   revealing any more: Harrison, 294.
160   "very close, indeed": Harrison, *TAT*, 414.
160   to another prison: Harrison, 419.
161   in a few days: Harrison, 421.
161   "under different conditions": Harrison, 421.
161   "approaching real Socialism": Harrison, 421.
162   clownish shoes: Harrison, 423.
163   in a Russian prison: Harrison, 424.
163   "out of her convent": Harrison, 425.
163   "modernizing Russia": Harrison, *MIM*, 298.
163   secretary of state: Gray to Secretary of State, August 2, 1921, MID files, NARA.
164   at great risk: Harrison, *TAT*, 424.
164   attention to her answers: Young, *Surgeon's Autobiography*, 455.

164 easily have forgotten: Harrison, memo, August 4, 1921, MID files, NARA.
165 left for London: Harrison, memo.
165 embraced in silence: Harrison, *TAT,* 428.
165 "the Harding regime": Harrison, 433.
166 published in the *Sun: Baltimore Sun,* October 1921.
167 chief of staff: Harrison, *TAT,* 431.
167 she would never return: Harrison, 433.
167 Asia into Europe: Harrison, 436.

CHAPTER 16: CHANGES

171 Naval Armaments: *New York Times,* October 2, 1977.
171 growing arms race: Washington Naval Conference 1921–1922, Office of the Historian Milestones, history.state.gov.
172 "preparing for it": Andelman, *Shattered Peace,* 281.
172 "has yet seen": Andelman, 281.
172 "is to disarm": "The Limitation of Naval Armaments," *Atlantic,* February 1922.
173 go to college: He felt he was too old to attend Princeton and was angry that he had been sent to school in Switzerland. Author interview with Nancy Harrison.
174 write up a report: Agent Starr, Department of Justice, Bureau of Investigation, New York, December 21, 1921, FBI files, NARA.
175 "to be a cowboy": Harrison, *TAT,* 438.
176 "I referred to": MID files, NARA.
177 "interests of the United States": Fath, *Intrepidity, Iron Will.*
177 in the Far East: MID files, NARA.
178 as a spy: Harrison, *TAT,* 431.
179 being a Jew: Harrison, 141.
179 "'supreme' in Asia": Harrison, 441.

CHAPTER 17: DRAGONS AND BEARS

180 "eighteenth century prints": Harrison, *TAT,* 445.
181 Major Winder: Harrison, *TAT,* 446–47.
181 report it to Washington: Burnett to Washington, memo, August 13, 1922.
182 "acting collectively": Harrison, *TAT,* 449.
182 "appealed to me": Harrison, *Red Bear,* 27.
183 "conditions on the spot": Harrison, 63.
183 more than two years: Harrison, 63.
184 "and weak tea": Harrison, *TAT,* 454.
184 destroyed her film: Harrison, lecture, 1942, FBI files, NARA.
184 "no matter what": Chekhov, *Sakhalin Island.*
185 "in New York": Harrison, *Red Bear,* 67.
185 could have been worse: Harrison, 70.
185 "more unique experience": Harrison, 73.

185   "this guarded smile": Einstein, *Travel Diaries.*
186   "by force if necessary": Harrison, *TAT,* 457.
186   "leaves tomorrow": Harrison, *Red Bear,* 74.
187   that had taken place: Harrison, *TAT,* 459.
187   "on Russian soil": Harrison, 459.
187   "it will be worse": Harrison, *Red Bear,* 83.
188   "hardships and adventure!" Harrison, *TAT,* 462.
189   "kiss me quick": Harrison, 465.
189   on the floor: Harrison, *Red Bear,* 91.
189   "to know everything": Harrison, 92.
190   "Far Eastern Republic": Harrison, 94.
191   "wildflowers": Harrison, *TAT,* 471.
191   "do without them": Harrison, 476.
192   RED AGENT: *Japan Advertiser,* August 24, 2022.
192   "emotions and enthusiasm": D. C. Poole to Phillips, memo, August 31,
      1922, MID files, NARA.
193   set her free: Harrison, *TAT,* 479.
193   "of shifting overnight": Harrison, *Red Bear,* 112.
193   "as a soap bubble!" Harrison, *TAT,* 483.
194   woman informed her: Harrison, *Red Bear,* 121.
194   "Siberia went Red": Harrison, 123.
194   "at Vladivostok": Harrison, 124.

CHAPTER 18: A STIFF UPPER LIP

196   "into a well": Harrison, *Red Bear,* 136.
197   ever to interview him: Harrison, *TAT,* 493.
197   "very much mistaken": Harrison, *Red Bear,* 138.
198   gloomy hotel: Harrison, 138.
198   ex-wife and daughter: Harrison, 141.
198   allowed in also: Harrison, *TAT,* 499.
198   "intrigue in the Far East": Harrison, *Red Bear,* 143.
199   rest of the night: Harrison, *TAT,* 495.
200   "with one another": Somerset Maugham, *Chinese Screen,* 32.
200   stalk the earth: Andrews, *Heart of Asia.*
201   red lips: Harrison, *Red Bear,* 149.
201   "Chinese politics": Harrison, 151.
201   "very long time": Franck, *Wandering in Northern China,* viii.
202   "for centuries": Harrison, *Red Bear,* 269.
202   "will eventually win": Harrison, 268.
203   "I yielded": Harrison, *TAT,* 500.
204   "the Gobi Desert": Harrison, "Russia Under the Bolsheviks."
204   Walk in peace: Harrison, *TAT,* 505.
205   celibate men: Harrison, 575.
205   "not particularly odiferous": Harrison, 575.
205   "the same space": Andrews, *Under a Lucky Star,* chap. 16.

206   "Catherine the Great": Harrison, *Red Bear,* 200.

206   "road was on me": Harrison, 200.

207   "phosphorescent green eyes": Harrison, *TAT,* 522.

207   "rubber tub": Harrison, 525.

207   "to go home!": Harrison, 529.

208   "just beginning": Harrison, *Red Bear,* 223.

209   thick black veil: Cheka files.

209   "You are arrested": Harrison, *Red Bear,* 228.

209   "when you get there": Harrison, 229.

209   "stiff upper lip": Harrison, *TAT,* 538.

210   "revived against me": Harrison, 539.

CHAPTER 19: RETURN

211   in secret: Harrison, *TAT,* 540.

212   at Delmonico's: Harrison, *Red Bear,* 231.

212   "afraid anymore": Harrison, *TAT,* 540.

212   "anything so horrible": Harrison, 541.

213   "ghastly experience": Harrison, 542. The illness was diagnosed by a doctor
       as erysipelas.

214   softened her ways: Harrison, 545.

214   "as my roommates": Harrison, 545.

215   until she died: Harrison, 551.

215   Far Eastern Republic: Harrison, 552.

215   "she is a spy": Cheka files.

217   "Au revoir, madame": Harrison, *TAT,* 553.

217   sent to Siberia: Harrison, 555.

217   "old man of the sea": Harrison, 556.

218   He smiled: Harrison, *Red Bear,* 249.

218   edition of *Vogue:* Harrison, 255.

218   "new despotism": Harrison, *TAT,* 560.

218   "ruthlessly suppressed": Harrison, 561.

218   Mogilevsky again: Mogilevsky died in a plane crash in the Caucasus in
       1925.

CHAPTER 20: SOMEWHERE, ANYWHERE

221   "never to be forgotten": Harrison, *Asia Reborn,* 102.

223   "footage they shot": Maghdsoulou, *Grass: Untold Stories;* Cooper, inter-
       view by Brownlow, 120.

223   "get away again": Harrison, *TAT,* 366.

223   "connected with her": Ames to Christian Herter, March 28, 2934, MID
       files, NARA.

224   wanted her own name cleared: Newsome to Hurley, Confidential State
       Department memo, March 5, 1923, MID files, NARA.

224   "get no help": Maugham, *Ashenden.*

225   "Ruhr for myself": Harrison, *TAT,* 563.

226   "led to Hitlerism": Harrison, 564.

226   "face of the earth": Harrison, 564.

226   "the next time": Ames to Herter, March 28, 1923, MID files, NARA.

226   "irresistible": Harrison, *TAT,* 565

228   reserves of oil: Harrison, 567.

229   get in the way: Schoedsack, interview by Brownlow.

229   "they were never personal": Harrison, *TAT,* 572.

230   more romantic: Harrison, 577.

230   "with a vengeance": Harrison, 576.

231   "domes and minarets": Cooper, *Grass.*

232   "in its history": Harrison, *Travel* magazine, October 1924.

232   little information: Harrison, *TAT,* 578.

234   "choked to death": Harrison, 582.

234   celebrated Christmas: Cooper, *Things Men Die For,* 72–74.

235   "still in the heavens": "Whirling Dervishes," *Asia* 24, 541–43.

235   "jailbirds": Harrison, *TAT,* 583.

236   "its hospitality": Harrison, 584.

236   "It was snowing!": Cooper, *Grass,* 110.

236   "in snow drifts": Harrison, *TAT,* 586.

237   and galloped away: Harrison, 588.

237   "moth-eaten lot": Harrison, 589.

238   "picture unbelievable": Cooper and Schoedsack, interview by Brownlow, YouTube.

CHAPTER 21: FRIENDSHIP

239   their kitchen refrigerator: Wallach, *Desert Queen,* 181.

239   "in the world": Wilson, "Bakhtiaris."

240   "peace with them": Wallach, *Desert Queen,* 197.

240   "in my life": *New York Times,* June 1926.

241   "official blush": Gertrude Bell to Hugh Bell.

241   "great success": Gertrude Bell to Hugh Bell, March 16, 1924.

242   "wharf at Kut": *New York Times Magazine,* March 1, 1925.

CHAPTER 22: WILD MEN

243   "bloodthirsty": Layard, *Early Adventures in Persia,* 343.

244   "at his camp": Harrison, *TAT,* 597.

244   music on Broadway: Harrison, 598.

244   pay any duties: Harrison, 599.

245   "ate ravenously": Harrison, 599.

246   "call them 'Bears'": Harrison, 603.

247   "peace and contentment": Harrison, 606.

247   "feeling fatigued": Harrison, 606.

247   "I had forgotten!": Harrison, 606.

248   all for himself: Harrison, 606.

248   his forceful jaw: Harrison, 606.

249   impression was isolation: Sackville-West, *Twelve Days,* 90.

249   "cast iron pancakes": *New York Times,* August 31, 1924.

250   "place of women": Harrison, *TAT,* 612.

250   "can do that": Cooper, *Grass,* 146.

250   "recovered completely": Harrison, *TAT,* 616.

251   "patients died": Harrison, 617.

CHAPTER 23: WHERE THE SOUL FLOWS

253   five thousand miles away: Harrison, *TAT,* 622.

253   synonymous with "robber": Maghsoudlou, *Grass,* 198.

254   "the opposite bank": Harrison, *TAT,* 622.

255   "have ever seen": Cooper, *Grass,* 204.

255   "always heeded": Harrison, *TAT,* 624.

256   "debt of gratitude": Harrison, 572.

256   "my morale": Harrison, 573.

257   "shoot him dead": Harrison, 625.

257   the next day: Harrison, 626.

258   "no bananas today": Cooper, *Grass,* 250.

259   "decent feeling": Harrison, *TAT,* 628.

CHAPTER 24: DISILLUSION

261   "stood still for two thousand years": Harrison, *TAT,* 635.

263   "altogether delightful": *New York Times,* December 6, 1926.

263   "ancestral memories": Harrison, *TAT,* 643.

264   "faiths and races": Harrison, 646.

264   "taken their places": Harrison, 646.

264   "not yet begun": Harrison, 647.

264   "confirmed wanderer": Harrison, 647.

264   "in the world": Harrison, 651.

CHAPTER 25: TRANSFORMATION

267   a bad mother: Harrison, *TAT,* 647.

267   life of their own: *Washington Evening Star,* October 3, 1924.

267   "natural manner": Harrison, *TAT,* 648.

268   "collaborate with them": Harrison, 648.

268   "ever produced": *New York Herald Tribune,* April 5, 1925.

268   "motion picture camera": Vaz, *Living Dangerously,* 136.

268   in the desert: Harrison, *TAT,* 650.

269   Barnard College: Zanglein, *The Girl Explorers.*

269   scientific world: Harrison, *TAT,* 650.

270   "a thing apart": Harrison, 652.

270   "I had no share": Harrison, 651.
271   "touch me again": Harrison, 651.
271   never occurred to her: Harrison, 652.
271   or in Asia: Harrison, 651.
271   "or ignored": Harrison, 652.
273   "soul has found peace": Harrison, 664.
273   "climate and geography": Harrison, *Asia Reborn*, 1.
273   drank too much: Author interview with Susan Richards, Marguerite's great-granddaughter, October 19, 2022.
276   "how the rise and fall": Harrison, *TAT*, 23.

Bibliography

ARCHIVAL SOURCES

American Relief Administration, Russian operational records, Hoover Institution Archives, Stanford University Archives.

Kevin Brownlow Collection, Harold B. Lee Library, Brigham Young University, Provo, Utah.

Cheka Files P47767, P28578, Central Archive of the Federal Security Bureau, Moscow, Russia.

Department of State RG 59, National Archives and Records Administration (NARA), College Park, Maryland.

Federal Bureau of Investigation Files 00-HQ-40298, Marguerite Elton Baker Harrison Blake.

National Archives and Records Administration (NARA), College Park, Maryland.

Maryland Historical Society, Baltimore, Maryland.

Military Intelligence Division Record Group 165, National Archives and Records Administration (NARA), College Park, Maryland.

Museum of Modern Art Film Library, New York, New York.

Society of Women Geographers records, Library of Congress, Washington, DC.

PUBLISHED WORKS BY MARGUERITE HARRISON

Asia Reborn. New York: Harper & Brothers, 1928.

Fair Play for Russia. Pamphlet, Foreign Policy Association, May 1922.

Heart of Asia. New York: Duell, Sloan and Pearce, 1952.

Marooned in Moscow: The Story of an American Woman Imprisoned in Russia. New York: George H. Doran, 1921.

Red Bear or Yellow Dragon. New York: George H. Doran, 1924.

"Russia Under the Bolsheviks," *Annals of the American Academy of Political and Social Science* 100 (March 1922): 1–4.

There's Always Tomorrow: The Story of a Checkered Life. New York: Farrar & Rinehart, 1935.

Unfinished Tales from a Russian Prison. New York: George H. Doran, 1923.

BOOKS AND ARTICLES

Amory, Copley. *Persian Days*. New York: Houghton Mifflin, 1929.

Andelman, David A. *A Shattered Peace*. Hoboken, NJ: Wiley, 2008.

Andrews, Roy Chapman. *Across Mongolian Plains*. New York: Appleton, 1921.

———. *Under a Lucky Star*. Garden City, NY: Blue Ribbon Books, 1945.

Anglein, Jayne. *The Girl Explorers*. Chicago: Sourcebooks, 2021.

Baedeker, Karl. *Berlin and Its Environs*. Leipzig: Baedeker, 1908.

Balabanoff, Angelica. *My Life as a Rebel*. New York: Greenwood Press, 1968.

Berkman, Alexander. *The Bolshevik Myth*. New York: Boni and Liveright, 925.

Bidwell, Bruce. *History of the Military Intelligence Division, Department of the Army General Staff: 1775–1941*. Frederick, MD: University Publications of America, 1986.

Bird, Isabella L. *Journeys in Persia and Kurdistan by Mrs. Bishop*. London: John Murray, 1891.

Brownlow, Kevin. *"I'm King Kong!": The Exploits of Merian C. Cooper*, documentary, 2005.

Bryant, Louise. *Mirrors of Moscow*. New York: Thomas Selzer, 1923.

Cashman, Sean Dennis. *America in the Gilded Age*. New York: New York University Press, 1993.

Chekhov, Anton. *Sakhalin Island*. London: One World Classics, 2007.

Churchill, Major Marlborough. "'MID' and How It Works." *American Consular Bulletin*, vol. IV, no. 3, Washington DC, March 1922.

Cockfield, Jamie H. *Russia's Iron General: The Life of Alexsei A. Brusilov*. Lanham, MD: Lexington Books, 2019.

Cooper, Merian C. *Grass*. New York: G. P. Putnam's Sons, 1925.

———. *Things Men Die For*. New York: G. P. Putnam's Sons, 1927.

———, and Ernest Schoedsack, prod. and dir. *Grass: A Nation's Battle for Life*, 1925.

Creel, George. *How We Advertised America*. New York: Harper Brothers, 1920.

Curzon, George N. *Persia and the Persian Question*. London: Longmans, Green, and Company, 1892.

Dallin, David J. *Soviet Espionage*. New Haven, CT: Yale University Press, 1955.

Dalrymple, William. *In Xanadu*. London: Flamingo, 1990.

Davidann, Jon Thares. *Cultural Diplomacy in US-Japanese Relations 1919–1941*. New York: Palgrave MacMillan, 2007.

de Beaufort, M. *Behind the German Veil*. New York: Dodd Mead, 1917.

Dickinson, Frederick. *World War I and the Triumph of a New Japan*. Cambridge: Cambridge University Press, 2013.

Dillon, E. J. *The Inside Story of the Peace Conference*. New York: Harper & Brothers, 1920.

Dwight, H. G. *Constantinople and Istanbul: Old and New*. New York: Kegan Paul, 2002.

Einstein, Albert. *The Travel Diaries of Albert Einstein 1922–1923*. Edited by Zev Rosenkranz. Princeton, NJ: Princeton University Press, 2018.

Elon, Amos. *The Pity of It All*. New York: Metropolitan Books, 2002.

Fath, Matthew H. *Intrepidity, Iron Will and Intellect: General Robert L. Eichelberger and Military Genius*. Verdun Press, 2015.

Fithian, Floyd J. "Dollars without the Flag: The Case of Sinclair and Sakhalin Oil." *Pacific Historical Review* 39, no. 2 (May 1970): 205–22.

Francis, David R. *Russia from the American Embassy*. New York: Scribner's Sons, 1921.

Franck, Harry. *Wandering in Northern China*. New York: Century, 1923.

Freely, John. *Istanbul*. New York: Penguin Books, 1998.

Gay, Peter. *Weimar Culture: The Outsider as Insider*. New York: Norton, 2001.

Goldman, Emma. *Living My Life*. New York: Knopf, 1931.

Griggs, Catherine M. *Beyond Boundaries: The Adventurous Life of Marguerite Harrison*. PhD diss. (unpublished), George Washington University, 1996.

Haffner, Sebastian. *Defying Hitler*. New York: Picador, 2000.

Hall, Clayton Colman, ed. *Baltimore: Biography*. New York: Lewis Historical Publishing Co., 1912.

Hanioglu, M. Sukru. *Preparation for a Revolution: The Young Turks 1902–1908*. New York: Oxford University Press, 2001.

Harding, Stan. *Underworld of State*. London: Allen & Unwin, 1925.

Hastings, Selina. *The Secret Lives of Somerset Maugham: A Biography*. New York: Arcade Publishing, 2009.

Hecht, Ben. *A Child of the Century*. New York: Donald I. Fine, 1985.

Heilbrun, Carolyn G. *Reinventing Womanhood*. New York: Norton, 1979.

Herter, C. A. "The Paris Peace Conference, 1919." *Military Intelligence Reports on Political Conditions in Germany*. Papers Relating to the Foreign Relations of the United States, vol. 12, Parispeaceconf.862.00/344. Available at https://history.state.gov/historicaldocuments/frus1919Parisv12/ch3.

Hicks, Granville. *John Reed: The Making of a Revolutionary*. New York: Macmillan, 1936.

Higham, John. *Strangers in the Land*. New York: Atheneum, 1963.

Hodder, Edwin, and Lt. Col. C. M. MacGregor. *Simla*. London: Forgotten Books, 1871.

Hole, Frank, and Sekandar Amanolahi-Baharvand. *Tribal Pastoralists in Transition: The Baharvand of Luristan, Iran*. Ann Arbor: University of Michigan Press, 2021.

Hutton, Marcilline. *Resilient Russian Women in the 1920s and 1930s*. Lincoln, NE: Zea Books, 2015.

James, Henry. *The American Scene*. New York: Penguin, 1994.

———. *The Portrait of a Lady*. London: Penguin Books, 1984.

Johnson, Thomas M. *Our Secret War: True American Spy Stories 1917–1919*. Indianapolis, IN: Bobbs-Merrill, 1929.

Jones, Howard. *Crucible of Power: A History of U.S. Foreign Relations Since 1897.* Lanham, MD: Rowman & Littlefield, 2001.

Jones, Mark. *Founding Weimar: Violence and the German Revolution of 1918–1919.* Cambridge: Cambridge University Press, 2016.

Kahn, David. *The Reader of Gentlemen's Mail.* New Haven, CT: Yale University Press, 2004.

Kessler, Count Harry. *Berlin in Lights: The Diaries of Count Harry Kessler.* New York: Grove Press, 2002.

King, Melanie. *The Lady Is a Spy.* London: Ashgrove Publishing, 2019.

Kinghorn, Jonathan. *The Atlantic Transport Line.* Jefferson, NC: McFarland, 2012.

Knightley, Phillip. *The First Casualty: The War Correspondent as Hero and Myth Maker.* Baltimore: Johns Hopkins University Press, 2004.

Koch, Scott A. "The Role of U.S. Army Military Attachés Between the World Wars." *Studies in Intelligence* 38, no. 5.

Kollwitz, Käthe. *The Diary and Letters of Kaethe Kollwitz,* edited by Hans Kollwitz, translated by Richard and Clara Winston. Evanston, IL: Northwestern University Press, 1955.

Larson, Erik. *Dead Reckoning.* New York: Penguin Random House, 2015.

Layard, Austin Henry. *Early Adventures in Persia, Susiana and Babylonia,* vol 1. London: John Murray, 1887.

Leong, Sow-Thong. *Sino-Soviet Diplomatic Relations 1917–1926.* Canberra: Australian National University Press, 1976.

Lodge, Henry Cabot. *The Senate and the League of Nations.* New York: Charles Scribner's Sons, 1925.

Lorenz, Edward. *The New Mediterranean Traveler.* New York: Fleming H. Revell, 1922.

MacAdams, William. *Ben Hecht: A Biography.* New York: Charles Scribner's Sons, 1990.

MacMillan, Margaret. *Paris 1919.* New York: Random House, 2003
———. *The War That Ended Peace.* New York: Random House, 2013.

Maghsoudlou, Bahman. *Grass: Untold Stories.* Costa Mesa, CA: Mazda, 2009.

Manners and Social Usages. New York: Harper & Brothers, 1887.

Maugham, W. Somerset. *Ashenden: Or the British Agent.* London: Heinemann, 1961.
———. *On a Chinese Screen.* London: Heinemann, 1922.
———. *A Writer's Notebook.* London: Heinemann, 1915.

McCullagh, Francis. *A Prisoner of the Reds: The Story of a British Officer Captured in Siberia.* New York: Dutton, 1922.

McNaughton, James C. *The Army in the Pacific: A Century of Engagement.* Washington, DC: Center of Military History, 2012.

Mencken, H. L. *Thirty-Five Years of Newspaper Work.* Edited by Fred Hobson, Vincent Fitzpatrick, and Bradford Jacobs. Baltimore: Johns Hopkins University Press, 1994.

Miller, Nathan. *Spying for America: The Hidden History of U.S. Intelligence.* New York: Paragon, 1989.

Moser, Michael J. *Foreigners Within the Gates.* New York: Oxford University Press, 1993.

Noble, H. G. S. *The New York Stock Exchange in the Crisis of 1914*. Garden City, NY: Country Life Press, 1915.

———. *The Second Oldest Profession: Spies and Spying in the Twentieth Century.* New York: Norton, 1987.

Olds, Elizabeth Fagg. *Women of the Four Winds*. Boston: Houghton Mifflin, 1985.

Papers Relating to the Foreign Relations of the United States, Publication no. 894. Washington DC: Government Printing Office, 1921, 1923.

Paterson, Thomas, et al. *War, Peace and Revolution in the Time of Wilson 1914–1920*, vol. 1. Boston: Cengage Learning, 2015.

Paterson, Thomas, et al. *American Foreign Relations: To 1920*, vol 1. Boston: Cengage Learning, 2015.

Pipes, Richard. *Russia under the Bolshevik Regime*. New York: Knopf, 1993.

Posse, Nils. *Handbook of School Gymnastics of the Swedish System*. Boston: Lothrop, Lee and Shepard, 1902.

Powell, E. Alexander. *By Camel and Car to the Peacock Throne*. New York: Century Company, 1923.

Pray, Eleanor L. *Letters from Vladisvostok 1894–1930*. Seattle: University of Washington Press, 2013.

Pritchett, V. S. *A Pritchett Century*. New York: Modern Library, 1997.

Ramsay, Alex. *The Peking Who's Who 1922*. Tientsin Press, 1922.

Randall, Steven J. *United States Foreign Oil Policy Since World War I*. Montreal: McGill-Queen's University Press, 2005.

Reinsch, Paul. *An American Diplomat in China*. New York: Doubleday, Page, 1922.

Remarque, Erich Maria. *The Road Back*. New York: Random House, 2013.

Rhodri, Jeffreys-Jones. *In Spies We Trust: The Story of Western Intelligence*. Oxford: Oxford University Press, 2013.

Richards, Susan. *Chosen by a Horse*. New York: Harcourt, 2006.

———. *Saddled: How a Spirited Horse Reined Me In and Set Me Free*. Boston: Houghton Mifflin Harcourt, 2010.

Rohmer, Sax. *The Insidious Dr. Fu Manchu*. New York: Mc Bride, 1913.

Root, Elihu, James Brown Scott, and Robert Bacon. *The United States and the War: Mission to Russia; Political Addresses*. Boston: Harvard University Press, 1918.

Ross, Elizabeth N. MacBean. *A Lady Doctor in Bakhtiari Land*. London: Leonard Parsons, 1921.

Russell, Bertrand. *Autobiography of Bertrand Russell 1914–1944*. New York: Bantam Books, 1969.

Sackville-West, V. *Twelve Days: A Journey Across the Bakhtiari Mountains*. London: Hogarth Press, 1928.

Sayers, Michael, and Albert E. Kahn. *The Great Conspiracy Against Russia*. New York: Boni & Gaer, 1946.

Schoedsack, Ernest. "Grass: The Making of an Epic." *American Cinematographer* (February 1983): 40–44, 109–14.

Schonpflug, Daniel. *A World on Edge*. New York: Henry Holt, 2018.

Scott, J. W. Robertson. *The Foundations of Japan*. London: John Murray, 1922.

Service, Robert. *Spies and Commissars: The Early Years of the Russian Revolution*. New York: Public Affairs, 2012.

Siegel, Katherine A. S. *Loans and Legitimacy: The Evolution of Soviet-American Relations, 1919–1933.* Lexington: University Press of Kentucky, 1996.

Snowden, Mrs. Philip. *Through Bolshevik Russia.* London: Cassell, 1920.

Sundaram, Chantal. "Manufacturing Culture." PhD diss., University of Toronto, 2000.

Talbert, Roy, Jr. *Negative Intelligence: The Army and the American Left, 1917–1941.* Jackson: University Press of Mississippi, 1991.

Theroux, Paul. *The Great Railway Bazaar.* New York: Mariner Books, 1975.

Thomson, James C., Jr., Peter W. Stanley, and John Curtis Perry. *Sentimental Imperialists.* New York: Harper & Row, 1981.

Tuchman, Barbara. *The Guns of August.* New York: Macmillan, 1962.

———. *Stilwell and the American Experience in China.* New York: Bantam Books, 1980.

Usden, Martin. *Times Past in Korea.* New York: Routledge, 2003.

Van Deman, Ralph H. *The Final Memoranda.* Edited by Ralph E. Weber. Wilmington, DE: SR Books, 1988.

Vaz, Mark Costa. *Living Dangerously: The Adventures of Merian Cooper, Creator of King Kong.* New York: Villard, 2005.

Von Bernstorff, Johann Heinrich. *My Three Years in America.* London: Skeffington, 1920.

Von de Golz, Colmar Freiherr. *The Nation in Arms.* London: Forgotten Books, 2018.

Wallach, Janet. *Desert Queen: The Extraordinary Life of Gertrude Bell.* New York: Nan A. Talese/Doubleday, 1996.

Weale, Putnam. *An Indiscreet Chronicle of the Pacific.* New York: Dodd, Mead, 1922.

Wheeler, Douglas, "Intelligence Between the Wars." *The Intelligencer: Journal of U.S. Intelligence Studies* 20, no. 1 (Spring/Summer 2013).

Wilson, Arnold. "The Bakhtiaris." *Journal of the Royal Central Asian Society* 13, no. 3 (1926).

Wise, Marsha Wright. *Catonsville.* Charleston, SC: Arcadia, 2005.

Yardley, Herbert. *American Black Chamber.* New York: Braunworth, 1931.

Yergin, Daniel. *The Prize: The Epic Quest for Oil, Money and Power.* New York: Simon & Schuster, 1991.

Young, George. *The New Germany.* New York: Harcourt, 1920.

Young, Hugh. *A Surgeon's Autobiography.* New York: Harcourt, Brace and Company, 1940.

Zia Bey, Mufty-Zade K. *Speaking of the Turks.* London: Stanley-Paul, 1922.

Index

Page numbers in *italics* refer to maps.

Middle East, map of, *xvi-xvii*
Mildred Pierce (Cain), 270
Military Intelligence Division (MID)
  Andrews works for, 200
  arrest of Marguerite in Moscow and,
    114, 116–17, 120, 140, 156
  Cipher Bureau, 167
  downgraded after WW I, 167
  Far Eastern Section, 177
  leaks reveal Marguerite as spy for,
    114, 224
  Marguerite hired by, 17, 20–21
  Marguerite returns to work for, 76
  Marguerite's relationship with,
    223–24
  Marguerite's release from Russian
    prison and, 162, 166–67
  Marguerite's reports on anti-
    Semitism and, 63
  Marguerite's reports on Berlin and,
    26, 28–31, 34, 43–45, 56
  Marguerite's reports on Japan and
    Far East and, 177–78, 192–93
  Marguerite's reports on Minor and
    Seidel and, 69
  Marguerite's reports on Poland,
    Danzig and Silesia and, 59
  Marguerite's reports on Russia and,
    81, 84–85, 90–91, 104, 109–10, 112,
    116–17, 120, 122–24, 127, 131–32
  Marguerite's reports on Weimar
    and, 36
  mole in, 85
  pogroms vs. Jews in Poland denied
    by, 90
  Van Deman and, 66
Mill, John Stuart, 19
Minor, Robert, 37–38, 65, 67–71, 80,
  90, 121
Minsk, *xiii*, 91, 92
Mitsubishi Bank, 181
Modern Library, 137
Mogilevsky, Solomon, 113–15, 118–21,
  131, 133, 135–36, 138, 148–49,
  160–61, 174, 215–18
Mohammad Reza, Shah of Persia, 262

Mohammed (Persian interpreter), 247,
  252, 253
Mohammerah, *xvii*, 241–43
Mona Lisa (Schilling), 41
Monarchist Russian zone (Siberia),
  192–94
Monet, Claude, 107, 110
Mongolia, *xv*, 172, 200, 202–8
Montessori method, 98
Moore, Mr., 181
Morgan, J.P., 15, 48, 75
Moscow, *xiii*, *xiv*, 2, 37–38, 76, 79, 84,
  164
  arrest of Marguerite in, and forced to
    spy for Russians, 112–20
  art, music, and literature in, 107–11
  children in, 98–99
  executions in, 89, 121
  health and education problems in,
    98–99
  Marguerite first travels to, for MID,
    90–91, 94–96
  Marguerite's final departure from,
    218
  Marguerite's interviews in, 98–101,
    104–6
  Marguerite returns to, after arrest in
    Siberia, 213–14
  Marguerite's social life in, 109–11
Moscow Art Theatre, 108–10
Moscow Conservatory, 108
Moscow Soviet, first session of 1920,
  101–5
Moscow Symphony Orchestra, 108
Moser, Frank, 137, 138
Mosse Brothers (Berlin), 33
Mosul, *xvii*, 3
Mother Earth, 121
Mount Hallyday, 89
Mukden, Manchuria, *xv*, 196–97,
  199
Munich, *xii*, 64
  assassination of Eisner in, 38–39
Museum of Modern Art, 276
Museum of Modern Western Art
  (Shchukin, Moscow), 107, 110

Muslims, 240
  Shiite vs. Sunni, 240
Muslim Turks, 272
Mussorgsky, Modest, 79

Nanook of the North (documentary),
  227
Nansen, Fridtjof, 127, 160
National Hotel (Moscow), 121
nationalism, 29–30, 59, 65, 71, 90, 276
Nazi Party, 64, 225
Near East Relief Society, 271–72
Nebuchadnezzar, 233
New Economic Policy, 213, 218
New York City, 172–73, 226, 264,
  268–71
New York Herald, 178
New York Herald Tribune, 268
New York Post, 90
New York Stock Exchange, 52–53, 173
New York Sun, 44, 137
New York Times, 175, 228, 262, 276
New York World, 36, 133, 134, 171
Niaz Ali (Persian servant), 252, 255, 259
Nicholas II, Czar of Russia, 80, 213
Nikolaevsk, *xv*, 172, 183, 186–88, 199,
  215–16
Niles, Blair, 269
Nizhny Novgorod, *xiii*, 132
Nolan, Dennis, 44, 59
North, Frank, 127, 136
Noske, Gustav, 37, 42–43
Novgorod, 213
Novinsky Hospital Prison for Women,
  157–60
Novo-Nikolaevsk, Siberia, 211

Odessa, 103
Offenbach, Jacques
  Tales of Hoffmann, 10
oil, 227–28, 240, 275
Olga (Russian prisoner), 154
Omsk, *xiv*, 213
O'Neill, Eugene, 121

Open Door Policy, 176
Oriental Conference, 141
Orient Express, 1, 222, 231
Orlando, Vittorio Emanuele, 22
Otaru, *xv*, 184
Ottoman Empire, 19, 52, 221–22, 227,
  242, 272, 275
Outer Mongolia, *xv*, 2, 202

Paderewski, Ignacy, 57, 89
Pak, Mr., 195
Palais de Danse (Berlin), 42
Pale of Settlement, 91
Palestine, British Mandate, *xvi*, 222,
  263–64
Pan-Arabists, 240
pan-Germanism, 28
Pani (Polish prisoner), 154
Paris, *xii*, 21–23, 66, 164
Paris Exposition of 1900, 79
Paris Peace Conference, 21–23, 32, 34,
  42–44, 59, 66. *See also* Versailles
  Treaty
Payne, Mabel, 68
Peel, Captain, 243–44
Peking, *xv*, 199–202, 209, 215
Penn, William, 18
People's Theatre (Berlin), 41
Pera Palace Hotel (Constantinople),
  231
Perm, Russia, 213
Persia, *xiv*, *xvii*, 227–28, 237, 240–64,
  275
Persian Gulf, 253
Persian khans, 243
Peter Ibbetson (Du Maurier), 152
Peter the Great, Czar of Russia, 79
Petrograd, 121, 135, 165
Pettit, Walter, 84–85
Pfitzner, Hans
  Der Arme Heinrich, 41
Philharmonie Theater (Berlin), 33
Philippines, 177
Pickford, Mary, 227
Pilsudski, General, 89

Illustration Credits

PAGE 6

Top: Library of Congress
Bottom left: Album / Alamy Stock Photo
Bottom right: Album / Alamy Stock Photo

PAGE 7

Top: Masheter Movie Archive / Alamy Stock Photo
Bottom: All rights reserved

PAGE 8

Top: Academy of Motion Picture Arts and Sciences Merrick Library
Bottom: All rights reserved